PREY

PREY

IMMIGRATION, ISLAM, AND THE EROSION OF WOMEN'S RIGHTS

AYAAN HIRSI ALI

HARPER

An Imprint of HarperCollinsPublishers

HarperCollins books may be purchased for educational, business, or sales promotional use. For information, please email the Special Markets Department at SPsales@harpercollins.com.

FIRST EDITION

Designed by Bonni Leon-Berman

Library of Congress Cataloging-in-Publication Data
Names: Hirsi Ali, Ayaan, 1969- author.
Title: Prey : immigration, Islam, and the erosion of women's rights / Ayaan Hirsi Ali.
Description: First edition. | New York, NY : Harper, [2020] | Includes
    bibliographical references and index.
Identifiers: LCCN 2020010264 (print) | LCCN 2020010265 (ebook) | ISBN
    9780062857873 (hardcover) | ISBN 9780062857897 (ebook)
Subjects: LCSH: Women's rights—Europe. | Sexual harrassment—Europe. |
    Women—Crimes against—Europe. | Muslims—Europe. | Muslim men—Europe. |
    Europe—Emigration and immigration—Social aspects.
Classification: LCC HQ1236.5.E85 H57 2020 (print) | LCC HQ1236.5.E85
    (ebook) | DDC 305.42—dc23
LC record available at https://lccn.loc.gov/2020010264
LC ebook record available at https://lccn.loc.gov/2020010265

21 22 23 24 25   LSC   10 9 8 7 6 5 4 3 2 1

To Niall

This is a trigger warning for the entire book.
Reading it, you should be triggered.

CONTENTS

PART IV:
SOLUTIONS, FAKE AND REAL

INTRODUCTION

This book is about mass migration, sexual violence, and the rights of women in Europe. It is about a colossal failure of the European political establishment. And it is about solutions to the problem, fake and real.

In recent years the debate on immigration, integration, and Islam in Europe has intensified. This has been in response to terrorist attacks, big and small; the preaching of radical Islam in some mosques and Islamic centers; the reemergence of extreme-right-wing and populist parties; and the recent arrival of large numbers of immigrants from the Middle East, Africa, and South Asia, especially (but not only) in 2015 and 2016. Even though the flow of migrants has abated in the past few years, there are still large numbers attempting to cross the Mediterranean or to reach Europe by other routes. One consequence of all this has been a change in the position of women in Europe. That change is the subject of this book.

The increase in the numbers of men from Muslim-majority countries has brought to the surface a problem: their attitude to women. Though not all Muslim men feel and express contempt for women, some do. In countries such as France, Germany, the United Kingdom, Sweden, and others with considerable numbers of Muslim immigrants, we have seen a rejection of women's freedoms by some of these men and sometimes by their children, too. For a few decades, discussion has focused on how some men treated their own relatives: wives, sisters, cousins, nieces, and others. The forms of violence justified in the name of honor—including murders, beatings, and incarcerations—are by now familiar or should be. In Europe, as in the rest of the West, it has taken a lot of activism and some high-profile cases to bring these issues into the open and to expose the numerous cases when sharia tribunals have endorsed child marriages, forced marriages, polygamous marriages, wife beating, and unjust divorce settlements. Survivors have been accused of lying; those who sided with the victims have been accused of various forms of bigotry. Even to acknowledge that Muslim women were being denied their rights in the name of culture and religion, often by their own families, has been difficult. Often the victims have simply been ignored.

However, men who feel contempt for women do not confine it to those women with whom they share a background. Some Muslim men feel contempt for all women—including European women, who had taken it for granted that they had achieved a level of emancipation that set them apart from Muslim women. And this problem concerns not only the new arrivals seeking asylum in Europe; the men discussed in this book include some who were born and raised in Europe, the sons and even grandsons of immigrants.

This raises a fundamental question: Why does this book focus only on Muslim men and not on all men, when sexual violence and contempt for women are universal phenomena? After all, when the Red Army invaded Germany between 1944 and 1945, Soviet soldiers committed many more crimes than those described in this book, raping countless German women in a semiorganized campaign of retaliation. In the Bosnian war of the 1990s, it was Muslim women who suffered at the hands of Serbian paramilitary rapists. Men who have recently arrived in Europe, North America, and Australia from Cuba, Argentina, Serbia, and South Sudan—to name just four countries with very small Muslim populations—have been guilty of sexual misconduct of all kinds. The leading sex-trafficking rings in the world today are led by non-Muslim criminal gangs in various parts of Asia, Russia, and Central and South America. Moreover, it would seem that the consumers of the most sordid products of the sex "industry"—notably child pornography—are mainly from the West. If several million mostly young men had arrived in Europe from any part of the world, there would almost certainly have been an increase in sexual crimes against women.

In this book, nevertheless, I focus on Muslim men's attitudes and behavior for three reasons:

1. The scale of the migration from Muslim-majority countries to Europe, as well as its likely continuation and the associated growth of Europe's Muslim population.
2. Its political salience. Put simply, evidence of sexual misconduct by some Muslim immigrants provides populists and other right-wing groups and parties with a powerful tool to demonize all Muslim immigrants. If we bring this issue out of the taboo zone, discussion will cease to be monopolized by those elements.
3. Frank discussion also challenges the Islamists, who recognize the problem but propose a remedy that would set back all women.

I am well aware of the difficulties of this undertaking. Talking about violence by Muslim men against European women is unfashionable in an age of identity politics, when we are supposed to operate within a partly historical matrix of victimhood. It is even harder when the topic is a favorite of Russian agents of disinformation as well as "alt-right" trolls. Russian president Vladimir Putin's government is engaged in a campaign intended to destabilize liberal democracy in Europe as well as the United States. Directly or indirectly through credulous or malicious Western websites, the Russians spread fake news—for example, the claim that the perpetrators in the case of a gang rape in Spain were Arabs, when in fact they were Cuban,

Argentinian, and Spanish. Even without the Russians, extreme-right-wing groups are highly effective in exaggerating or wholly fabricating anti-immigrant stories. Anyone who seeks to write in a serious fashion about negative aspects of immigration is almost certain to be accused of legitimizing the alt-right and its accomplices. Yet I am convinced that a book such as this can provide far more effective arguments against those people than a strategy of denial, which would seem to be the alternative preferred by many liberals and progressives. Only by clarifying what has gone wrong in Europe in recent years can one make a truly credible case for effective integration of immigrants. For that—not the exclusion and repatriation favored by the populists of the Right—is the only feasible way forward.

You may ask why, if the problem is as serious as I claim, it has taken so long to bring it into the open. Part of the answer is that in the West, all things related to immigration and Islam are talked about with great difficulty, if they are talked about at all. Another part of the answer is that this is also an issue of class as well as religion or race. Most of the crime and misconduct against women takes place in low-income neighborhoods. The women who could afford to move to safer neighborhoods have done so, along with their families. Those stuck in the poor zones are the less well off. And somehow, in the era of #MeToo, their predicament arouses much less sympathy than that of Hollywood actresses subjected to sexual harassment by predatory producers.

In my life, I have experienced, in mild forms, the sexual discrimination, harassment, and violence that are commonplace in Muslim-majority countries such as Somalia and Saudi Arabia, as well as in some Muslim communities in the West. I have also, on more than one occasion, had to fend off the unwanted attentions of sexually overbearing Western men. I can tell you which problem is the worse one. Indeed, telling you that is a large part of the purpose of this book.

Another reason this book needs an introduction is that its publication was postponed from June 2, 2020 to February 9, 2021, due to the global COVID-19 pandemic. The postponement has had six consequences.

First, the delay of publication means that some of the numbers used in the book are now more dated than would be usual in a new work. Updating the data after the book had been typeset has been challenging. Moreover, I noticed that even while I was writing, statistics were constantly being updated and retroactively adjusted; no doubt this process will continue after the book goes to press.

Second, due to the COVID-19–related restrictions imposed by various European governments or voluntarily adopted by citizens, the frequency and dynamics of encounters between people have changed. With lockdowns and social distancing, it is logical to expect fewer attacks of all kinds on women. I say "fewer," not zero, however. In May 2020, a 48-year-old Naples woman was raped while waiting for a bus. With the city in lockdown and few people about, a Senegalese man allegedly sexually abused her for 45 minutes. According to the victim, her attacker said "absurd things, as in a litany: I kill you, I have to purify you, I remove the fire inside you. You have to strip yourself of everything, get dressed and comb your hair like I say." The following month, on the night of June 28, 2020, on a street in Bordeaux, three women were approached by a Libyan man with a knife and assaulted. The man, who was apparently in France illegally, stabbed one of the women nine times, while the others suffered attempted rape and assault. He was taken into custody and awaits trial. The statistics for 2020 will almost certainly show a significant decline in the numbers of sexual assaults by strangers, but this should not be interpreted to mean that the problem identified in *Prey* has gone away.

Crime in general went down in many countries as a result of pandemic measures. However, domestic violence went up—a predictable consequence of confining families to their homes for prolonged periods of time. According to Hans Kluge, the World Health Organization's regional director, European Union member states are "reporting up to a 60 percent increase in emergency calls by women subjected to violence by their intimate partners in April this year, compared to last. Online enquiries to violence-prevention support hotlines have increased up to five times." There have been reports of a "shadow pandemic" of increased domestic violence from Belgium, Cyprus, France, Germany, Ireland, Italy, Spain, and the United Kingdom, as well as from Afghanistan, Argentina, Australia, Brazil, Canada, China, the Russian Federation, Singapore, and the United States. The United Nations Population Fund (UNPFA) has warned that there could be "an extra 31 million cases of gender-based violence if lockdowns were to continue for six months." Overall, the UNPFA assumes an average 20 percent increase in violence during a three-month lockdown in all 193 UN member states. In addition to violence, there have been significant increases in underage marriage as well deaths in childbirth.

A third important point to acknowledge is that *Prey* is about a threat that is primarily directed against girls and young women, whereas COVID-19 disproportionately kills old men. Still, the two crises have much in common. In the first half of 2020, the authorities in many European countries bungled the handling of the pandemic in much the same way they mishandled the migration crisis discussed in *Prey*. In the case of coronavirus, many governments were in denial at first; they wasted precious time that could have been used to contain the contagion. In much the same way, governments ignored (and continue to ignore) the lack of assimilation of migrants coming into Europe and the fact that women were losing their safety bit by bit. On coronavirus, many policy makers avoided taking responsibility and instead told us to "listen to the experts"; this was exactly what they did in the face of a wave of crimes against women after 2015.

With COVID-19, we have seen some governments prioritizing economic stability while risking the lives of their people, especially senior citizens in care homes. Why were we surprised by this kind of incompetence? In *Prey*, we see governments prioritizing the avoidance of xenophobia toward immigrants while neglecting women's rights and freedoms, particularly in high-risk areas such as the poorer neighborhoods of big cities. In Germany, the arrival of a convicted rapist could have been prevented if a pilot refused to allow the criminal on the plane he was employed to fly. In the UK, a senior police officer admitted that "his force ignored the sexual abuse of girls by Pakistani grooming gangs for decades because it was afraid of increasing 'racial tensions.'" The government commissioned a study of the characteristics of grooming gangs but then refused to release its findings.

New figures suggest that we are fast approaching the de facto decriminalization of rape in the UK. The number of individuals prosecuted for and convicted of rape fell in 2019–2020 to the lowest level since records began. In all, police recorded 55,130 rapes in England and Wales, but there were only 2,102 prosecutions and just 1,439 convictions—a mere 1.4 percent. I do not expect these shocking figures to elicit much political reaction. When it became clear that women in many immigrant communities were subject to abuses like child marriage, honor violence, and female genital mutilation, most European governments behaved in much the same way as when confronted in early 2020 with the death statistics for nursing homes during the pandemic.

Fourthly, *Prey* is about a cultural problem that migrants bring from Muslim-majority countries to Europe. Even though the principal victims are women, it is still difficult in today's increasingly intolerant "cancel culture" to write on this subject. My view is that foreclosing certain avenues of inquiry ex ante is the antithesis of the scientific method. It makes little sense to insist that immigrants cannot be seen to be overrepresented in sex crime statistics and that it is better not to publish such statistics rather than risk exacerbating anti-immigrant feeling. Such obscurantism never ends well.

Fifth, as well as significantly reducing the opportunities for sex crimes in the public sphere, the pandemic has of course slowed migration, legal and illegal. But that does not mean this book is already obsolete, even before its publication. The pandemic will pass, as infection rates rise and a vaccine arrives, bringing societies closer to something like herd immunity. In addition, migration into Europe was only temporarily interrupted in March–April 2020 and is certain to revive due to the negative economic consequences of COVID-19 in Africa, the Near East, and South Asia. While, according to Frontex data, "In the first seven months of this year, the number of illegal border crossings at Europe's external borders fell by 15 percent from a year ago to 47,250 . . . reaching record lows in April due to restrictions related to COVID-19," migration through some routes actually went up in the first half of 2020, despite the pandemic. More than 6,900 people came along the Western Balkan route in the first five months of 2020, a 50 percent increase over the same period in 2019. Between January and May, almost three times as many people came from Libya and Tunisia across the Mediterranean to Italy and Malta compared to the same period in 2019. Most came from Bangladesh, Sudan, and the Ivory Coast. Since the peak of COVID-19 in April, traffic through other routes has also picked up. Moreover, the European Union's asylum agency has warned that the pandemic could ultimately trigger more arrivals in the future, "particularly if it leads to food shortages and more turmoil in the Middle East and North Africa."

Indeed, it is possible that the next wave of migration could be even larger than that of 2015–2016, even if Europe's politicians today are unlikely to be as welcoming as they were five years ago. Given the complex web of treaties, laws, agencies, and national restrictions that now govern immigration in Europe, there are still plenty of opportunities for people-smugglers and rejected asylum-seekers to find their way into the EU. The United Nations High Commissioner for Refugees (UNHCR) estimates that around 70 percent of those crossing from Libya to Europe are unlikely to qualify for asylum when they arrive. Yet, as *Prey* shows, Europe is very far from having the "fair and equitable return mechanism" the UNHCR suggests is necessary to avoid "the entire asylum system [being] called into question."

Finally, it is worth noting that, even if migration stopped completely tomorrow, we would still confront the problems described in *Prey*. Nothing that has happened since the manuscript of this book was completed last year has changed my view that the top priority for policy makers—not only in Europe but throughout the West—must be to assimilate the immigrants already residing in these countries. If we fail to make a success of this, women will disproportionately be the losers, while right-wing populists and Islamists will be the beneficiaries—so that liberal democracy itself will be the ultimate loser.

August 21, 2020

PREY

PART I

The Unsafe Streets

Chapter 1

THE CLOCK TURNS BACK

We in the West are used to seeing women everywhere around us. We see them as colleagues in the office, sitting next to us on the bus, as patrons in restaurants, jogging on the streets, and working in shops. We are also seeing more women than ever in leadership positions as prime ministers, politicians, chancellors, directors, and bosses. Women born in the West in the 1990s onward take this as a given. They do not consider that walking to school or sitting in a café is a triumph of liberalism. But in some parts of Western cities and towns these days, you may notice something strange: there are simply no women around—or very few.

Walking in certain neighborhoods in Brussels, London, Paris, or Stockholm, you suddenly notice that only men are visible. The shop assistants, waiters, and patrons in cafés are all men. In parks nearby, it is only men and boys playing soccer. In the communal areas of apartment buildings, it is men talking, laughing, and smoking. On the continent to which millions of tourists travel each year to see the female body as an object of art or wearing the latest fashions, this seems a little strange. What happened to the women? Why are they no longer sitting at sidewalk cafés or chatting in the streets?

The answer is that some women have removed themselves from those neighborhoods, others have been hounded out, and still others are at home, out of sight. As more women erase themselves from public places in such neighborhoods, the few who remain are exposed, drawing the attention of men inhabiting the area. There is no formal segregation, but a feeling of discomfort and vulnerability is enough to make any woman walking alone shudder and think "I won't come this way again."

Women in such areas are harassed out of the public square. Some men call out to them, "Hey, baby, give me your number" or "Nice ass" or "What are you doing here?" Whatever their age or appearance, if they are female and especially if they are alone, they get the same treatment. A persistent harasser might follow a woman up the street, touch her, and block her path. If a woman looks vulnerable, some men will go further: they pick her as a target, they encircle and intimidate her, groping her, pulling at her clothes, and occasionally doing worse.

Such incidents are becoming more common. Women and girls across Europe speak of being harassed walking to the shops, at school and university, in swimming pools, in nightclub bathrooms, in parks, at festivals, in parking lots. They say that local streets and public places are no longer safe. And their assailants have no shame about perpetrating their harassment in public.

Finding robust data about this phenomenon is notoriously difficult. My research assistants and I have spent two years combing through the available sources—crime statistics, court reports, police reports, government accounts, academic sources—and none of them offer a complete picture. We know that only a small fraction of women report being sexually assaulted after they have suffered it and even fewer report sexual harassment, which most women shrug off as being part of the course of their daily lives. Frustratingly, many of the relevant experiences of ordinary women rarely make it into the public domain, beyond isolated posts on social media.

In speaking to European women, however, I have come to see that the problem goes much deeper and wider than the stories that appear in the news. Their testimony has convinced me that we are living through a quiet but significant erosion of women's rights in some neighborhoods in Europe. If this trend continues, it will affect more and more places in Europe; more and more streets will become unsafe for women. For now, these neighborhoods have two things in common: low income and a large number of immigrants from Muslim-majority countries.

A CHANGE FOR WOMEN IN EUROPE

As a Somali arriving in the Netherlands in 1992, I was shocked to see young women alone on public transport and in bars and restaurants. I had grown up knowing that to step outside the house without covering my head and body, or without a male relative to escort me, would make me a target for harassment and assault. But in Holland, women freely walked the streets at night without men to chaperone them, their hair uncovered, wearing whatever they pleased.

Of course, there were exceptions. There were assaults, rapes, and occasionally murders of women, even in Holland. But those cases were so exceptional that they made national news for weeks. As I acclimated to life in a Western city, I learned that the position of women there was radically different from what it was in the world I had come from. Today, two decades later, that can no longer be said with the same confidence. A growing number of European women are questioning their safety. Cases of rape, assault, groping, and sexual harassment in public places seem to have become more numerous.

It is no secret—though it is considered impolite or politically incorrect to point it out—that the perpetrators are disproportionately young immigrant men from the Middle East, South Asia, and various parts of Africa. Often operating in groups, they are making it increasingly unsafe for women to venture into a growing number of neighborhoods in European cities.

It is a truism to say women have always suffered the threat of sexual violence. But for at least the last four decades in Europe, it was the exception, not the rule. In the 1990s, I assumed that developing countries would gradually become more like Europe. Back then, few people would have predicted that parts of Europe would begin to take on the attitudes and beliefs of cultures that explicitly downgrade women's rights. But I believe that is what is happening. We are witnessing a challenge to the rights that European women once took for granted. I do not think it is coincidental that this challenge has followed a significant increase in immigration.

Approximately 3 million people have arrived illegally in Europe since 2009, the majority of whom have applied for asylum.[1] Roughly half arrived in 2015. Two-thirds of the newcomers were male. Eighty percent of asylum applicants were under the age of 35. In the most recent years, a third were (or claimed to be) under 18.

The overwhelming majority of these young men have arrived from countries where women are not regarded as equals or near equals, as they are in Europe. In some of the countries of origin, for example, boys and girls are separated in the household from the age of 7. They are discouraged from mixing, and sex education is taboo. They come from a context that does not give equal rights to women and discourages them from working, remaining single, or following their own aspirations.

Of course, this is not an entirely new phenomenon. Migrants from the Muslim world have been settling in western Europe since the early 1960s. However, those earlier periods of settlement were rarely associated in the public mind with violence against women. That was because few Europeans noticed the way women and girls were treated inside the immigrant families. People like me tried to shed light on the honor violence, female genital mutilation, and forced marriage to which many girls and women were subjected. But it was assumed that within a generation or two those cultural behaviors would go away as the liberties enjoyed by Western women spread to migrant communities. For too many women within those communities, that simply has not happened.

This book came about because I was curious to investigate why women were retreating from the public space in some neighborhoods. My hunch was that women were ceding their access to public places in a trade-off for personal safety. That is what life is like for many women in Muslim-majority countries. It is also how many women in immigrant communities have continued to live in the West for the last five decades: they are confined to their homes for a significant part of their lives, and their outside movements are policed by a network of family and community members. It seemed logical to ask how far increasing numbers of men from societies where this dynamic between men and women exists might be imposing their norms on other women in their proximity.

In the years leading up to Europe's migrant crisis in 2015, I had noticed occasional reports of sexual assault in the media. Each instance had been reported as an isolated, individual case. At first glance, they did not add up to a bigger picture. Generally, the assault involved a woman attacked by a stranger on her way home from a night out. It later transpired in some cases that the perpetrator was an immigrant, or maybe he had been born in Europe and lived in a poorly integrated immigrant community. But the cases did not seem numerous enough to constitute a pattern.

Beginning in late 2015, however, this changed. Reports of such sexual assaults, as well as rapes and cases of harassment, snowballed. As I looked further into the phenomenon, it became apparent to me that the escalation in the number of sex crimes was occurring in the western European countries that had opened their borders to unprecedented numbers of migrants and asylum seekers from highly patriarchal, predominantly Muslim societies. In 2015 alone, close to 2 million people, mainly men, arrived in western Europe from Syria, Afghanistan, Iraq, Pakistan, Nigeria, and other countries with large Muslim populations. However, the language differences among the various European societies and the parochialism of their media reporting meant that people in countries as geographically close as Sweden, Germany, France, and Austria did not appreciate that what was being reported by women in their country was also happening elsewhere.

It is important to state unambiguously that there is no racial component to my argument. A certain proportion of men of all ethnicities will rape and harass women. According to the World Health Organization, 35 percent of women worldwide "have experienced either physical and/or sexual intimate partner violence or non-partner sexual violence."[2] But the rates are markedly lower in Europe than in other parts of the world. In some societies, men are brought up to respect women's physical autonomy, whereas in others predatory behavior is not proscribed with the same severity.

BEFORE YOU OBJECT . . .

Let me state this up front: being Muslim, or being an immigrant from the Muslim world, does not make you a threat to women. Rape, sexual assault, and sexual harassment seem to be universal. In numerous periods of upheaval, large-scale population movements have been associated with increases in sexual violence against women. It would be easy to fill an entire book with such gruesome episodes, and it would quickly become apparent that they occur in a wide variety of geographical and cultural settings. Indeed, as I have already said, nothing that occurred after 2015 can remotely compare with the horrific campaign of rape waged against German women by the Red Army at the end of World War II.

The point of this book is not to demonize migrant men from the Muslim world. Rather, it is to better understand the nature and significance of the sexual violence that has occurred in so many parts of Europe in the recent past. As I was researching for this book, the #MeToo movement shone a light on sexual abuse and exploitation in the upper echelons of North America. I found myself wondering why an equally bright light was not being shone on the often more serious crimes against women in lower-income neighborhoods in Europe.

Time and again in my career I have come across authorities and commentators—including self-described feminists—who are prepared to look the other way when it comes to the harassment and abuse of immigrant women at the hands of their own men. It now looks as if the same people are applying the same double standards when it comes to the harassment and abuse of native-born women. In some cases, I have even heard European victims of sexual assault make excuses for their attackers. Afraid of being called racist, these women strike an apologetic tone on behalf of those who assaulted them, some even apologizing for bringing them to justice.

Authorities understate the incidence of assaults and harassment of women. In the interest of political expediency, politicians play down the threat and encourage the police to do the same. Excuses are made for criminal behavior. Judges hand out light sentences to perpetrators. And the media self-censor their reporting—all in order, it is said, to avoid stoking racial and religious tensions or providing ammunition for right-wing populists.[3]

This conspiracy of silence, or at least of understatement, has had predictable beneficiaries: none other than the right-wing populists such as the National Front (now National Rally) in France, the Party for Freedom in the Netherlands, the Alternative für Deutschland in Germany, and all the other parties whose core policy pledge is to restrict immigration, and particularly Muslim immigration.

I was once an asylum seeker. I am an immigrant twice over, first to the Netherlands, then to the United States. Fleeing to Holland helped me avoid a forced marriage and gave me opportunities I would never have enjoyed had I remained in the Somali society into which I was born. So the last thing I want to see is more obstacles put in the way of those who seek to escape religious oppression, civil war, and economic collapse and to make better lives for themselves, taking advantage of the freedoms of the West. I am writing this book not to help the proponents of closed borders but to persuade liberal Europeans that denial is a self-defeating strategy. If I can also persuade some populists to give integration a chance, so much the better.

Many authors have written about the clash of cultures between Islam and the West. They look at economics, demography, language, religion, values, and geopolitics. Some mention women's rights as an example. But I believe women deserve to be the central focus of discussion. For nothing else so clearly distinguishes Western societies from Muslim societies today than the different ways they treat women. In this book I therefore concentrate on how women's rights are being negatively affected by immigration from Muslim societies, what we can expect in the future if things continue as they are, and what we might do differently to avoid a dangerous backlash.

The very idea of women being equal to men is a historical anomaly. It has appeared only in the West and only very recently. (The propaganda claims about sexual equality in Communist regimes belied a reality that was quite different.) If we zoom out and consider the whole planet, we see that it is still only a fraction of women who have the wonderful rights and liberties that have been achieved in the West. But these rights are fragile and are at risk of being eroded by men who view independent women—women who enjoy the same rights as men—as prey.

Chapter 2

THE FIFTH WAVE

A NEW *VÖLKERWANDERUNG*

Since 1945, western Europe has experienced several waves of mass migration.[1] The first wave saw a westward exodus of peoples displaced by the Second World War and the concomitant redrawing of national borders from 1945 to 1956. The displaced included Jewish Holocaust survivors; East Prussian, Pomeranian, Silesian, and Sudeten expellees; Estonians, Latvians, and Lithuanians; anti-Communist Russians and Ukrainians; former European forced laborers; and legions of demobilized soldiers. The second wave covered the migration of "guest workers" and their families from former European colonies, from *pieds-noirs* and *harkis* fleeing the newly independent Algeria to the "Windrush" generation seeking economic opportunities in Great Britain. In a third wave, the Germany of the *Wirtschaftswunder* sought to meet labor shortages by inviting guest workers from Turkey. During the economic slowdown of the 1970s, even as the demand for labor ebbed and resentment toward immigrants grew, it became clear that the majority of the supposed guests had no intention of returning home. A significant number of migrant communities from Muslim-majority countries—Algerians in France, Pakistanis and Bangladeshis in Great Britain, Turks in Germany—had put down deep roots in that period.

The fourth wave was a surge of mass migration resulting from the dissolution of the Communist regimes in eastern and central

Europe, the violent disintegration of Yugoslavia, and the enactment of new pan-European policies (such as the Schengen Agreement) to manage European borders. Among the new arrivals in this period were Muslims from Bosnia and Somalia, countries ravaged by civil war. Those newcomers—I among them—came seeking asylum or refuge. Not all—indeed, disappointingly few—were absorbed into the labor forces of the countries that accepted them.

The fifth wave has been the largest in scale since the post-1945 period. In the past ten years, according to the European Border and Coast Guard Agency, Frontex, there were around 3.5 million illegal border crossings into the European Union.[2] Eurostat recorded just under 5.8 million first-time asylum applications.[3] Three-quarters of the illegal entries and two-thirds of the applications for asylum occurred between 2015—the peak year—and 2018.

Each wave has reached the shores of an evolving and enlarging Europe. What began with the Treaty of Rome of 1957, which created a six-member club focused mainly on reducing trade barriers, is now a twenty-eight-member European Union with a mixture of federal and confederal elements and ties to non-EU countries such as the four members of the European Free Trade Association (EFTA: Iceland, Norway, Switzerland, and Liechtenstein).

A number of international accords, EU agreements among member states, and directives from Brussels outline the responsibilities of European governments toward migrants and refugees:

- The Geneva Convention Relating to the Status of Refugees (1951) and its supplementary protocol (1967) outlined the legal definition of a refugee and the obligations of sovereign states toward refugees. Article 33 established the *jus cogens** principle of *non-refoulement*, in which refugees cannot be returned to a country

---

* A peremptory norm in international law from which no derogation is permitted.

where they can expect to receive an unfair trial, persecution, torture, or death.

- The Schengen Agreement (1985) abolished the internal borders among a number of European states (originally five, now twenty-six) and created a common visa policy for EU member states.
- The Dublin Regulation (1990; amended 2003 and 2013) established that asylum seekers must be processed at their first EU state of entry.
- The Treaty of Amsterdam (1997) transferred national powers of immigration legislation, foreign policy, and security policy to the European Union.
- The Treaty of Lisbon (2007) created a legally binding Charter of Fundamental Rights. The charter includes, among other things, a right to asylum.
- We must also be careful to distinguish among:
  ○ *Authorized* or *legal immigrants*: noncitizens with residency status in a European nation for a period of longer than twelve months. Asylum applicants granted refugee status and asylum seekers given subsidiary protection status fall into this category.
  ○ *Asylum seekers*: noncitizens who have applied for asylum in an EU member state under the procedures of the Dublin Regulation. Persons in this category are temporarily protected from deportation while their asylum applications are being processed. Those whose applications are processed successfully acquire refugee status and the right to live, move, and work in the European Union.
  ○ *Unauthorized* or *illegal immigrants*: noncitizens living in their country of residence without a residency permit. Persons who have overstayed their visas, have refused deportation orders, have entered an EU member state without proper authorization,

or are awaiting the final status of their asylum applications fall into this category. As many European nations still retain the *jus sanguinis* principle of citizenship, children born in Europe to unauthorized migrants do not necessarily become EU citizens, unlike in *jus soli* nations such as the United States. Immigrants who obtained residency papers with fraudulent identities do not technically fall into this category.

In the period after 2008, the volume of illegal migrants and asylum seekers entering the European Union surged, reaching a peak in 2015 due to the confluence of a number of factors.

The intensification of the Syrian civil war was the largest proximate cause for the migrant influx. The beginning of direct Russian military involvement in September 2015 tipped the strategic balance of a multifaceted conflict that had hitherto been going badly for Syria's incumbent president, Bashar al-Assad. In eastern Syria, the apogee of the Islamic State, along with the multifactional conflicts among Kurdish forces, Hezbollah, "moderate" Syrian rebels, Iranian-backed Shiite militias, and Turkish proxies were powerful "push" factors encouraging ordinary Syrians and Iraqis to brave the treacherous journey toward safety in Europe. In addition to refugee traffic originating in the Middle East, the toppling of Muammar al-Qaddafi's regime in 2011 removed a roadblock across the migration and human-trafficking routes originating in sub-Saharan Africa.

The official data on this most recent *Völkerwanderung* must be read with care. The "illegal border crossings" data count entry attempts, so some individuals appear multiple times. Not all migrants who enter the European Union illegally later apply for asylum. Some migrants counted in "illegal border crossings" are more or less immediately sent back to their home country or transit country (e.g., Turkey). Others try to stay below the official "radar" and prefer to avoid applying for asylum. For others, there is a lag between the recording of their illegal entry into the European Union and their application for asylum. Migrants often apply for asylum only after they have reached their preferred destination country. Some migrants enter the European Union legally and apply for asylum once in Europe.

The European Union's Dublin III Regulation requires asylum seekers to apply in the first safe country they reach. But those who have their application rejected in one country can take advantage of the borderless Schengen Area and try again in a neighboring country. To access any government support such as housing, health care, and social assistance, a migrant must have an active asylum application. Thus, when Italy withdrew its social assistance for failed applicants, many migrants moved on to Germany via Switzerland and Austria.[4] The numbers of those who double- and triple-dipped were significant. The German Federal Office for Migration and Refugees (Bundesamt für Migration und Flüchtlinge, or BAMF) says that one-third of asylum applications in Germany are "Dublin cases."[5] In just the first six months of 2018, Germany had 30,000 applicants who had already applied in Italy, France, or Greece.[6] Similarly, many asylum applicants in the Netherlands and Sweden had already applied in Germany, Italy, or France.[7]

Using only Eurostat records, the French demographer Michèle Tribalat tracked the flow of asylum seekers. Tribalat found that as the numbers decreased in Germany and Sweden, they increased in France. On average, 30 percent of asylum seekers in France had already filed a request (for asylum) in another EU member state.[8] The French Office of Immigration and Integration (Office Français de l'Immigration et de l'Intégration, or OFII) acknowledged that France was attracting failed applicants from other jurisdictions by providing social services even to the asylum seekers it rejected. In

France, Afghans have a better chance of being approved than else-where, and there are fewer restrictions on family reunification.[9]

To estimate the net inflow of people into Europe over the past decade is therefore far from easy. The Frontex figure of 3.5 million illegal border crossings in 2009–2018 is no more reliable than the Eurostat figure of 5.8 million first-time asylum applications, as both totals include individuals counted more than once.

The number of asylum applications was trending upward from 2009 and still remains far above its long-term average. But the year 2015 was an exceptional one for illegal border crossings, with 1.8 million recorded, more than half of the total for the decade 2009–2018. European agreements with Turkey and Libya have brought the number of illegal border crossings back to pre-2015 levels, and the figures for the first half of 2019 showed another 30 percent drop relative to 2018. New entries are projected to be around 100,000 for the whole year of 2019.[*] The number of new asylum applications is falling less rapidly as migrants from the 2015 wave are still being processed by authorities.

Because Frontex began recording the gender and age of persons illegally crossing the border only in 2018, the sole way to estimate these things is to look at asylum applications. The statistics show a clear preponderance of men over women. On average over the last ten years, 67 percent of asylum seekers were men. Roughly 80 percent of asylum applicants were under the age of 35. The share younger than 18 rose from 25 percent in 2009 to 32 percent in 2018. In the case of Germany, the country that attracted the largest number of asylum seekers, 60.5 percent were aged between 15 and 39, and men out-numbered women in this age group by a ratio of 2.81 to 1.[10]

Where do the migrants come from? Countries afflicted by war and terrorism—in particular Syria, Afghanistan, and Iraq—are the

---

[*]   Total detected illegal border crossings were in fact above 140,000.

most important sources of illegal entrants (see Table 1). However, a significant number come from Pakistan and Nigeria.

Table 1: Illegal Entrants into the European Union, 2009–2018, Principal Source Countries

	Afghanistan	Iraq	Nigeria	Pakistan	Syria
2009	14,539	4,168	1,824	1,592	613
2010	25,918	3,625	559	3,878	861
2011	22,994	1,361	6,893	15,375	1,616
2012	13,169	1,213	826	4,877	7,903
2013	9,494	537	3,386	5,047	25,546
2014	22,132	2,079	8,706	4,115	78,886
2015	267,485	101,155	23,605	43,310	594,059
2016	54,366	32,044	37,811	17,973	88,551
2017	7,576	10,158	18,310	10,015	19,452
2018	12,666	10,025	1,611	1,017	14,378
TOTAL	450,339	166,365	103,531	107,199	831,865

Source: Extracted from Frontex, https://frontex.europa.eu/along-eu-borders/migratory-map/.

How many of the migrants are Muslims? Frontex does not collect data on the religion or cultural attributes of asylum seekers, but it does report their citizenship. The statistics imply that the great majority of the newcomers in the past decade were Muslim, as they came from countries with Muslim majorities ranging from just over 50 percent (Nigeria) to between 92 and 99 percent (Afghanistan, Iraq, Pakistan, and Syria, as well as Algeria, Libya, and Tunisia).[11] In all, approximately 2.4 million asylum applications were lodged in Europe by people from nine Muslim-majority countries between 2015 and 2018.[12] Some of the 2.3 million doubtless belonged to non-Muslim minorities or were not strict believers in Islam, but they can have been only a small fraction. If we assume that there were also Muslims from Muslim-minority countries, we can probably take the totals in the table below as a fair proxy for Muslim migration.

Table 2: Asylum Applications to European Union Countries
from Selected Muslim-Majority Countries

	2015	2016	2017	2018	2015–2018
Syria	368,357	339,246	105,077	83,720	896,400
Afghanistan	181,423	186,604	47,905	45,920	461,852
Iraq	124,969	130,100	51,696	44,735	351,500
Pakistan	48,015	49,916	31,857	29,045	158,833
Nigeria	31,243	47,777	41,017	25,880	145,917
Iran	26,574	41,396	18,467	25,085	111,522
Eritrea	34,132	34,469	25,116	15,585	109,302
Bangladesh	18,867	17,245	20,838	15,145	72,095
Somalia	21,048	20,062	14,085	12,905	68,100
TOTAL	854,628	866,815	356,058	298,020	2,375,521

Source: Extracted from Eurostat, https://ec.europa.eu/eurostat/databrowser/,
accessed on July 23, 2018.

Another way to arrive at a similar conclusion is to note that nine of the top-ten "sender" countries are Muslim-majority countries.

Table 3: Principal Country of Origin of Asylum Seekers in the European Union, 2015–2018

Syria	896,400
Afghanistan	461,852
Iraq	351,500
Pakistan	158,833
Albania	148,380
Nigeria	145,917
Iran	111,522
Eritrea	109,302
Russia	82,055
Bangladesh	72,095
Somalia	68,100
Ukraine	54,895

Turkey	54,725
Guinea	52,710
Georgia	46,495
Venezuela	42,440
Ivory Coast	40,350
Mali	35,775

Source: Extracted from Eurostat, https://ec.europa.eu/eurostat/databrowser,
accessed on July 23, 2018.

The scale of the influx of migrants to Europe is well documented, but where the migrants have ended up is less well understood. We can begin with the countries in which asylum seekers made their initial applications.

Table 4: Numbers of Asylum Seekers by Principal Destination Country, 2009–2018

Germany	2,169,860
France	729,880
Italy	571,835
Sweden	504,105
United Kingdom	327,490
Austria	273,035
Belgium	255,230
Greece	252,670
Switzerland	227,960
Netherlands	204,625
Spain	143,020

Source: Extracted from Eurostat, https://ec.europa.eu/eurostat/databrowser,
accessed on September 3, 2019.

However, this is only the beginning of a complex process. Around a third of asylum seekers in France, for example, have already filed a request in another EU member state, and are supposed to be sent back to the state where they first applied.

Across Europe, 61 percent of those applying for asylum in 2015–2016 were granted refugee status.[13] Others may have been given temporary protection, allowing them to stay but with limitations such as fewer welfare benefits and no access to the labor market until their residency was reassessed. A third category, "humanitarian status," is for migrants whose asylum application was rejected but who were not sent home.

In 2015, there were an estimated 2.2 million migrants illegally present in Europe, half a million of whom had been ordered to leave. The following year, the number of illegal migrants had dropped to 984,000, half of whom had been told to leave.[14] Official sources say that in both 2015 and 2016, fewer than half of those ordered to go did so. By 2018, according to Eurostat, the number had dropped to 601,500 illegals in the European Union, the majority living in Germany (134,125), France (105,880), and Greece (93,365). Of the rejected asylum seekers still in Europe in 2018, the highest proportion were Iraqis, Albanians, Syrians, and Pakistanis.

However, a November 2019 study by the Pew Research Center found that at least 3.9 million and as many as 4.8 million unauthorized immigrants lived in Europe in 2017, compared with 3 million to 3.7 million unauthorized migrants in 2014, implying an increase in the population of illegal immigrants of around a million.[15] In proportional terms, unauthorized immigrants account for less than 1 percent of the population of the EU and EFTA nations combined. Among the approximately 24 million resident noncitizens in Europe in 2017, about one-fifth were unauthorized immigrants, the majority of whom (12 to 16 percent) were without pending asylum claims. But clearly the Pew data omit those whose asylum applications were granted or who in other ways were given the right to remain in a European country. The term "newcomers" is appropriate, though it clearly does not apply to communities created in earlier waves of migration. In 2017, some 56 percent of illegal immigrants in Europe had lived in their nation of residence for less than five years.[16]

Together, Germany, the United Kingdom, Italy, and France account for 70 percent of Europe's unauthorized migrants. Pew estimates that the population of unauthorized migrants is 1 million to 1.2 million in Germany, 800,000 to 1.2 million in the United Kingdom, 500,000 to 700,000 in Italy, and 300,000 to 400,000 in France.[17] The number of unauthorized immigrants roughly doubled between 2014 and 2016.

Though the number of illegal immigrants in the United Kingdom is high in absolute terms, that country did not see as large an influx in 2015 as did Germany, for the simple reason that it is much harder to reach the United Kingdom by sea from North Africa and the Middle East. By contrast, Italy has seen a sustained flow of unauthorized immigrants since 2014, as has Greece. Tighter border restrictions

Table 5: Third-Country Nationals Illegally Present in the European Union, by Citizenship

	2014	2015	2016	2017	2018
Albania	32,195	50,125	36,130	40,175	34,810
Afghanistan	48,550	409,250	151,760	35,395	30,980
Syria	118,865	858,940	212,965	39,315	31,115
Iran	8,465	44,780	33,475	13,090	16,235
Iraq	10,275	185,285	92,945	36,375	36,475
Nigeria	16,410	20,400	20,535	19,380	16,520
Pakistan	24,005	81,850	46,525	33,575	24,895
Eritrea	50,795	41,570	23,260	17,870	13,090
Bangladesh	10,145	21,575	10,370	8,520	7,975
Guinea	3,115	4,810	6,675	10,440	17,290

Source: Extracted from Eurostat, https://ec.europa.eu/eurostat/databrowser, accessed on June 6, 2019.

put into place by France, Switzerland, and Austria have tended to deter migrants from trying their luck by pushing north over the Alps, leaving Italy as a kind of last resort for unsuccessful asylum seekers. France has a lower share of unauthorized migrants relative to its population, perhaps because some unauthorized migrants have been able to gain legal residency more easily.

It is easy to forget that although the wave of asylum seekers has dominated headlines in recent years, ordinary migration from Muslim countries also continued apace. Between 2010 and 2016, 2.5 million Muslims migrated to Europe outside the asylum system. They entered to work or to study or for family reunification. The United Kingdom, France, and Italy were their top destinations, whereas asylum seekers were more likely to head to Germany. Overall, Muslims made up more than half of all migration to Europe between 2010 and 2016. Their movements increased Europe's Muslim population from 19.5 million, or 3.8 percent, in 2010 to 25.8 million, or 4.9 percent, by 2016.[18]

To set the most recent wave of migration in historical perspective, it makes sense to look more closely at the German case. The most recent inflow of asylum seekers exceeded the exodus of citizens of the former German Democratic Republic to the Federal Republic between 1989 and 1990 (as a result of German reunification), which totaled almost 600,000, roughly 3.7 percent of the population in the region of the former GDR (apart from East Berlin).

True, the recent influx was smaller than the 6 million to 7 million ethnic Germans who were expelled from eastern Europe and territory annexed from the German Reich between 1944 and 1946, the overwhelming majority of whom settled in what became the Federal Republic of Germany. However, the expellees—like those who crossed from east to west after the fall of the Berlin Wall—were Germans. Today's newcomers to Germany are overwhelmingly Muslim in religion and are drawn from all over North Africa, the

Middle East, and South Asia, as well as the Balkans. In that sense, the relevant parallel is the *Gastarbeiter* program of the 1960s, which over slightly more than a decade (1961–1973) brought a total of 2.6 million workers to West Germany for what was supposed to be temporary employment in the country's booming industries. Although initially intended to recruit other Europeans, the program was extended to Turkey. Within a short time, Turks became the most numerous "guest workers" in the country. When the program was terminated in the economic hard times of 1973, the majority stayed. Today, as a consequence, the number of German residents with origins in Turkey (i.e., at least one Turkish parent) is around 3 million (according to the 2011 census), or approximately 3.7 percent of Germany's population.

Such was the fifth wave of modern immigration to Europe. Now, what were its consequences?

Chapter 3

SEXUAL VIOLENCE BY NUMBERS

A WORLD OF VIOLENCE AGAINST WOMEN

Violence against women is a global problem. In the words of former UN secretary-general Ban Ki-moon, "There is one universal truth, applicable to all countries, cultures and communities: violence against women is never acceptable, never excusable, never tolerable." As the World Health Organization (WHO)'s first comprehensive report on the topic in 2013 noted, violence against women is not only a fundamental violation of human rights but also a significant public health problem.[1] It still goes on, everywhere.

The WHO report defined "violence against women" as violence by an intimate partner or stranger, physical abuse, rape, sexual assault, female genital mutilation, honor killing, and trafficking. The report leaned heavily upon self-reported and household surveys to assess women's exposure to intimate-partner violence. For non-intimate-partner violence, external data such as police reports as well as previous academic studies were used. As the authors of the report conceded, however, "definitions may vary between studies, and not all forms of sexual violence are well documented."[2] As previously mentioned, according to the WHO, 35 percent of women worldwide "have experienced either intimate partner violence and/or non-partner sexual violence."[3] Of this violence, the large majority was committed by intimate partners or persons otherwise known to the victim. (Globally, 7.2 percent of women have been sexually assaulted by someone other than a partner.) Women who have been physically or sexually abused tend to have significant health problems as a consequence. They are 16 percent as likely to have a low-birth-weight baby, some 1.5 times more likely to contract HIV in some regions, almost twice as likely to suffer from depression, and more than twice as likely to have an abortion or to abuse alcohol. Sexual violence can result in mental health problems such as anxiety, post-traumatic stress disorder, eating disorders, substance abuse, and suicidality; physical problems such as musculoskeletal, genital, and soft-tissue injury; and chronic and debilitating bowel and pelvic pain.[4]

While the WHO report emphasized the global nature of violence against women, it also revealed significant regional variations (see Table 6), though the lack of data on non-partner violence in the "eastern Mediterranean" region is a notable deficiency, as this is the region from which most recent migrants to Europe came.

Table 6: Regional Prevalence of Violence Against Women 15 Years of Age and Older

WHO Region	Lifetime Prevalence Rate of Intimate-Partner Violence (%) [CI = 95%]	Lifetime Prevalence Rate of Non-Intimate-Partner Violence (%) [CI = 95%]	Compositional Notes
Africa	36.6	11.9	Includes Madagascar, Comoros, and Mauritius. Excludes Morocco, Tunisia, Libya, Egypt, Sudan, South Sudan, and Somalia. No data reported for Western Sahara.
Americas	29.8	10.7	North America, South America, Central America, and the Caribbean.
Eastern Mediterranean	37.0	N/A	Morocco, Tunisia, Libya, Egypt, Sudan, South Sudan, Somalia, Israel, Palestinian Territories, Lebanon, Syria, Jordan, Saudi Arabia, Yemen, Oman, Bahrain, Qatar, UAE, Kuwait, Iraq, Iran, and Pakistan. No data reported for Afghanistan.

Europe	25.4	5.2	Geographical Europe (i.e., west of the Urals), all CIS states, Cyprus, and Turkey.
High income	23.2	12.6	United States, Canada, Great Britain, Ireland, Norway, Denmark, Faroe Islands, Sweden, Finland, Estonia, Germany, Netherlands, Belgium, Luxembourg, France, Portugal, Spain, Andorra, Italy, Malta, Switzerland, Austria, Poland, Czechia, Slovakia, Slovenia, Croatia, Japan, South Korea, Australia, and New Zealand.
Southeast Asia	37.7	4.9	India, Sri Lanka, Bangladesh, Nepal, Bhutan, Burma, Thailand, Indonesia, and East Timor.
Western Pacific	24.6	6.8	Mongolia, China, Vietnam, Laos, Cambodia, Malaysia, Bhutan, Philippines, Taiwan, South Korea, Japan, Papua New Guinea, Australia, New Zealand, and minor Oceania islands. No data reported for North Korea.
Global Average	30.0	7.2	

Source: World Health Organization, *Global and Regional Estimates of Violence against Women: Prevalence and Health Effects of Intimate Partner Violence and Non-Partner Sexual Violence* (Geneva: World Health Organization, 2013), Figure 1 and Table 4.

The highest rates of intimate-partner violence against women were in Southeast Asia (37.7 percent), the eastern Mediterranean (37.0 percent), and Africa (36.6 percent). By contrast, the rate for Europe was 25.4 percent, and the overall rate for high-income countries was even lower (23.2 percent). The WHO report hypothesized that the lower rates in the developed world reflected a higher female social standing due to women's greater economic attainment, favorable social norms, and enforceable legal penalties. Puzzlingly, however, the non-intimate-partner rate for the high-income countries (12.6 percent) was even higher than for Africa (11.9 percent), despite the notorious prevalence of rape in African conflict zones. For Europe, the figure was below the global average (5.2 percent), though not as low as for Southeast Asia (4.9 percent).

Such survey data provide an important corrective to official data on sexual violence, which are derived mostly from national criminal justice system records. But surveys, too, have their limitations. Much depends on how questions are phrased, as well as on the context in which they are posed. In a report published as part of the EU Gender Equality Index, 33 percent of women said they had experienced physical and/or sexual violence since they were age 15, a figure not inconsistent with the WHO data in Table 6.[5] Among those women, however, 13.4 percent had never told anyone about it. In addition, 55 percent said they had experienced sexual harassment. Yet who is to say that all those surveyed were perfectly candid? If one in ten had never previously told anyone about her experiences of sexual violence, how many were still remaining silent?

IS SEXUAL VIOLENCE ON THE RISE OVERALL?

It is a well-known fact that official crime statistics capture a mere fraction of the sexual violence taking place. Nevertheless, we can learn something from them, though it is not easy. Crime statistics are easy to misinterpret. Police records are the main source of data for national and regional statistics, but because sexual violence is underreported to the police, the records need to be read alongside other sources, such as the international surveys cited in the previous section and the national surveys discussed below. It should also be remembered that there are significant lags in the processes of data collection and publication. For example, Eurostat releases crime data eighteen months after a crime is recorded by police. For most countries, the data for 2017 were published only as this book was being written.

Comparing statistics among countries is especially hard. Different jurisdictions use different definitions of crimes such as sexual assault, and those definitions often change over time, as do reporting methods. Eurostat's definition of sexual violence covers "unwanted sexual acts, attempts to obtain a sexual act, or contact or communication with unwanted sexual attention without valid consent or with consent as a result of intimidation, force, fraud, coercion, threat, deception, use of drugs or alcohol, or abuse of power or of a position of vulnerability." It excludes "acts of abuse of a position of vulnerability, power or trust, or use of force or threat of force, for profiting monetarily, socially or politically from the prostitution or sexual acts of a person, coercion, prostitution offences, pornography offences and other acts against public order, sexual standards such as incest not amounting to rape and exhibitionism, assaults and threats, slavery and exploitation not amounting to injurious acts of a sexual nature, trafficking in human beings for sexual exploitation, harassment and stalking."[6] However, France, Spain, Greece, Denmark, and Sweden include sexual harassment in their official figures on sexual violence. It is even difficult to compare statistics for a single country from one year to another because of rapidly changing legal definitions, police methods, and public behavior.

What do the official European statistics tell us? The headline figures on sexual violence show that in the five years between 2008 and 2013, sexual violence offenses increased slightly, by 3.9 percent.[7] However, as Table 7 shows, there were significant increases in several regions and countries (England, Wales, Denmark, and Sweden) after 2015, which surely cannot all be explained away by technicalities. Can a doubling in the number of crimes of sexual violence in the space of just three years—as appears to have happened in England—be attributed solely to bureaucratic factors?

Table 7: Sexual Violence in Europe, 2014–2017, Selected Countries

	Absolute numbers				Per 100,000				2014–17	
	2014	2015	2016	2017	2014	2015	2016	2017	change in rate	% change in absolute numbers
Austria	3,564	3,479	4,391		41.9	40.6	50.5			
(consistent data)		(-2.4%)	(+26.2%)							
Belgium	6,897	6,742	7,273	7,177	61.7	60.0	64.3	63.22	1.5	4%
(2019 figures)*		(-2.3%)	(+7.8%)	(-1.3%)						
Denmark	2,368	2,611	3,793	4,795	42.1	46.1	66.5	83.4	41.3	102%
(2019 figures)**		(+10.2%)	(+45.2)	(+26.4)						
England & Wales**	78,787	95,853	110,037	134,292	137.8	166.3	189.3	229.3	91.5	70%
(2019 figures)		(+21.6%)	(+14.8%)	(+22%)						
France	30,959	33,283			47.0	50.1				
(2018 figures)		(+7.5%)								
France			37,595	41,751			56.4	62.5		
(2019 figures)			(+12.9%)	(+11.1%)						
Germany	34,959	34,265	37,166	34,815	43.3	42.2	45.2	42.19	-1.1	
(consistent data)		(-2.0%)	(+8.5%)	(-6.7%)						
Hungary	773	1,686	600	588	7.8	17.1	6.1	6.0	-1.8	
		(+218%)	(-281%)	(-2.0%)						
Italy	4,754	4,511	4,513	5,115	7.8	7.4	7.4	8.4	0.6	8%
(2019 figures)***		(-5.3%)	(+0.04%)	(+13.3%)						
Spain	9,468	9,869			20.4	21.3				
(2018 figures)		(+4.2%)								
Spain			10,844	11,692			23.4	25.1		
(2019 figures)			(+9.8%)	(+7.8%)						
Sweden	16,910	15,237	17,681	18,874	175.3	156.3	179.5	188.83	13.5	12%
(consistent data)****		(-10.9%)	(+16.0%)	(+6.7%)						

*Belgium's historical sexual violence figures were revised downward in 2019, but rape and sexual assault were revised upward.
**In Denmark, France, England, and Wales, the 2018 figures across all three categories of police data (sexual violence, rape, and sexual assault) were revised upward in 2019. In Denmark, the increase from year 2015 to year 2016 is in connection with changes in the police registration practice.
***Italian historical sexual violence figures were revised upward from 2018 to 2019, but rape and sexual assault data were not available.
**** Data refer to reported offenses regarding rape (including attempted), sexual coercion, exploitation, abuse, etc., and sexual molestation, but exclude indecent exposure.
Sexual violence figures typically include rape and sexual assault but not sexual harassment (although Denmark, Greece, Spain, France, and Sweden do include harassment in their data).

Source: Extracted from Eurostat, http://appsso.eurostat.ec.europa.eu/nui.

Bearing in mind that differences in crime rates between countries are primarily a reflection of differences in the law and its enforcement, we should concentrate more on changes over time within a country. For the specific crimes of rape and sexual assault, there are, once again, differences in definitions from place to place. Some countries, to give just one example, distinguish between rape with physical force and rape without it. Table 8 is not telling us that one is nine times more likely to be raped in England and Wales than in Germany. It is telling us that rates of either rape or sexual assault went up between 2014 and 2017 in every European country for which data are available and that in some countries—notably Denmark and England—they went up a lot, roughly doubling in the case of Denmark.

National crime data offer a more detailed picture. In Denmark, sexual offenses remained stable or slightly decreased from 2010 to 2014, then steadily rose. Danish law expanded the definition of rape in 2013, it is true, but between 2014 and 2017, the number of rapes (based on the new definition) more than doubled.[8] All sexual offenses reported in Denmark also doubled between 2015 and 2017.

England and Wales saw a 15 percent increase in rapes in the year to March 2017 and an 8 percent increase in sexual assaults from the year before.[9] Survey data show that more than a third of UK women felt at risk of harassment on public transport and 23 percent had been victims of groping or unwanted sexual contact.[10]

France's national statistics also point to an increase in sexual violence. Between 2017 and 2018, the French Interior Ministry reported a 17 percent increase in rapes and a 20 percent increase in other forms of sexual violence, including harassment.[11] The ministry suggested that this could be explained by increasing awareness of and resistance to sexual harassment under the influence of the #MeToo movement. A French survey estimated that 3 million women had been subjected to unwanted sexual advances in public.[12] Inter-

Table 8: Rape and Sexual Assault in Europe, 2014–2017, Selected Countries (per 100,000 people)

	Rape				Sexual Assault			
	2014	2015	2016	2017	2014	2015	2016	2017
Austria*	13.68	13.18	14.17		24.91	23.43	32.46	
(consistent data)						(+6.3%)	(+38.5%)	
Belgium	28.51	28.59	29.49	30.14	33.17	31.4	34.81	33.09
(2019 figures)						(-5.6%)	(+10.8%)	(-5.2%)
Denmark	14.87	18.57	29.42	31.36	27.21	27.56	37.04	52.05
(2019 figures)						(+1.3%)	(+34.4%)	(+40.5%)
England & Wales	51.40	62.81	71.37	92.08	61.07	71.74	79.15	95.05
(2019 figures)						(+17.5%)	(+10.3%)	(+20.1%)
France	18.44	19.28			28.51	30.78		
(2018 figures)						(+7.9%)		
France			22.31	25.17			34.11	37.33
(2019 figures)							(+10.8%)	(+9.4)
Germany**	9.09	8.65	9.64	10.07	34.19	33.55	35.59	32.12
(consistent data)						(-2.0%)	(+6.1%)	(-10.8%)
Hungary	3.22	3.86	6.08	6.00	2.3	2.45		
Italy					7.00	6.58		
(2019 figures)								
Spain	2.66	2.65	2.69	2.98	17.69	18.6	16.1	17.36
(consistent data)						(+5.1%)	(-15.5%)	(+7.8%)
Sweden***	65.26	56.88	64.06	69.72	105.89	95.61	111.32	115.11
(consistent data)						(-10.7%)	(+16.4)	(+3.4%)

* The law changed for data reported in 2016. That explains the significant change from previous years.
** The recent revision of the German Penal Code with regard to rape and other sexual offenses will be considered only in the subsequent years.
*** Sexual coercion, exploitation, abuse, etc., and sexual molestation (excluding indecent exposure).
Rape: Sexual penetration without valid consent or with consent as a result of intimidation, force, fraud, coercion, threat, deception, use of drugs or alcohol, abuse of power or of a position of vulnerability, or the giving or receiving of benefits (varies by country if they include things like statutory rape, rape without force, and sexual penetration with physical force).
Sexual assault: Sexual violence not amounting to rape. It includes an unwanted sexual act, an attempt to obtain a sexual act, or contact or communication with unwanted sexual attention not amounting to rape. It also includes sexual assault with or without physical contact including drug-facilitated sexual assault, sexual assault committed against a marital partner against her/his will, sexual assault against a helpless person, unwanted groping or fondling, harassment and threat of a sexual nature.

Source: Extracted from Eurostat, http://appsso.eurostat.ec.europa.eu/nui.

pol figures for sexual assault in France—which include coercion, groping, harassment, and indecent exposure—steadily increased after 2014, from 28.5 incidents of sexual assault per 100,000 people to 32.4 per 100,000 just two years later.[13] The most recent figures from the National Observatory of Crime and Criminal Justice (Observatoire National de la Délinquance et des Réponses Pénales, or ONDRP) show that 220,000 women were sexually harassed on public transport in 2014 and 2015. The incidents ranged from kissing and flashing to groping and rape.[14]

In Germany, there was a striking increase in rape cases after 2015. The number of victims of rape and sexual coercion (*Vergewaltigung und sexueller Nötigung*) had ranged between 7,000 and 9,000 a year between 2000 and 2015, with no discernible trend. In 2016, it was 8,102, but in 2017, it was 11,444—a 41 percent increase.[15] According to German police crime statistics (see Table 10), a marked rise in criminal offenses against "sexual self-determination" was recorded between 2014 and 2018, from just under 47,000 to nearly 64,000. The biggest jumps occurred in 2017 (up 18 percent year on year) and 2018 (up 14 percent).

Finally, Sweden's crime statistics show that sex offenses against women were at relatively stable levels between 2005 and 2011 but trended upward after that and doubled between 2014 and 2016.[16] True, the definition of rape was changed after 2013 (it was changed many times, most recently in 2019), but that alone is unlikely to explain the subsequent rise. In all, 20,300 sex offenses were reported in 2016, a 12 percent increase from the year before.[17] The rate of sexual harassment also rose after 2014. In 2015, 4.7 percent of Swedes said they had been harassed; the following year it was 5.5 percent.[18] Unusually, more than half of sex offenses in Sweden in 2016 took place outdoors, suggesting a relatively low level of domestic sexual violence.[19]

THE EVIDENCE FROM SURVEYS

A major deficiency of the data on sexual violence is that official statistics generally lump all kinds of perpetrators together. They do not differentiate sexual violence perpetrated by people the victims knew from opportunistic assaults by strangers. Since the 1990s, feminists have focused on the more prevalent phenomenon of "acquaintance rape," that is, rape by a spouse, boyfriend, family member, friend, or acquaintance of the victim.[20] But we need to know how many rapes are committed by strangers. The United Kingdom estimates that 13 percent of rapes are committed by strangers; in Germany it is 20 percent and in Denmark 32 percent.[21] By way of comparison, the United States puts the figure at 22 percent. Here the disparity between official sources and self-reported data is especially striking. Sweden's National Council for Crime Prevention (Brottsförebyggande Rådet, or Brå) says that only 12 percent of rapes are by strangers but its National Safety Survey, which uses different definitions of strangers and acquaintances, puts it at 35 percent.[22] It seems clear that women are more likely to report to the police an act of sexual violence by a stranger than one by someone they know, whom they may want to protect from criminal proceedings.

Recent research in Germany provides an illuminating baseline for violence against women in Germany as it is perceived by women themselves. In 2004, the German Federal Ministry for Family Affairs, Senior Citizens, Women and Youth (Bundesministerium für Familie, Senioren, Frauen und Jugend, or BMFSFJ) published *Health, Well-Being and Personal Safety of Women in Germany: A Representative Study of Violence Against Women in Germany*. Like the WHO report, this study was based on a large ($n > 10,000$) representative sample size, standardized interviews, and written questionnaires. The main data set consisted of 10,264 interviews conducted among women aged 16 to 85 in Germany over a period from February to October 2003. Reflecting the already changing demographic composition of the nation, the study included immigrant women residing in Germany, with Russian- and Turkish-language surveys and research personnel proficient in those languages. Traditionally marginalized women such as prostitutes, prison inmates, and asylum seekers were also included in the study.

Health, Well-Being and Personal Safety classified violence against women under four headings: physical violence, sexual violence, sexual harassment, and psychological abuse. The category of physical violence is by far the broadest, encompassing acts from light slapping to battering, choking, and the use of a weapon. The category of sexual violence was deliberately limited to explicitly criminal forms of violence, including rape, attempted rape, and forms of sexual coercion involving the use or threat of physical force. The category of sexual harassment was comparatively vague. The category of psychological abuse included acts ranging from yelling to threats and "psycho-terror."[23]

Using the study's generous definition of physical violence, 37 percent of all interviewees had experienced at least one form of physical attack or sexual violence since the age of 16. Using the study's strict definition of sexual violence, 13 percent had done so. In all, 42 percent of all interviewees had experienced at least one instance of psychological violence, while 58 percent reported at least one form of sexual harassment. Two-fifths (40 percent) of respondents had experienced either physical or sexual abuse or both, though when instances of abuse were limited to current or previous partners, the proportion fell to 25 percent. Partners and former partners were blamed for approximately half of cases of physical violence and sexual abuse.[24] People unknown to the victim made up 19.5 percent of perpetrators of physical violence and 14.5 percent of sexual abusers.

These figures on prevalence were, according to the report's authors, to be seen as "conservative minimum estimates."[25] They put Germany near the top of European rankings for physical violence against women, as rates in other European countries derived from similar studies ranged from 14 to 30 percent, whereas for sexual violence Germany lay somewhere between Iceland (5 percent) and Sweden (34 percent). Needless to say, the survey data implied a much higher level of violence against women than the official German crime statistics do.

There are a number of other noteworthy points. First, as roughly half of the perpetrators were domestic partners, the location of violence against women was very often their own homes. By contrast, the authors noted, "Public places such as streets and parks, typically places where women feel afraid, were named much less often as sites of violence, at 26% for physical and 20% for sexual attacks respectively."[26] Second, prostitutes, prisoners, and female refugees ($n = 65$) were affected by physical violence and sexual assault to a noticeably higher degree than the German women in the general representative study. Among immigrant women, Turkish ($n = 397$) and Russian ($n = 862$) women reported incidents of psychological violence and sexual harassment at roughly the same rate as their native German peers. However, the frequency of physical violence was greater among both immigrant groups. Turkish women reported somewhat lower frequencies of sexual violence than did their eastern European peers.[27] On the other hand, they reported staggeringly high rates of partner physical violence, with 38 percent reporting violence, as opposed to 25 percent in the general German female population, including specific forms of physical violence at the extreme end of the spectrum, such as beatings, strangulations, and murder threats.[28] In other words, even before the great *Völkerwanderung* of 2009–2018, there was already reason to be concerned about violence against women within Germany's Muslim community.

Since the publication of *Health, Well-Being and Personal Safety* in 2004, no nationwide study of comparable scope and methodological rigor has been published. There is therefore a considerable gap that will remain until a new study using similar methods is published. The nearest comparable work was done in 2018 by Deborah F. Hellmann, Max W. Kinninger, and Sören Kliem on the basis of 2011 data from the Criminological Research Institute of Lower Saxony (Kriminologisches Forschungsinstitut Niedersachsen, or KFN).[29] The KFN data were drawn from a representative sample of German women ($n = 11,428$), albeit those aged 21 to 40 years. The authors found that the rate of violence against women reported in the 2011 KFN study was substantially lower than in the earlier BMFSFJ study: lifetime prevalence for experiencing sexual violence was 5.4 percent. They also found that "physical and sexual abuse during childhood as well as being divorced, separated, or widowed" were "the most informative constellation of risk markers, increasing the five-year prevalence rate of experienced sexual violence victimizations up to 17.0%."[30]

In short, like all European countries, Germany was hardly free from violence against women prior to the major influx of migrants and asylum seekers around 2015. The crucial question is: How far did that influx lead to an increase in the incidence of violence against women?

CORRELATION OR CAUSATION?

The claim that immigration has driven up violent crime—and especially crimes of a sexual nature—has repeatedly been made by right-wing populists in recent years. We also know that Russian agencies engaged in "information warfare" sought to bolster that claim: there were around three hundred Russian-sourced Instagram posts featuring the word "rapefugee" in 2016.[31] As a 2018 report in *Der Spiegel* made clear, however, websites such as Rapefugees.net and Truth24.net systematically exaggerate the responsibility of migrants for sex crimes.[32] In about one-third of the 291 cases the magazine investigated from the year 2016—95 cases, to be precise— the suspects or perpetrators were indeed refugees. In a further third (84) of the cases, the assailants were unidentified. The remainder were foreigners with unresolved residency status, EU citizens, or, in 22 cases, German nationals. The Rapefugees.net site listed 205 of the 291 incidents as cases of rape, whereas rape was suspected in only 59 of the cases. In 47 cases, the authorities determined that the incident did not meet the criteria to be considered a criminal offense. Eighteen refugees were convicted on charges of rape, and courts also convicted (or upheld rulings against) 51 refugees for sexual abuse or sexual assault in more than half of the cases. An additional 18 foreigners were convicted who were not refugees but whose residency status remains unresolved, including Turks, Afghans, Serbs, an Azerbaijani, and a Ukrainian tourist. A number of the crimes for which refugees were convicted took place in refugee camps and were perpetrated against other refugees.[33]

Yet the fact that populist websites exaggerate a problem does not mean that the problem is wholly imaginary. Alternative für Deutschland deputy leader Beatrix von Storch claimed that, in 2017, 447 killings and murders were committed by illegal migrants in Germany. According to the German Interior Ministry, to be sure, illegal migrants committed or attempted to commit just 27 murders in 2017. But when all asylum seekers and refugees were counted, the number of homicide victims was indeed 447.

We have seen that there was a surge in illegal border crossings and asylum applications in Europe, especially in the years 2015 and 2016, and we have seen that the majority of people who entered were young and male and that relatively few of them subsequently left Europe, even if their asylum applications were rejected. We have also seen that there was an increase in crimes of sexual violence in a number of the countries to which a significant proportion of the migrants went. But is there a causal connection between the increase in migration and the increase in sex crime? Or is this just alt-right propaganda?

In most European countries, police statistics do not report the migration status, ethnicity, or religion of criminals. We may know their age and occasionally details about their state of mental health, but their motivations tend not to make it into official data, either. However, in the countries that do collect data on migration status— and, crucially, make this information available—we do see evidence of a causal relationship between increased migration and increased sexual violence.

Austria's Federal Ministry of the Interior does publish the migration status of suspects in its crime statistics. Since 2009, sex offenses increased by 11.8 percent. Of the 936 rape cases reported in 2018, more than half of the suspects (55 percent) were not Austrian citizens. In 2017, asylum seekers were suspects in 11 percent of all reported rapes and sexual harassment cases in Austria, despite making up less than 1 percent of the total population.[34] The more general category of "foreigners"—which includes other non-Austrian citizens, who make up around 19 percent of Austria's population—were suspects in almost a third of rape and sexual harassment cases.[35]

Denmark's national statistics agency, Statistics Denmark, breaks down convictions according to whether perpetrators were of non-Western origin or descent. The evidence is striking: "non-Western" immigrants and their descendants account for a high proportion of convictions for sex offenses—around two-fifths of rape convictions and between a quarter and a third of groping convictions—even though they make up less than 13 percent of the population.[36]

**Table 9: Share of Sex Offenses in Denmark Perpetrated by
"Non-Western Immigrants and Their Descendants"**

	2014	2015	2016	2017	2018
% of rape convictions: non-Western immigrants and their descendants	47%	32%	42%	45%	39%
% of groping convictions: non-Western immigrants and their descendants	21%	26%	28%	35%	18%
% of all sexual offenses: non-Western immigrants and their descendants	14%	14%	16%	21%	11%

Source: "STRAFNA4: Persons Guilty in Crimes Aged 15–79 Years by Type of Offence and Country of Origin," Statistics Denmark, https://www.statbank.dk/statbank5a/SelectVarVal /Define.asp?MainTable=STRAFNA4&PLanguage=1&PXSId=0&wsid=cflist.

In neighboring Sweden, data are also collected on the migration status of criminals. However, they have not been released to the public for more than a decade. One set of data released in 1996 found that those with a migrant background were 4.5 times more likely to commit rape than native Swedes.[37] The most recent official study, carried out in 2005, found that immigrants were five times more likely to be sex-crime suspects than native Swedes.[38] When pressed on the issue in 2015, Sweden's minister of justice refused to release updated data.[39] Adding to the opacity in Sweden, court records are not systematically published, so information about convictions can be obtained only by requesting individual case records at each courthouse. The Swedish National Council for Crime Prevention has recently updated the migration status of *victims* of sex crimes. In its 2017 Swedish Crime Survey, people born in Sweden to two migrant parents were significantly more likely to be victims of sex crimes (4.4 percent) than those with only one migrant parent (1.5 percent) or two native Swedes as parents (2.5 percent). We shall return to the phenomenon of "migrant-on-migrant" crime below. In late 2019, a privately financed study of sex-crime perpetrators was published by the sociologist Göran Adamson, based on data obtained from Brå. It concluded that the overrepresentation in sex crimes for first-generation migrants had fallen, although it was fairly stable if second-generation migrants and unregistered foreigners were included. For rape, the immigrant share of perpetrators appeared to fall, though that may have reflected changes in the legal definition of rape. In response to public pressure, Brå has announced that it will compile and publish new data in 2021.

Frustrated by this lack of transparency about the perpetrators of sex crimes, one Swedish newspaper did track down the 58 individual gang rape cases heard in Swedish courts between 2012 and 2017.[40] It found that, of the 112 males convicted, 70 percent were under 20 years of age, three-quarters had been born overseas, and 41 percent of those were asylum seekers.[41] Swedish public television aired a documentary on the immigrant share of convicted offenders of sex crimes based on court rulings between 2012 and 2017. In all, 58 percent were foreign-born. Of 129 convicted for assault rape, 110 were foreign-born. Of 94 gang rapists, 70 were born outside Europe.[42]

After a spate of assaults at the "We Are Sthlm" music festival in 2015, the head of events of the Stockholm city administration admitted, "In the cases where we were able to apprehend suspects, they were with a foreign background, newly arrived refugees aged 17–20, who had come to Sweden without their families."[43] Piecing together reports of harassment from the 2015 festival, the Swedish newspaper *Expressen* revealed that fifteen of the sixteen perpetrators were of Middle Eastern, South Asian, or African background.[44]

In France, the Interior Ministry acknowledges that foreigners are overrepresented among sex offenders. Though they account for only 7 percent of the population, they are suspects in 14 percent of sex crimes. In 2018, 9 percent of those convicted of sexual offenses were of African origin.[45]

Figures from the German Federal Criminal Police Office (Bundeskriminalamt, or BKA) show that, since 2014, the proportion of non-German suspects in the crime statistics has risen to over 30 percent, when one excludes crimes related to immigration processing and administrative irregularities.[46] The share of non-Germans among suspects in cases of sexual violence rose from 18 percent in 2014 to 29 percent in 2018. The new category of "rape, sexual coercion and sexual assault in especially serious cases including resulting in death" was introduced in 2016. That year and

Table 10: Sexual Crimes in Germany, Most Serious Categories, and Non-German Perpetrators, 2014–2018

offence or offence category	2014		2015		2016		2017		2018	
	recorded cases	non-German suspects (%)	recorded cases	non-German suspects (%)	recorded cases	non-German suspects (%)	recorded cases	non-German suspects (%)	recorded cases	non-Germ suspects (%)
sexual murder	18	5.9	13	9.1	9	57.1	8	9.1	8	20.0
offences against sexual self-determination in total	46,982	18.4	46,081	20.5	47,401	25.9	56,047	28.7	63,782	29.4
rape, sexual coercion, and sexual assault in especially serious cases, including resulting in death				.	7,919	38.8	11,282	37.0	9,234	38.5
sexual assault and sexual coercion, especially serious cases									1,119	34.6
sexual assault, sexual coercion, and rape resulting in death									9	37.5
sexual harassment							9,619	45.9	13,742	43.5
offences from within groups									47	66.7
sexual abuse	22,422	15.2	21,860	18.0	22,674	23.2	20,601	22.8	21,454	23.2

Source: Extracted from BKA, https://www.bka.de/EN/CurrentInformation/PoliceCrimeStatistics/police crimestatistics_node.html.

in the succeeding two years, non-Germans were suspects in nearly two-fifths of all cases. In 2017 and 2018, more than two-fifths of the suspects in the new category of sexual harassment cases were non-Germans. And although the number of sexual abuse cases remained constant at around 22,000 a year, the share of non-German suspects rose from 15 percent in 2014 to 23 percent in 2016, 2017, and 2018.

True, the term "non-German" covers a wide range of categories, including (for example) nationals of other EU member states. But we can be more precise. In Germany's police crime statistics, the category *Zuwanderer* (immigrant) was used until 2016 to identify suspects who had applied for asylum, failed asylum seekers, and illegal residents. This definition was expanded in 2017 to include successful asylum seekers, who had previously been counted under a more general category. Other official German statistics do not use the term *Zuwanderer*; rather, they use the category *Schutzsuchende* (person seeking protection) to indicate asylum seekers, whether their application has been decided upon, they have temporary protection, or they have been directed to leave the country. This means that the figures before and after 2017 are not strictly comparable with the most recent figures, as the migration status of asylum applicants may have changed. For my purposes, however, the status of their asylum claim does not matter. All that matters is that the proportion of those suspected or convicted of sex crimes who were asylum seekers has clearly risen. Though they made up only 1 or 2 percent of the German population from 2015 onward, asylum seekers were disproportionately responsible for the sex crimes included in the statistics, making up nearly 12 percent of suspects by 2018.

When it comes to particularly grievous sex crimes, such as rapes, the figures are even higher, with 16.3 percent perpetrated by *Zuwanderer* in 2018 (see Table 12).

Table 11: *Zuwanderer* as a Proportion of Sex Offenders in Germany, 2013–2018

	2013	2014	2015	2016	2017	2018
Number (percentage) of solved sex crimes (including attempts) committed by *Zuwanderer* (defined as asylum seekers, failed asylum seekers, and illegal residents)*	599 (1.6%)	949 (2.6%)	1,683 (4.6%)	3,404 (9.1%)	5,258 (11.9%)	6,046 (11.8%)
Number (percentage) of *Zuwanderer* suspects in sex crimes*	N/A	879 (2.7%)	1,548 (4.8%)	3,329 (9.9%)	4,852 (12.2%)	5,626 (12.4%)
Schutzsuchende as percentage of German population**	0.76%	0.92%	1.28%	1.94%	2.04%	

Note: In 2017, the definition of an immigrant in these statistics was changed to include successful asylum seekers as well. At that time the definition of sex offenses was broadened to include sexual harassment.

Sources:

*PKS, "Polizeiliche Kriminalstatistik 2017 and 2018 Ausgewählte Zahlen in Überblick."

**"Schutzsuchende nach Schutzstatus," Statistisches Bundesamt, "Schutzsuchende Ergebnisse des Ausländerzentralregisters," Fachserie 1, Reihe 2.4, 28.

Table 12: *Zuwanderer* as a Proportion of Serious Sex Offenders in Germany, 2016–2018

	2016	2017	2018
Cases of rape, sexual coercion, and assault in exceptionally severe cases with a deadly outcome	7,919	11,282	9,234
Suspects who were *Zuwanderer*	N/A	1,495 (13.3%)	1,316 (14.3%)

Source: PKS, "Polizeiliche Kriminalstatistik 2018 Ausgewählte Zahlen in Überblick," 14, category 111000, and PKS reports from earlier years.

A report titled *Bundeslagebild Kriminalität im Kontext von Zuwanderung 2017* ("National Situation of Crime in the Context of Immigration 2017") was released by Germany's Federal Criminal Police

Office in 2017. It found that across all categories of crime, asylum seekers made up 8.5 percent of suspects.[47] The figure was slightly higher for sex crimes, where *Zuwanderer* were suspects in 9 percent of cases.[48] In Table 13, we can see the nationalities of *Zuwanderer* suspects over the years. As is immediately apparent, Syria, Afghanistan, and Iraq account for a very large proportion of the total.

Table 13: Nationalities of *Zuwanderer* Suspected in Sex Crimes in Germany, 2014–2018

	2014	2015	2016	2017	2018
Syria	47	171	716	1,203	1,271
Afghanistan	95	189	679	1,031	1,180
Iraq	57	97	313	475	572
Pakistan	57	101	172	228	209
Eritrea			77	157	203
Iran		37	159	172	178
Nigeria			64	119	173
Somalia			69	125	162
Morocco		51	110	125	115
Algeria		60	120		
Gambia				78	102
Kosovo	20				
Albania	8				
Serbia	48				

Source: "Polizeiliche Kriminalstatistik 2017—Bedeutung, Inhalt, Aussagekraft," Bundeskriminalamt, May 8, 2018, https://www.bka.de/DE/AktuelleInformationen /StatistikenLagebilder/PolizeilicheKriminalstatistik/PKS2017/pks2017_node.html.

Regional data tell a similar story. The Bavarian interior minister, Joachim Herrmann, announced shortly before the German federal election of September 2017 that the number of rapes and serious sexual abuses in Bavaria had risen by 48 percent during the first half of the year. In all, 126 of the 685 crimes could be attributed to immigrants (including successful asylum seekers), 91 percent more than in the same period the previous year.[49] In Lower Saxony—the fourth highest receiver of asylum seekers among German states—a 10.4 percent increase in violent crime occurred between 2014 and 2016, according to a BMFSFJ-commissioned study published by the Zurich University of Applied Sciences. This reversed a decline in violent crime dating back to 2007. In the same period, the number of registered refugees in Lower Saxony had more than doubled. By the end of 2016, around 750,000 of the state's 8 million residents were not German citizens, and about 170,000 of them had applied for asylum. Between 2014 and 2016, the number of rape cases in Lower Saxony involving asylum seekers as suspects quintupled, whereas the number of rape suspects from other segments of the population fell: German suspects by 11.5 percent and non-Germans (i.e., other foreigners who were not claiming asylum) by 13.5 percent. More than 92 percent of the increase in violent crime was attributable to a small but violent minority of the newcomers, with young (14- to 30-year-old) men from Morocco, Algeria, and Tunisia notably over-represented among the perpetrators. (Afghans, Iraqis, and Syrians were underrepresented, the authors hypothesized, because their chances of being granted asylum were perceived to be higher.) In nine out of ten murders and three-quarters of cases of grievous bodily harm, the victims were other migrants. But in 70 percent of robberies and 58.6 percent of rape and sexual assault cases, the victims were German.[50]

The last statistic is perhaps the most striking. However, the most recent scholarly investigation of the subject—published in 2019 under the auspices of the Institute of Labor Economics (Institut zur Zukunft der Arbeit, or IZA)—casts doubt on the relationship between the migration surge and increased sexual violence. "Our results," wrote Yue Huang and Michael Kvasnicka, "do not support the view that Germans were victimized in greater numbers by refugees as

measured by their rate of victimization in crimes with refugee suspects."[51] Huang and Kvasnicka focused on "actual rates of victimization of natives by refugees or foreigners," filtering out crimes by
and against foreigners, crimes by and against natives, and crimes by
natives against foreigners. They based their study on county-level
statistics on the regional distribution of refugees; their gender
composition, age structure, and type of accommodation, based on
the statistics for asylum seekers' benefits; and on special data extracts
from the Police Crime Statistics of the Federal Criminal Police Office. Decentralized accommodation of refugees tended to reduce the
crime rate, they observed, while refugee sex ratios exerted no effect.
They did "not find . . . any evidence for a systematic link between
the scale of refugee immigration . . . and the risk of Germans to become victims of a crime in which refugees are suspects."[52] In short,
"refugee inflows do not exert a statistically significant effect on the
victimization rate."[53] That central result, they concluded, "holds true
not only for total crimes with victim recording in police crime statistics, but also for sub-categories of such crimes, such as robbery (economic crimes), bodily injury (violent crimes), and rape and sexual
coercion (sex crimes)."[54]

Yet there are some important difficulties with Huang and Kvasnicka's approach. As they acknowledged, "If one allows for non-
linearities . . . a one standard deviation increase in refugee inflows
raises the county-level crime rate by . . . 1.67% from the level it
had in 2014, and the county-level victimization rate by . . . an increase of 2.27% on its 2014 value."[55] The principal weakness of their
study, however, is that it focuses largely on the changes between
2014 and 2015, whereas (as we have seen) the real jump in sexual
violence came in 2017. To be precise, their key dependent variable
was "the change from 2014 to 2015 in the county-level number of
Germans victimized in crimes with at least one refugee suspect."[56]

They asserted that on the basis of their regressions, "there is . . . no indication that Germans were put at higher risk of victimization by refugees when refugees settled in greater numbers in their county of residence in the wake of the 2015 refugee crisis." But the refugee crisis only *began* in the second half of 2015—to be precise, in late August, when Chancellor Angela Merkel opened the German border to refugees (see chapter 7). The changes in the crime rate between 2014 and 2015 therefore tell us almost nothing about what happened "in the wake of the 2015 refugee crisis."[57] Even the addition of 2016 data in the final pages of the paper does not satisfactorily address the evidence that 2017 and 2018 appear to have been the peak years of violent crimes—and especially sexual crimes—by refugees.

The joke originates in Victorian England that there are "lies, damned lies, and statistics." As we have seen, the statistics on immigration, crime—especially sexual crime—and the role of immigrants in crime are too fraught with difficulty for any argument about policy to rest solely on them. Nevertheless, we can see here a prima facie case for the view that the surge of immigration into Europe around the year 2015 led to a significant increase in sexual violence in the countries that accommodated the largest numbers of migrants. But why was this? What was going on?

Chapter 4

TAHARRUSH GAMEA
(THE RAPE GAME)
COMES TO EUROPE

In the pages that follow, I set out brief summaries of some of the individual cases of sexual assault and harassment I have come across. These were all reported locally by police and sometimes in the media; most of the cases, though by no means all of them, ended up in court proceedings and sentences. These individual tragedies are intended as a sample rather than as a definitive list of sexual assaults and harassment. In fact, the full extent of this problem is something we are unlikely ever to know, as I shall explain further on.

I proceed country by country. I begin in Germany, where the largest number of asylum seekers were received between 2015 and 2018, and then turn to Italy, France, Sweden, Austria, Hungary, and Denmark.

I or my research assistants traveled to each of these countries in the course of researching this book to see for ourselves how far published accounts could be corroborated. We also experienced the phenomenon of harassment for ourselves. On one trip to Munich, our translator was groped by a tall African man as she crossed the street. The man hit her upper thigh and squeezed it while walking past. She said it felt proprietary rather than sexual. He had let her know that walking in that street was something she could do only on his terms. She came away more or less unscathed, but that was not the case for the unlucky women whose experiences are chronicled in what follows. It makes for harrowing reading, but I urge you not to turn away, as many have.

A SELECTION OF CASES

In 2016, a 45-year-old woman jogging in a Munich park was attacked from behind. Her assailant strangled her so tightly with her headband that he lacerated her neck and she collapsed unconscious. He raped her, then left her in a bush. By a fluke spot check at the attacker's workplace, police identified his DNA. This evidence also implicated him in a rape the year before of a 19-year-old woman jogging in nearby Rosenheim. The rapist was a 28-year-old asylum seeker known in court as Emrah T. Initially claiming to be Syrian, Emrah T. was in fact a Kurdish Turk who had applied for asylum in Germany in 2015, along with his pregnant wife and young son.[1]

The following September 2017, another woman jogging near a Rosenheim lake was knocked over and molested. This time the woman was 23 years of age and her assailant a 34-year-old Nigerian who had been hunting joggers since the day before. In court it was revealed that the man had committed previous offenses, and despite the rejection of his asylum application, he was living in asylum-seeker accommodation nearby. He was sentenced to five years in prison.

Earlier in July, a 39-year-old woman walking near a riverside path in Garmisch-Partenkirchen, near the Austrian border, was attacked from behind and sexually assaulted by a 20-year-old Iraqi asylum seeker.[2]

In separate incidents in 2017, two German women were followed as they left after visiting acquaintances at local asylum-seeker facilities. The first was a 43-year-old woman in Bamberg.[3] She was beaten and raped by a 17-year-old Somali resident of the facility who followed her to a nearby pedestrian underpass.[4] The second victim was a 16-year-old girl who was followed from an asylum-seeker center in Höhenkirchen-Siegertsbrunn near Munich. As she walked to a nearby train station, she was raped by three Afghan men between 17 and 27 years of age, one of them a rejected asylum applicant.[5]

The opportunistic nature of these assaults is striking. Four Eritrean asylum seekers raped a 56-year-old woman in Dessau that same year. She was collecting recyclable bottles behind a school near where the men were drinking. They lured her with the promise of giving her their bottles to recycle, but instead they smashed one of the bottles, cut her face with it, and gang-raped her. During their trial the men showed no remorse toward their victim, who was hospitalized for days. Two of the perpetrators sought a reduced sentence by claiming to be underage, but the court proved their culpability as adults over 18 years.

The same seemingly spontaneous style of assault was reported in January 2019 by the Hamburg police. A 29-year-old woman was sexually assaulted by a "black African man" in his 20s near a church on a Sunday morning. The man grabbed his victim from behind, pushed her to the ground between two parked cars, and assaulted her.[6]

In August 2018, a 19-year-old Somali broke into a retirement home in Halle, Central Germany. He sexually assaulted one of the residents, a 74-year-old woman, simply "because he wanted sex." He threw his victim onto the bed and beat and choked her, pulling his trousers down in order to rape her, but she managed to call for help. The man was arrested days later for a separate burglary and received a seven-year juvenile sentence.[7]

Eighteen-year-old Franziska W. left a Freiburg nightclub in October

2018 with a Syrian asylum seeker she had met inside.[8] What she did not know was that her new acquaintance was wanted by police for drug offenses and as a suspect in a gang rape. Majid H. was 21 at the time. It appears that he drugged the girl, dragged her behind a row of hedges, and raped her. He then phoned his friends, inviting them to join him. According to the court prosecutor, Majid told them there was a woman outside "who can be fucked." Over several hours, eleven men—eight Syrians, one Iraqi, one Algerian, and one German—between 19 and 29 years of age either raped or provided cover for the rapists.[9] Of the eleven, eight were sentenced to prison terms of between three and four years, two received suspended sentences of four and six months, and one was acquitted.

The German media tend to report such crimes in isolation, with each attack a single atomized moment of tragic violence. Having watched this issue for years, however, I do not believe these crimes are solitary one-offs. Consider the worst (and therefore most reported) cases: the murders.

Four young German women—two of them mere girls—were murdered by asylum seekers between 2016 and 2018. The first case was the brutal rape and murder of a 19-year-old medical student, Maria Ladenburger, by Hussein Khavari. As Maria was riding home from a party in Freiburg in 2016, Khavari pushed her off her bicycle, bit her, choked her, and raped her, leaving her on a riverbank, where she drowned. When he had arrived in Germany the year before, Khavari had claimed to be an unaccompanied minor from Afghanistan; he had been placed with a German host family and been sent to school. Investigations later revealed that he was in his 20s and more likely from Iran. He had previously been convicted of attempted murder in Greece before arriving in Germany but had not been jailed. Giving evidence at his German trial, Greek police noted that he had been unremorseful. Replying to their question about his having pushed a woman off a cliff, Khavari replied, "That's just a woman."[10] He received a fifteen-year prison sentence.[11]

Susanna Maria Feldman's body was found in a wooded area in Mainz near Frankfurt in June 2018. The 14-year-old girl had been raped and strangled. The man convicted of her murder was Ali Bashar, a 20-year-old Iraqi living in an asylum-seeker center near where she was found. Bashar's family had already had their application for asylum rejected, as they were judged to be economic migrants, not refugees. Yet the German authorities had not deported them. At Bashar's sentencing, the judge noted that Bashar had grown up in northern Iraq in a family with strict rules about gender, and once he had entered Germany, "he then had the opportunity to access women, including sexual contacts, and deliberately sought after very young, still insecure girls."[12] Echoing Khavari's story, Bashar was suspected of previous crimes, including armed robbery and the gang rape of an 11-year-old at the asylum center where he was living. His alleged accomplice was a 35-year-old Turkish man also living in nearby asylum-seeker accommodation.

Six months before Susanna Feldman's murder, a 15-year-old Afghan asylum seeker named Abdul D. stabbed his ex-girlfriend Mia V. to death in a drugstore. The murder took place in a small town called Kandel near the French border. Because Abdul was a minor, his court case was closed to the public and he received a juvenile sentence of eight years and six months in prison.

In 2015, Ahmad S. arrived in Germany, claiming to be an underage Afghan seeking asylum. His application was denied, but he stayed on in an asylum center in Flensburg near Germany's northern border. In March 2018, he stabbed to death his 17-year-old ex-girlfriend Mireille for starting a new relationship. The judge who sentenced Ahmad to life in prison for the murder commented that "he no longer recognized Mireille as an independent personality; in his eyes she was his."[13] During the trial, expert analysis put his age at 29 years, and police gave evidence that he was an Iranian crane driver and had been implicated in, but acquitted of, another murder.

These are the extreme cases, of course. But the striking thing is that, like the cases of rape I previously described, they have undeniable similarities. The locations may be different, but the circumstances of the men involved are the same: arriving in Germany among the migrant wave, claiming asylum in order to acquire residency, having a history of violent crime, and eluding the attempts of the authorities to enforce the law and remove them from the country. Now they reside in German prisons, except one who committed suicide in his cell.

Though Germany took in the largest numbers during the "migrant crisis," its neighbors in the borderless Schengen Area experienced the same phenomenon of newly arrived young men preying on unsuspecting women, although in Italy the perpetrators tend to be recently arrived from Africa rather than from the Middle East.

In March 2017, a 27-year-old Nigerian living in an asylum reception center in Bagnoli near Naples sexually assaulted a 41-year-old woman. In 2018, a 20-year-old Somali, who had just received a subsidiary protection permit from the Italian authorities, sexually assaulted a 68-year-old woman sunbathing at a beach.[14]

Reports of gang rape by migrants have also surfaced in Italy. In August 2017, four immigrants from West Africa, Nigeria, and Morocco aged between 15 and 20 were convicted for gang-raping a Polish tourist after beating up her husband on a beach at Rimini, on Italy's Adriatic coast. Four months later, a 16-year-old girl was raped by two Moroccan migrants in an alley in a village near Avezzano, about fifty miles from Rome.[15] The following year, 16-year-old Desirée Mariottini was gang-raped and killed near Rome's Termini station. Two Senegalese and one Nigerian man were arrested.[16]

Following the migrant wave in France, there were similar cases. In 2016, a 38-year-old Pashtun interpreter who was translating for a journalist was raped at knifepoint in the notorious Calais refugee camp known as "the Jungle" by a group of Afghan men.[17] In 2017, a woman walking home from work at a Calais hotel was dragged into a grove by a 22-year-old Eritrean migrant who threatened her with a knife and raped her.[18] In July 2018, a 28-year-old Moroccan migrant—whose asylum application had previously been rejected in both Germany and the Netherlands—was convicted of sexually assaulting an 11-year-old girl in a grocery store in Croisilles, France.[19] He received six months in prison. In 2017, a 26-year-old Sudanese migrant sexually assaulted two 14-year-old girls in broad daylight on a street in Sin-le-Noble near Lille.[20]

Among many similar cases in Sweden, two stand out for the feeble responses of the authorities. One involved a 17-year-old Somali named Mohomed who followed a 13-year-old girl into a shopping center bathroom in Borlänge.[21] Despite her screams, he pushed her down onto a changing table and raped her. Days later he called her a "fat, disgusting whore" and threatened to "cut her neck" and "jump on her head" if she reported him to police. He had made similar threats to another girl he had previously assaulted, spitting on her and threatening to kill her. In June 2018, Mohomed was convicted for numerous offenses, including theft, abusive behavior, sexual harassment, and child rape. However, the Swedish court found "no special reason" to imprison him as he was a minor, sentencing him to perform just 150 hours of community service and to pay modest compensation to his victims. In their report the police commented that Mohomed had bragged about being above the law.

The case of Arif Moradi, though less violent, also illustrates the leniency with which migrant men convicted of sex crimes are treated in Sweden. An Afghani, Moradi entered Sweden in 2014, one of

7,044 other unaccompanied minors hoping to receive asylum that year. His application was refused in 2016, and the Swedish government ordered him to leave the country. While waiting to appeal this decision, Moradi attended a Christian camp in Söderköping, where he sexually assaulted a 14-year-old girl. The case was heard in Norrköping District Court, where it was revealed that the camp leaders had permitted him to sleep in the same room as young girls. He had molested one of the campers and despite her protests had continued pawing her for more than thirty minutes, until she had run out of the room crying. According to the court report, the camp leaders had not taken the girl's complaint seriously, but Moradi was nevertheless convicted of sexual harassment and sentenced to twenty-one days in prison and a fine of SEK 7,000 ($800). Four months after his conviction, Moradi's asylum appeal was heard by the Swedish Migration Court. The court granted him a three-year residence permit and refugee status based partly on his conversion to Christianity. Even though the court was informed of his conviction for assaulting a 14-year-old, it decided not to take that into consideration on his residency status.

Following the news of his successful appeal, Arif's Swedish friends congratulated him with adoring posts and love heart emojis on Facebook; they have since been removed, but I screenshotted them for posterity. They read:

"Welcome back to us"

"Hi, welcome back to freedom Arif 🖤 🌱 ☺ 🦵"

"Finest, finest role model Moradi Arif 🖤"

"Fantastic! Welcome to us 🖤"

"Beloved friend 🖤🖤🖤🖤"

"Not a day too early"

"Finally 🖤🖤🖤"

One final Swedish case illustrates how slowly the wheels of European justice can turn. In August 2015, a Swedish woman was raped by three men as she left a pub near Strängnäs. Two perpetrators living in a nearby refugee shelter were convicted that December. But only in November 2019 was the third man arrested.[22]

Austrian women, too, have suffered. In September 2015, a 72-year-old woman walking her dog near a river in Schwechat on the outskirts of Vienna was thrown to the ground and raped.[23] In 2018, a 19-year-old Afghan named Ziyaoddin O., who had arrived seeking asylum three years before, lured a 20-year-old Albanian woman into a forest, where he raped her and threatened to kill her. After he was charged with sexual assault, it was revealed that, like so many others, he had a prior sex conviction.[24]

Danube Island is a popular Viennese leisure spot, with numerous restaurants and places to sit and enjoy the river. A Vienna police spokesperson reported that a mother pushing a baby carriage there in 2017 was grabbed around the neck by a 17-year-old Afghan asylum seeker. He threw her to the ground and got on top of her, but as he tried to kiss her, she fended him off by biting him on the nose. The police eventually caught him with the help of CCTV and sniffer dogs.[25]

"They do not respect the same things we do," said one lawyer defending an Afghan man for the rape of a Turkish student in an Austrian park in 2016.[26] Among the "things" the perpetrators clearly do not respect are women's rights to physical safety and sexual self-determination.

Similar stories can be found in other European countries, too. For the sake of brevity, I will mention just two more cases. In Hungary, an 18-year-old Afghan was charged with three sexual assaults in 2018, including the rape of a woman in a fast-food restaurant bathroom on a Sunday morning.[27] Also in 2018, a 14-year-old girl was followed into a shopping center bathroom in Esbjerg in Denmark and raped by a 17-year-old Afghan. He later claimed that the girl had initiated the attack and that "Satan" had led him on.[28]

A TYPOLOGY OF SEXUAL VIOLENCE

The above is just a selection from the much longer list of sexual assaults I have compiled. Let me offer some tentative generalizations, based on my entire sample.

First, there is a wide range in the gravity of the offenses. Some of the incidents I have studied were at the lower end of the scale of sexual violence: calling out obscenities and sexual slurs, ogling, wolf whistling, and shouting insults. Such behavior is offensive, but only in some countries is it illegal. The next tier of harassment included following victims, stalking, and ignoring their attempts to evade or rebuff them. Some perpetrators exposed themselves to unsuspecting women but did not attempt to touch them. Some cases were outright sexual assault: the men touched women's breasts and genitals, put hands down their underwear, and forcibly groped them. Other cases involved more violent acts, including slapping, punching, pulling hair, strangling, kicking, and using brute force to immobilize the victims. As we have seen in the previous section, some cases progressed to rape of a victim, some were gang rapes, and, at the furthest end of the scale, a few women were murdered after they had been raped.

You may well ask how, if at all, these cases differ from cases of harassment, assault, rape, and sexual murder in all societies, including those with few immigrants. So I have also looked for commonalities among the perpetrators.

Aside from being migrants from Muslim-majority countries, the perpetrators were mostly quite young men. Some acted alone, while others hunted in pairs or coordinated groups. Many perpetrators were later found to have committed lower-level crimes before, such as theft, drug and driving offenses, or other assaults. A striking difference between these cases and conventional cases of sexual violence is that the perpetrators were mainly "strangers," in that they did not have a prior relationship with their victims or were only loosely acquainted. In most instances of violence against women, as we have seen, the accused has an existing relationship with his victim.

Another striking feature of the data is the lack of any pattern in the characteristics of the victims: their ages, their looks, their other attributes. Girls as young as 12 have been assaulted, as have teenagers, adult women, and mothers with babies in baby carriages, but also elderly women in their 70s and 80s. Women and girls are attacked while wearing party dresses, tracksuits and athletic shoes, swimwear, school uniforms, winter coats, and hijabs; their attire does not appear to be a determinant. It is not accurate to say that the men targeted white or European women, as some victims in my sample were themselves immigrants or descended from earlier generations of migrants. They appear to have been much more opportunistic and to have targeted any woman who looked like easy prey: alone, drunk, incapacitated, or in some other way vulnerable.

Nor is there any clear pattern in the timing of the attacks, which took place at various hours of the day and night. More tended to occur in the summer, when women are outside more often, but winter weather proved to be no obstacle for some perpetrators. I also tried classifying the locations of attacks, but here, too, there is not much of a pattern. Sexual assaults happened in large cities and small towns, on trains and buses, in transit stations, on streets and road underpasses, in hedges and groves, between parked cars, in schools, in shopping centers, in parks, in recreation areas, along riversides and jogging tracks, in bathrooms, behind buildings, at concerts, in retirement homes and asylum-seeker centers, and in workplaces. The one obvious common factor is that nearly all the attacks occurred in public places and not in women's homes. But there was no typical public place where attacks were more likely to occur.

Chapter 5

HOW WOMEN'S RIGHTS ARE BEING ERODED

THE RISE OF SEXUAL HARASSMENT

The various sex crimes described in the previous chapter are, clearly, the worst manifestations of an attitude held by some men that women are available for their sexual satisfaction whether they consent or not. This attitude can also express itself in ways that have tended not to be criminalized in most countries until quite recently, if at all.

Now, I am *not* claiming that sexual harassment is a vice unique to immigrants from Muslim-majority countries. On the contrary, part of my reason for writing this book was to make sense of the changing attitudes of women toward sexual harassment, which have come to be associated around the world with the #MeToo movement. For me, it is a puzzle that in the United States and other Western countries, countless pages and copious airtime have been devoted to the misdeeds of a few hundred prominent figures in the entertainment industry, politics, education, and finance but much less has been written about the far more numerous acts of rape, assault, and harassment perpetrated by recent migrants to Europe.

A key question is how far changing female attitudes are behind the increase in cases of sexual harassment and assault. In the United

Kingdom, a 2018 government inquiry into sexual harassment sought anonymous submissions from the public. British women detailed their experiences of unwelcome interactions with men. Their accounts made it clear that harassment occurs throughout British society. A mother of two hit the nail on the head in her submission:

> . . . in my experience, I could be wearing scruffy clothes and still be attacked. It's not the clothes or the makeup; it's the fact that I am very obviously female in what is perceived as male spaces. . . . It's not even about attracting a sexual partner; it never is, because the men are so disrespectful and aggressive. It's about asserting power and dominance over what they see as the "weaker" sex, it feeds egos and a sense of entitlement and it helps them if women are dehumanized into sexual objects, created for the gratification of men.[1]

This kind of open discussion of sexual harassment has been one of the most invigorating social changes of the past decade. It may in part be explained by a relatively new cultural milieu in which women feel empowered to come forward and speak out. Social media provides platforms where women can share their experiences, though their unverified format can lead to doubt being cast on the veracity of some of the women's claims. Another reason we are hearing more about sexual harassment is that, for the first time in history, a critical mass of women are in positions of authority and are willing to take such complaints seriously—though, as we shall see, female politicians have played their part in underestimating the consequences to women of the great *Völkerwanderung*.

Frenchwomen, too, report high levels of sexual harassment in the streets and on public transit. Parisian women complain of men rubbing their genitals against them on the Métro and following them in

supermarkets to grope them.[2] A 2018 case in the 19th Arrondissement of Paris was captured on video. Marie Laguerre told a man to
shut up in response to his sexual comments and suggestive hissing
as she walked by him. Outraged, he retaliated by throwing an ashtray into her face. Marie shared the video on social media, and police caught the man, who was later tried. Yet although the story was
covered by media globally, few reported that the man was a Tunisian
immigrant who had lived in Paris since his childhood.[3]

Following the mass sexual harassment of women in German cities on New Year's Eve 2015 (see below), the German government
introduced new laws against sexual harassment and group offenses.[4]
Before then, such behavior was not outlawed. New laws against sexual harassment and street harassment were also passed in Belgium
in 2014 and in France in 2017. But was that because harassment had
not previously happened on such a scale? Or because there had been
a sea change in women's attitudes?

In Sweden, certainly, there is a heightened awareness of sexual
coercion in the workplace by male superiors, which seems attributable to the #MeToo movement. But Swedish authorities were unprepared for harassment in the workplace by males in positions of
bureaucratic inferiority. In a 2017 report by the Swedish Migration
Agency (Migrationsverket), female employees reported 15 cases of
sexual harassment by asylum seekers whose applications they were
administering. Staff reported 279 threats by applicants in the year to
August 2016.[5] In some cases, female workers were targeted as they
left the office, then harassed and threatened with rape or murder on
their evening commute.[6] Librarians, too, were targeted by "unruly"
young migrant men, who viewed them as symbols of the Swedish
state.[7]

As noted above, the targets of harassment by migrants are not always white women. Though a minority among the migrants, female

asylum seekers have also been subjected to harassment and sexual assault.[8] Girls as young as 9 have reported being groped, hissed at, and sexually harassed in the kitchens and hallways and even in their beds in hostels for refugees. Fearing retaliation or because of distrust of authorities, however, few asylum-seeker women report their mistreatment.[9]

Looking back on my own time living in an asylum shelter in Lunteren, Holland, in 1992, I recall one chilling experience. A Somali man tried to attack me while I was riding a bicycle in the complex. He said I was on a bicycle with my legs parted, so I was "asking for it." The woman in charge of the shelter asked him if she was also asking for it, as she, too, like most Dutch women, rode a bicycle every day. He answered unequivocally, "Yes." That was almost thirty years ago.

SILVESTERNACHT

Sexual violence in public places—especially that orchestrated by gangs of men—had come to be seen as an aberration in most of Europe until very recently. The rates of rape and sexual assault had been falling for decades. It was widely acknowledged that most sexual violence occurred within established relationships. Having grown up in societies where violence was rare and gender equality more advanced than at any other time in history, Europeans were unprepared for what was coming.

A reckoning came in the German city of Cologne on New Year's Eve, December 31, 2015. Around fifteen hundred men, mostly newly arrived asylum seekers of Arab and North African backgrounds, converged in the area between Cologne Central Station and the city's famed Gothic cathedral to see in the new year on what Germans call *Silvesternacht*, after the fourth-century pope

Saint Sylvester. The men were drunk, unruly, and—as soon became clear—beyond the control of the city's police. They mobbed together to entrap women in the square, sexually harassing and assaulting any they could get their hands on, often stealing their wallets and mobile phones in the process. In the following months, 661 women reported being victims of sexual attacks that night.[10]

Alice Schwarzer, one of Germany's leading feminists and a Cologne local, investigated the events of that evening, interviewing many of the women who had been attacked. They described being separated from their husbands and male friends and pushed inside "hell circles" of young migrant men. The men groped women and girls, no matter their age, appearance, or circumstances, grabbing their breasts and between their legs. One woman described several men trying to insert their fingers into her vagina. The only thing blocking them was the thick winter tights she was wearing. Some women were held by swarms of men for thirty minutes of continual assault. When they were eventually spat out of the crowd, some reported, the police had deliberately looked away. Many women reported ongoing trauma and fear many months after the event. Yet those who have spoken about what happened to them in public forums have been labeled "racist" for pointing out the ethnicity or migration status of their perpetrators and now often use pseudonyms when speaking about their experiences.[11]

The response of the authorities was bewildering. On New Year's Day, the Cologne police issued a statement that the evening had been "largely peaceful." Only an outpouring of reports on social media left the authorities—and the mainstream media—no choice but to discuss the attacks publicly and release information on their level and severity, as well as the background of the perpetrators. Within a week, the original police statement was retracted and the police chief was dismissed. Leaks later revealed that the police had been unprepared to cope with the sheer scale of sexual violence that evening and had been incapable of enforcing the law.

It later emerged that similar, if smaller, attacks by Arab and North African migrants had occurred on the same night in Hamburg, Stuttgart, Düsseldorf, and Bielefeld.[12] In the words of Chancellor Angela Merkel (more about her later), "The events of New Year's Eve have dramatically exposed the challenge we're facing, revealing a new facet that we haven't yet seen."[13] This "new facet" was less surprising for some. Asked by Alice Schwarzer whether there had been any warning signs, "Helin" (a pseudonym adopted by a woman of Turkish descent from Stuttgart) explained that the atmosphere had changed months before New Year's Eve. She had noticed groups of Arab and African men hanging around the streets, often drunk. They regularly harassed her and other women nearby, suggestively calling out and trying to touch them. She soon became wary of walking the streets alone.

I find it difficult to accept the claims by German authorities and police that they were "taken by surprise" with regard to these attacks, for the tactics used by the young men were not new to Germany. Just seven months before, in May 2015, German women and girls had reported being encircled by groups of migrant men, groped, and robbed at a Berlin street festival known as "Karneval der Kulturen."[14] That same month, girls had been subjected to the same treatment at a music festival in Darmstadt, where they had been encircled by groups of around ten men and groped. Police later apprehended three suspects, including two Pakistani asylum seekers.[15] Two months later, in July 2015, police in Bremen had arrested six suspects, "predominantly refugees of Afghan origin," for the same form of group sexual harassment at an open-air festival called "Breminale."[16] In August of the same year, just north of the German border on the Danish island of Langeland, police had arrested three asylum seekers for groping nine women and girls, including a 16-year-old, at a festival. In short, by December 2015, there had been enough of such attacks at public events to put German police on notice.

Soon after the Cologne case, the Swedish police admitted to a cover-up of their own. A mob of fifty young male asylum seekers, mainly Afghans and Moroccans according to police, had sexually assaulted women in the same way at the "We Are Sthlm" summer festival in 2015. Police had found that they did not have the resources to stop them returning and reoffending during the event. Police issued a statement that the event had seen "relatively few crimes" and hid the fact that thirty-eight sex offenses had been reported on girls as young as 14. Six months later, fearing a backlash like the one that had followed the events in Cologne, Swedish police came clean.[17] Revealingly, Södermalm police chief Peter Ågren said that one reason for the cover-up was to avoid provoking racism or "play into the hands of the Swedish Democrats," Sweden's right-wing populist party.[18]

We shall return in Part II to this remarkably pervasive mentality of "see no evil, hear no evil, speak no evil" within Europe's forces of law and order and explore its profoundly adverse unintended consequences.

THE CHANGING STREET

I am not the only woman who worries that the hard-won gains women have made in liberal societies are being eroded by immigrants from places that do not grant such rights to women. Another is Nicola Frank, a 39-year-old editor and mother living in Oldenburg in northwestern Germany. When I spoke to Nicola, she was sitting side by side with her husband, Stefan, in their neat living room, with their young son playing on the floor.[19] They appeared to me to be quintessentially modern Europeans: the husband sharing in child care and supportive of his wife's career, Nicola in a blue sweater and floral shirt, her auburn hair pulled up into a chignon. I asked her what had changed in her life.

"As a young girl," she told me, "I never worried about feeling harassed or unsafe in my surroundings. For me, this started to change in 2015. It is a recent phenomenon that women are not safe here during the day. It's a problem all over the world that women are not safe at certain times of night. But here during the daylight, being harassed and receiving disrespectful sexual remarks didn't happen to me before. All the German cities I know have changed. Two guys harassed me while I was visiting Bonn, my hometown, this summer. They were very young, certainly under twenty-five, and clearly immigrants. In this situation I would normally show a clear response—perhaps even an aggressive one—but I was with my two-year-old son, I didn't want to provoke them further, so I just gave them the finger. They laughed and moved on to harass other women walking near us."

"Are all men behaving in this way now in Germany?" I asked.

Nicola's face became strained; she was visibly uncomfortable answering. "Sadly, no. I have to say for me it is a consequence of migration. It's hard to articulate. It's a problem with culture and the attitudes of Arab men to women."

Her face creased further, and she wriggled in her seat, even more uncomfortable. "Until a few years ago, I was a real leftist here in Germany. My political view was that we should always be tolerant and respect other cultures. In high school, I worked for antiracist groups."

She rubbed her brow. "I didn't dare to come forward and talk about these things with my leftist friends. I didn't want to be called a racist.

"I don't speak about these things much. I have friends who are left-ist types, and they won't discuss it. For instance, I go to a toddlers' and parents' group here in Oldenburg, and one day I made a remark about a very gruesome murder that took place at the end of Ramadan in May. There was a fight between two men downtown, one Arab and one Kurd. The fight was in front of many people, including children. The Arab man suddenly pulled a knife and slit the Kurd's neck and chest. He died on the street. At the play group I remarked, 'This isn't something that would have happened here ten years ago.' And the other parents responded that it always happens and isn't a problem caused by migration and culture. They were uneasy about the conversation, so I backed down and we've since avoided the subject of migration and violence in our town."

Like her friends, Nicola seemed uncomfortable articulating the migration status of the men harassing her. I got the sense she almost wished they were white Germans so that the problem would be easier to discuss.

I asked, "Has your daily routine changed because of this?"

Nicola nodded. "Now when I have to do shopping downtown, I make detours. I postpone morning walks with my son for an hour to avoid walking in the dark; this is in winter and summer. I no longer walk through the big city park. At certain times of the day, I don't buy in some supermarkets in certain neighborhoods. I used to enjoy walking along the canal, but after an unpleasant incident a few months ago, I stopped going there."

"What happened?"

"It's a similar story. Two young Arab-looking men addressed me in broken German with the words 'You cunt.' It was a Sunday morning, I was walking with a stroller, and they continued following me for some time. There were joggers, cyclists, and other pedestrians around. I wasn't the only woman who had to endure that treatment. . . .

It's obvious that these men aren't afraid of anything and don't have any respect.

"On another occasion, I was sitting in a bus, it was nine o'clock on a workday. I witnessed the misbehavior of two drunk Arab-looking young men. When they had gotten off the bus, there was a discussion among us passengers and the bus driver, who had not dared to throw them out. He explained that if he had done so, they might file a complaint with his employer for 'racist' behavior. I left the bus with another female passenger; she was trembling as she lit a cigarette and said one of the men sat behind her and had played with her hair all the time during the drive."

Throughout our conversation, Nicola was matter-of-fact. She didn't appear angry or volatile. She wasn't railing to close the borders. In a sad way, she was simply describing the sudden way her life had changed.

She said, "I'm on my guard and have had to change or drop many habits. I always have pepper spray in my pocket. I didn't used to walk through Oldenburg like this, and I have known the city for twenty years."

As we have seen, Lower Saxony, where Nicola lives, is one of the rare regions in Europe where the link between immigration and crime has been rigorously investigated.[20] Her account confirms a key conclusion of the report regarding the "violence-legitimizing masculinity norms" the migrants have brought with them from their native lands.

For women living in this climate, being alone in public has become dangerous. I am not surprised by Nicola's observations. Shrinking from men, being on guard, avoiding drawing attention to oneself: this is the daily life of women in Africa and the Middle East. As girls growing up in Mogadishu and Nairobi, my sister and I covered ourselves with hijabs to conceal ourselves from public view. Today, women in Europe must consider what manner of dress will best deflect the attention of the increasing numbers of men on the prowl.

The Swedish journalist Paulina Neuding, whose reporting has bravely addressed the negative social consequences of immigration, explained to me, "People are changing their lives here in Sweden. There have been numerous reports of group assaults at public swimming pools, and many of them have had to employ security guards and bilingual 'hosts,' or put up cameras. The biggest swimming pool in Stockholm even introduced different time slots in its Jacuzzi after reports of assaults. But those are confined spaces. What does this do to women's freedom of movement in places where there are no 'hosts' or cameras? I used to walk down to the forest or bike with friends to swim in the lake where I grew up in a Stockholm suburb. But would you let a teenage girl go to the lake by herself, when swimming pools have to take such drastic measures in response to assaults?"[21] In one of her articles, she exposed the naiveté of Swedish authorities' response to the receding presence of women in the Stockholm suburb of Rinkeby. In the belief that it would encourage women to return to the town square, the local council had painted some benches in pink, intending to reserve them for women's use. The benches had soon been removed after it turned out that only men sat on them.

"THE STREET DOESN'T BELONG TO YOU. THAT'S HOW IT FEELS. I DON'T FEEL FREE."[22]

Women's complaints about an increase in sexual harassment are not confined to Germany and Sweden. In 2017, the La Chapelle–Pajol district of Paris became a contested "no-go zone" when a petition titled "Women: A Threatened Species in the Heart of Paris" received

20,000 signatures following an influx of migrants from the "Calais Jungle." [23] Local women reported that La Chapelle–Pajol had been transformed in the space of just a year. Speaking to the French newspaper *Le Parisien*, 38-year-old Aurélie said she no longer recognized the neighborhood she had lived in for fifteen years:

> The simple act of traveling has become problematic. The café, down from my home, a once-nice bistro, has turned into an all-male haunt and is always packed. I get my share of remarks when I pass by, especially since they drink a lot. A few days ago, the mere fact of going to my window triggered a flood of insults, and I had to lock myself in my apartment. Some time ago, I took the Boulevard de la Chapelle from Stalingrad, even late at night. . . . It is unthinkable today. [24]

The feeling that women are no longer safe on some Parisian streets was captured on film by Aziza Sayah and Nadia Remadna, the founder of Brigade des Mères, an organization that works with mothers to prevent radicalization of children. [25] Using a hidden camera, the two women recorded an exchange in Seine-Saint-Denis, a migrant-heavy suburb northeast of Paris. The streets and cafés were completely devoid of women. On entering a café, the two women were asked why they had entered:

VOICE-OVER: In this bar of men, they are not very welcoming.
PROPRIETOR: It is best to wait outside.
NADIA: Why?
PROPRIETOR: This place is for men.
NADIA: It's no problem. We live in a world where there are men and women. Are you crazy?
PROPRIETOR: No, you are.

VOICE-OVER: The bartender didn't feel like discussing it. The other men were shocked to see women.

NADIA: We will be discreet in a corner.

MAN IN CAFÉ: This is a place for guys.

MAN IN CAFÉ: We are in Sevran, not in Paris.

NADIA: Even in Sevran, this is France!

MAN IN CAFÉ: You are in the ninety-third here [a reference to the administrative number of Seine-Saint-Denis]!

NADIA: So what?

MAN IN CAFÉ: You are not in Paris! The mentality is different! It's like back home.

Indeed, it is "like back home." I could not believe that women would be unwelcome on the streets of a Paris suburb. Their experience sounded so much like mine—but not my experience of Europe—of my life in Nairobi or Mogadishu decades before. The man in the Parisian café was right: the 93rd may physically be in France, but in this respect it is in North Africa.

Parts of Brussels, too, have earned the reputation of being no-go zones for women. The sidewalk cafés along the streets of Koekelberg, not far from Molenbeek, are lined with men from Turkey and Morocco, sitting, relaxed, chatting to one another. They are unperturbed by the traffic and noisy buses going past. But their faces turn from puffing on cigarettes and sipping tea as any woman strides past. A number of them smirk, all eyes trained on the female pedestrian. In the nearby parks, young African men play soccer and the occasional Muslim woman, veiled in black from head to toe, hurries along the cobblestoned sidewalks carrying groceries. A few head scarf–wearing mothers walk by with young children. Otherwise, for the most part, women are conspicuous by their absence.

In Sofie Peeters's film *Femme de la Rue* (2012), a hidden camera follows her walking through the city center of Brussels dressed in a short-sleeved, knee-length dress and flat-soled leather boots.[26] To European eyes she is dressed unremarkably. But she is repeatedly leered at by men walking past. We see her reading on a park bench while eight young men stare intently at her as though a polar bear had just landed in the park. Sofie is not making a spectacle of herself; she is simply reading a book. As she walks along the city streets, she is approached by man after man, their comments ranging from sleazy compliments to insults and threats: "You're pretty, miss." "How are you?" "Are we going for a drink together? At my place, of course. Or a hotel. In bed. You know, no fuss." "You are sexy. You make me hot." As she passes a café with groups of men sitting outside, they make noises like cracking a whip and exaggerated kissing sounds. Someone calls out, "Nice ass!" and the other men laugh. She continues walking. One guy says "Slut" to her. Another casually calls over his shoulder as he walks past, "Whore." That is what the men in her neighborhood are seeing; to them, a woman who is not covered from head to toe is a "slut" who is "asking for it." Their perception applies to all women, not just the women in their own community. They do not excuse the appearance of European women on cultural grounds.

In the film, Sofie's female neighbors share their strategies for minimizing the harassment. They avoid eye contact, they change their clothes so as not to wear skirts outside, they find new routes to shops and transit, they listen to music on digital devices to block out the comments. At the end of the film, one of Sofie's female neighbors moves out because she is sick each day, as she leaves her home, of weathering sexist remarks such as "If I could, I would put it in your ass!"

"Once the film aired on TV, it was like a bomb went off," said Sofie when I spoke to her in 2018. "The guys in my documentary were mainly Moroccan, Tunisian, and Algerian, because Brussels has a very multicultural scene. Some perceived the film to be racist because we see only these guys doing the harassment."[27] But Sofie emphasized that her motivations were not anti-immigrant but pro–women's rights. She explained that she had simply filmed what was happening on the streets in her neighborhood, rather than trying to target a particular group. "I'm not racist at all. If anything, the #MeToo movement has shown that sexual harassment is everywhere. It is not exclusively limited to one culture, social class, or background. But that doesn't mean that culture can't play any role in stereotypical beliefs or sexist behavior." Eventually, she, too, moved out of Brussels. She was fed up with the sexual harassment that was consuming her life and the threats she was getting for having made the film.

There is nothing mysterious about the behavior of the men Sofie captured on film. As we shall see, they come from a gender-segregated society that abhors the free movement of women in public, and they see no reason to alter their views simply because they now live in western Europe. In response to her film, Hicham Chaib, a now-deceased spokesman for a Salafist group calling itself Sharia4Belgium, released a video saying that Sofie "walks the streets half-naked and dresses like a cheap prostitute. She has painted her face like a clown. She has done all this to attract the attention of men."[28] Chaib did not condemn the harassment or express shame for the men's behavior; he blamed Sofie. Though his politics proved to be extreme—he left to fight for ISIS in Syria the following year—his attitude to women is typical of many men from these parts of the world.

RUNNING THE GAUNTLET ON PUBLIC TRANSIT

When I lived in Holland, I would try to make myself physically shrink when Somali or other African men sat next to me on the train. They

behaved in a proprietary manner, as though I were theirs to be subjected to lewd comments. Now I see that it is not just Somali girls
editing themselves out of city streets. European women, too, are facing increased rates of sexual violence and harassment on public
transit and are adopting coping mechanisms similar to those used
by women in Africa and the Middle East.

With their free Wi-Fi and central heating, many European train
stations became makeshift migrant shelters during the peak influx
in 2015–2016. In 2016, Linz station in northern Austria was dubbed
a no-go zone by the tabloid press and required additional patrols by
riot police. In a letter to the regional authorities, a local father wrote,
"My daughter is 16 and is terrified when she has to come through
Linz train station in the evening."[29] Two years later, the migrants
were dispersed and with them the makeshift refugee services that
had been installed during the peak months of the "migrant crisis."
There are no gangs of listless men hassling bystanders. A couple of
young African guys smoke cigarettes in the park opposite the station
entrance, but they keep to themselves, quietly observing the passing
commuters. When asked, the rather bored-looking security guards
say there are fewer migrants and less trouble than before.

The same cannot be said of German train stations. In 2018, parents are still escorting their daughters to and from Sigmaringen station to avoid harassment by young male asylum seekers living in a
refugee reception center in the town.[30] The Muslim reformer and
women's activist Seyran Ateş has noticed that women and girls avoid
certain subway lines in Berlin's districts. Young women have told her
that they are reluctant to take the subway lines alone where many
young Muslim men are traveling. Sometimes they take detours because there are too many nuisances. Sexual assaults take place almost daily in certain subway lines.[31] She says that the situation for
women is getting worse. Rather than policing the trains after a spate

of sex attacks, in 2016, one German train company, Mitteldeutsche Regiobahn, introduced women-only carriages on its Leipzig-to-Chemnitz service.[32]

German public transit is losing its reputation for safety, even at fun fairs. In an almost comical incident, police in the northern German town of Steinfurt reported a group of ten immigrants harassing and groping teenage girls as they drove bumper cars at the village fair in March 2018.[33] It is farcical that even a dodgem ride is no longer safe for women in Germany.

Telltale signs of the speed of social deterioration are the small changes being made by many women. A 2017 Stanford study of "activity inequality" that analyzed smartphone data from more than 700,000 people found that women walk less than men in all 111 countries studied.[34] Though there are multiple reasons why people choose not to walk, the gender imbalance here is striking. Unsurprisingly, Arab countries had the largest disparities between the average distances that men and women walked, but the gender gap has recently become more pronounced in Europe. A 2014 report by the European Union Agency for Fundamental Rights found that almost half the 42,000 women surveyed had restricted their movement out of fear of gender-based violence.[35] The OECD's Better Life Index for 2017 reported that around a quarter of German and Swedish women do not feel safe walking home alone at night.[36] Street harassment is not a new phenomenon, of course; native-born European men are also capable of it. But a change in their behavior simply cannot explain the speed with which women have begun to feel threatened in the streets of Europe and to change their behavior in response.

Sociologists have a name to describe the strategies women use to avoid sexual predators in public: they call it "safety work."[37] But this term seems to me much too anodyne to convey the insidiousness of what is happening.

Under these circumstances, it is not surprising that many European women are taking matters into their own hands. After the migrant crisis reached its peak in late 2015, sales of firearms spiked in Austria and Germany. The number of permits for handguns doubled in Graz and quadrupled in Vienna.[38] Other entrepreneurs are capitalizing on women's newfound concern for personal safety. "No-go zone" and harassment map apps are now available. My researcher was surprised to find pepper spray for sale in Berlin pharmacies in 2018, sitting on shelves between ponytail holders and women's magazines, even though carrying pepper spray for self-defense requires a license in Germany.[39]

Perhaps the most bizarre manifestation of this new security consciousness is the appearance of anti-rape underwear and jogging shorts. The start-up AR Wear is crowdfunding the development of women's underpants that can be locked at the waist and legs.[40] Following the mass sexual assaults in Cologne in 2015—and after she herself narrowly escaped a gang rape while jogging—the German entrepreneur Sandra Seilz created "Safe Shorts," which can be bought for upward of €89.[41] Safe Shorts are padlocked onto the body with cut-resistant cords and feature a siren that activates if the pants are tampered with. Alternatively, for around the same price, women can adorn themselves with a Dutch-developed bracelet that emits an odor like that of a skunk when activated.

But that is not the only thing that stinks about this story.

Chapter 6

IS THE LAW AN ASS?

There is no shortage of people who want to deny the reality of what is happening in Europe. Part of the reason for this is, as we have seen, that sexual assault is often underreported by victims, wherever and whenever it happens. But it is also true that it is politically inconvenient for most European governments to acknowledge the existence of this particular crisis. Thus, much evidence remains wrapped in reams of red tape and buried under piles of bureaucratic paperwork. I encountered both these obstacles in my research for this book.

Estimates by official sources, including police statisticians, are that 80 to 90 percent of sexual offenses are not reported to police in Sweden.[1] In Germany, around 90 percent of sexual assaults are not reported.[2] The British Home Office estimates that 82 percent of sexual assaults and 80 percent of more severe rapes in the United Kingdom are not reported.[3] In Canada 90 percent and in Australia 81 percent of sexual offenses never make it to the police.[4] Of the cases that are reported, a majority are dropped somewhere during the legal process prior to conviction.[5] From this we can assume that the official data on sexual violence vastly understate the problem. Even in the most generous estimates, the quantity of sexual violence reported is only around one-fifth of what is taking place.

This may seem scandalous to anyone unfamiliar with the topic, but the reasons for such dramatic underreporting are myriad. One of the greatest deterrents for women to report an offense is that the reporting is often pointless. Of the 10 to 20 percent of sex crimes that are reported to police, most do not lead to a conviction. Police struggle to identify and arrest sex predators. Victims, too, often have trouble identifying their assailants. In Sweden in 2017, nearly two-fifths (39 percent) of reported rape cases were dropped without a suspect being identified, and in the United Kingdom the following year, police arrested suspects in only 43 percent of rape cases.[6]

Even with relatively recent legislation criminalizing street sexual harassment, the obstacles to reporting and prosecuting harassment are significant. No woman I know will want to linger near a man who just called her a whore or groped her bottom. Even if she reports him to the nearest police station, how helpful will the police be? And how likely is it that the police will immediately dash out the door to apprehend the offender? Police resourcing is another significant factor. Swedish police whistle-blowers admit that the rising volumes of homicide and other violent crimes have drawn resources away from investigating rapes.[7]

It is no wonder, then, that the majority of women do not report being assaulted. One telling example is a Frenchwoman who attended World Cup celebrations in Nantes in 2018. When she complained to police at the event that a man had masturbated against her leg, they said they were present only in case of terror attacks. She gave up on pressing charges, knowing that even willing police would not catch the perpetrator.[8]

Of the tiny proportion of cases that are reported to police with a suspect who is identified, many are not brought to court. Sometimes the police decide that the victim's claim is too weak to hold up in court, so they do not pursue it further.[9] Investigations in the United States in the early 2000s found that police sidelined difficult and time-consuming rape cases to improve their arrest records.[10] Even when prosecutions go ahead, convictions are hard to secure without physical evidence and reliable witness statements. Most sexual assaults happen away from onlookers. In the absence of witnesses, the victim's word is pitted against that of the perpetrator. Victims have been known to withdraw charges for fear of reprisals or out of pain and frustration with invasive legal processes that ask them repeatedly to recount the details of what they suffered. The number of unsolved sexual crimes is therefore depressingly high.

Altogether, 1,304 people filed a criminal complaint after the events of Silvesternacht in Cologne, among them 661 women who had been victims of sex crimes. By the spring of 2019, however, the Cologne Prosecutor's Office had investigated 290 persons and indicted fifty-two, mainly Algerians (seventeen), Moroccans (sixteen), and Iraqis (seven). Six out of forty-three cases were dropped because the whereabouts of the suspected perpetrator could not be determined. There were thirty-two convictions, mostly for theft. Only three men were convicted of sex crimes such as sexual assault, of which two received only suspended sentences. The three—an Iraqi, an Algerian, and a Libyan—were convicted only because they had taken selfies of themselves and their victims.

The fraction of cases that make it to court are typically decided by a judge (trial by jury is not part of continental criminal law systems). One such case in 2016 involved a 24-year-old German woman and a 35-year-old Moroccan man known in court reports as "Adil B." The woman and her two friends had been drinking at Hamburg's Christmas market before continuing to the Bar 99 Cent in the St. Pauli district of the city. At the bar, Adil B. made advances toward the group, touching them and at one point kissing the woman. She then turned her back on him, and all three ignored him. Later he followed the woman into the ladies' bathroom at the back of the bar. She told the court that he had locked her into a stall and raped her. She had cried and told him more than once she did not want to have sex with him.

As soon as she could escape, she had run to her friends with her pants down and said she had been forced to have sex. Sitting on the floor of the bar crying, her makeup running down her face, the woman had been completely distraught. Upon reporting the incident, she had identified Adil B. to police at the club, gone through a physical examination at a hospital, and recorded her video testimony.

When the matter was heard at Hamburg Regional Court six months later, however, the judge found that the woman had not shown sufficient signs of resistance and that therefore the sex had been consensual. Earlier in 2016, the German Parliament had tightened up the country's sexual assault laws. The new definition was based on a "no means no" model rather than requiring the victim to be coerced (Section 177 of the *Strafgesetzbuch*). But the new definition did not help the young woman. Nor did the fact that Adil B. was found to have been illegally residing in Germany after his asylum application had been rejected eight months earlier. Rather, he was acquitted and awarded compensation for the six months he had spent in custody waiting for trial. Cases like this one do eventually make it into official statistics, but not as instances of rape, as Adil B. was found not guilty.

CONCERNS ABOUT PRIVACY

In western European countries, the government collects enormous quantities of data on all aspects of their populations because the central government is more involved in providing public services than it is in the United States. Through multiple programs for housing, health, employment, education, and citizenship, governments collect abundant data on migrant social outcomes. However, they draw the line at using this information where crime is concerned. Data privacy provisions are invoked to prevent crime data from being dis-aggregated by migration status or ethnicity. The bureaucrats who prevent the public release of this data fear that the public they serve will conflate all asylum seekers with the minority who break the law. They doubt the population's ability to understand the difference be-tween criminals and law-abiding immigrants.

This creates problems, not least for social scientists. The Dutch researcher Ruud Koopmans found his empirical work being selec-tively edited when it was reported in the media or cited by policy makers. "My research findings became politicized," he told me from his office in downtown Berlin. "The research was no longer simply information to help solve social problems, the research itself became the problem."[11] Even though Koopmans is himself a Social Demo-crat, his work on the relationship between cultural background and integration outcomes was dismissed as "far right." Like many others, Koopmans found that the only acceptable collection and use of data on ethnicity or cultural background was to log incidents of discrimi-nation against minorities.[12] In my discussions with other researchers in Germany, Sweden, the Netherlands, and France, the same con-cern repeatedly arose.

The political scientist Valerie Hudson was appalled by the unwill-ingness of the Swedish government to look at its migration data in relation to sexual violence. "[This] has the potential to undo all of the progress we have made for women," she told me. "Women are no less important than immigrants, so why can't we ask these questions? It comes across as Alice in Wonderland when a society refuses to let its researchers answer a question with their own data."[13]

Falling down a rabbit hole was exactly what my researchers and I felt like we were doing when we tried to obtain crime data in Germany in 2018. With no publicly available case information for regional and lower criminal court cases, accessing court records on sex offenses was extremely difficult.[14] After many months of effort simply to acquire the numbering system for the cases we were looking for, unhelpful court clerks and media offices refused to make the corresponding court reports available. We enlisted the help of working journalists to make the requests on our behalf, but they, too, found their requests to German court press offices ignored or denied. We also applied for court records formally through academic channels, again without any response from the gatekeepers of the German justice system.

Increasingly frustrated, we attempted to track down a live case then going through the courts in Bavaria. A news story had reported that a Turkish asylum seeker known as "Emrah T." was being tried that day in a Munich district court for the brutal rape in late 2016 of a 45-year-old woman who had been jogging in a park.[15] Unfortunately for us, court lists are not published online in advance in Bavarian courts as they are in other countries. The only way to find out which court the case would be heard in was to apply in person at the courthouse that day.

My research team visited three district courts in Munich that morning to find the list identifying which courtroom the Emrah T. case would be heard in. Defensive press officers tried to divert us at every turn, and the police officers on duty could not help. In Munich's main court building, the imposing Justizpalast, the court clerk held a binder up to the glass window of his booth near the building entrance. That was the day's court list. There was only one copy. We awkwardly scanned the thirty or so pages of the printout through the thick security glass as lawyers and police flowed through the entrance next to us. No luck. The same in the second court building. We tried a third district court, the one in which more criminal cases were being held that day. Once through the airport-style security, we asked to speak to a court clerk to find a case listing, to no avail.

The only interlocutor available was a policeman, who pointed us to a dark corner of the lobby where a plastic binder was tied with string to a desk. Inside was a single printout of the court lists for the day. We joined a short line of others scanning through the pages for names, case numbers, and courtroom schedules. The printout listed the names of defendants, the category of crime they were being tried for, and the time of their hearing. The cases involving juvenile defendants were listed but redacted. Their hearings and the transcripts of those proceedings are never open to the public. At the end of each day, the printed court lists are destroyed. Emrah T. was not on any of the lists we were able to see.

We decided to sit in the public gallery of two courtrooms that afternoon. One case was a rape and the other an assault. The rape case proceedings were closed to the public while the witness was present, so we could learn little about the circumstances. The assault case did permit members of the public into the gallery. The defendant was a 32-year-old asylum seeker. Wearing jeans, a brightly patterned T-shirt, and flashy sneakers, he handed over his green immigration card as identification to the judge. Speaking through an Arabic interpreter, the defendant explained that he had been in Germany for three years but still required language assistance. The prosecutor told the court that the defendant had been banned from a Munich nightclub in 2015 following an incident with three women and three men. When the defendant had tried to gain access to the club again in 2017, the complainant had called the police, and while he was on the phone, the defendant had allegedly struck him on the head from behind. Just outside the courtroom before the case was called, we had noticed the complainant and defendant talking, and halfway through the hearing the complainant informed the court that he was dropping the charges. The prosecutor shot him a frustrated glance. The case was dismissed.

We spoke with one of the two other members of the public sitting in the gallery after the case, a tall, blond Bavarian lady in her late 60s. As a retiree, she told us, she enjoyed watching court cases and had seen a lot of them. We asked if the nature of the cases she watched had changed at all in the last three years. She immediately answered, "Yes." "There are a lot of asylum seekers and refugees, like the guy today, in court for assault," she said. She had noticed immigrants being tried for a whole list of crimes ranging from drugs and theft to violence and sexual assault. We asked the stony-faced court police officer the same question. He replied, "There are a lot of Arabic names on the court lists these days."

We retired to a café overlooking the courthouse entrance to continue our search for information, asking press officers and the court reporters at local newspapers to try to pin down where the Emrah T. case was being heard. We never found out. While seated at the café, we noticed temporary barricades being installed as a large scrum of journalists assembled with television cameras and recording devices. But the case they were reporting on was a murder trial with a neo-Nazi defendant. The case had an entire website devoted to it with articles translated into English and Turkish, encouraging members of the public to attend and watch the trial. No doubt a racially motivated murder deserved such coverage, but the contrast to the unrecorded and inaccessible sexual assault trial was striking.

Germans are renowned for being protective of their data and privacy. The country's internet privacy laws are among the tightest of any democracy's. My experience suggests that the German justice system is set up in the same way to protect privacy at any cost—including the public good. Eventually, I did manage to get access to the case records for some of the sexual assaults I was looking for, but only because they were sent to me months later by a sympathetic official inside the prosecutor's office in another jurisdiction. The official mentioned that it was sometimes impossible even for prosecutors to get access to court reports both within their state and in other jurisdictions.

What follows is based on the records of a rape case in Hamburg, where in 2018, 44 percent of suspects in sex-offense cases were foreigners.[16] Although it makes for distressing reading, the circumstances and the perpetrator's views are revealing.

LIGHTS OUT IN HAMBURG

Like many thousands of others, Ali D. borrowed money in his late 20s and set out to find work in the West. He left his wife and young children in Iraq and made his way via Greece to apply for asylum in Germany in September 2015. However, with only four years of primary schooling in Iraq, the 30-year-old struggled to find work in Germany.

On a Saturday night in November 2016, Ali D. joined two people from his temporary accommodation to drink and socialize with a group in Hamburg's central square, the Rathausmarkt. One of the group was a 13-year-old girl. They drank vodka and partied until the early hours. After 2:00 a.m., members of the group peeled off, and Ali D. walked to the Jungfernstieg train station with a few of them. Security cameras at the train station recorded him dragging the 13-year-old girl into a dark room—a temporary structure built as part of construction works taking place at the station. The low ceiling and angled corridors blocked visibility between the platform and passageways.

Ali D. pushed the girl to the floor, which was dusty and dirty. The court report spells out what happened next:

> The accused tried to kiss the joint plaintiff, and she turned her head away. He grabbed her breasts under her clothing,

pulled down his and her trousers and underpants, pulled her legs apart with force, pulled his penis out of his underpants, and penetrated vaginally into the body of the plaintiff, who had no previous sexual experience and, in particular, never had sexual intercourse before. The accused had unprotected intercourse with the joint plaintiff until ejaculation, while the plaintiff cried and screamed in pain.[17]

After the ordeal the girl sought help, and a police officer found her crying and trembling at the station. A gynecological examination confirmed that Ali D.'s sperm was present in her vagina. Six months later, the girl still suffered physical pain and struggled to interact with men, including her male schoolteachers. Ali D. fled Germany to avoid arrest, but the Hungarian authorities apprehended him and sent him back across the border to face trial.

In court Ali D. admitted to the rape but explained that it had been a spontaneous "knee-jerk reaction." He knew that the girl did not consent so covered her mouth to stop her calling for help. Ali D. said he was not concerned about the girl's virginity, as he was drunk. He was convicted and sentenced to three and a half years in prison. His sentence was reduced because he had been intoxicated on the night of the attack and his victim could not face him in court and therefore did not testify. After his release, Ali D. said he planned to work in Germany to earn money and return to Iraq.

So much had to go right to bring this incident to prosecution: security cameras, witnesses, a brave plaintiff, an accurate rape kit, foreign police, and a dedicated prosecution. It is rare for all these elements to come together. To repeat: most rapes do not make it to prosecution, so we do not read about them, and even when they do come to court, especially in Germany, such cases are effectively kept secret by an all but impenetrable bureaucracy.

PART II

The European Establishment Abrogates Responsibility for Women's Safety

Chapter 7

ACTIONS HAVE CONSEQUENCES

Never in history have women been more powerful than they are now. Sixty-three of the world's countries have had at least one female head of government or state in the past half century. At the peak of the refugee crisis (2015–2016), there were seventeen female presidents and prime ministers around the world. It is one of the rich ironies of early-twenty-first-century history that the single decision that has done the most harm to European women in my lifetime was made by a woman.

The origins of that decision can be traced back to a German television talk show in July 2015, when the German chancellor Angela Merkel reduced a young Palestinian refugee, Reem Sawhil, to tears by explaining that her family might have to face deportation. "You know that in the Palestinian refugee camps in Lebanon there are thousands and thousands," Merkel told her. "If we now say, 'You can all come.' . . . We just can't manage that" (*"Das konnen wir auch nicht schaffen"*). In an extraordinary scene, she crossed the room to comfort the weeping girl.[1]

Within six weeks, Merkel had opened the German border and was declaring "We can manage that" (*"Wir schaffen das"*). Arguing that the immigration crisis represented a bigger challenge for Germany than the eurozone financial crisis, on August 21, 2015, she suspended the Dublin Regulation requiring refugees to apply for asylum at their first point of entry to the European Union. On September 4, she announced that there was to be no upper limit on the number of asylum seekers who would be allowed to come to Germany. The result was the surge of migration described in chapter 2, with tens and then hundreds of thousands of people pouring across the German border, most of them via the Budapest-Vienna-Munich railway route. In a television interview on October 7, Merkel came close to advocating an open-border policy.

That was not something that could easily have been predicted from Merkel's previous statements on the subject of immigration. Referring to the Turkish "guest workers" of the 1960s in a speech to an audience of young CDU members in October 2010, she had said, "We kidded ourselves awhile, we said, 'They won't stay, sometime they will be gone,' but this isn't reality. . . . And of course, the approach [to build] a multicultural [society] and to live side by side and to enjoy each other . . . has failed, utterly failed."[2]

So what motivated the chancellor to open the gates? It was certainly not, as a few commentators guessed, an attempt to repair the damage done to Germany's international image by the Greek debt crisis. Some have speculated that her decision reflected her upbringing as a pastor's daughter in Communist East Germany. Others have seen it as an attempt to emulate Chancellor Willy Brandt's atonement for Germany's Nazi past, akin to his kneeling before the monument to the Warsaw ghetto uprising. A more plausible rationale is that she had learned from her predecessor Helmut Kohl, whose mismanagement of the refugee wave of the early 1990s Merkel had witnessed as a minister in his cabinet. Back then, the CDU/CSU's hardline approach against immigration had not paid off electorally; rather, it cost the party more than 7 percent of the vote in the federal elections between 1987 and 1994 and did not prevent the emergence of a new populist party, Die Republikaner, which managed to enter several state parliaments as well as the European Parliament.

Rather than out of high-mindedness or low political calculation, however, Merkel's decision was made in a fit of absence of mind, according to *Die Welt* reporter Robin Alexander. "The public debate in Germany at that time concentrated on whether it was a good or bad decision to open the border," he recalled. "But there was no decision at all. The border police were in position on the Alpine border between Austria and Germany, and an official thirty-page order to close the borders had been drafted." Alexander spoke with the government officials who had met in the Federal Ministry of the Interior, Building and Community (Bundesministerium des Innern, für Bau und Heimat) that day, September 12, 2015.

> At the last moment, no one, including the Chancellor, had the courage to sign off on the order. The government let it slip through their hands; it wasn't a policy or a strategy, it just happened. And at first, a huge majority of Germans were happy with what Merkel did. Germans cheered the refugees arriving at train stations waving signs saying "Refugees welcome here." . . . And then the refugees kept coming, ten thousand a day for weeks. It became clear that the government [had] lost control.[3]

It is important to remember that within less than a year of Merkel's decision, Germany, along with other European countries, suffered the first of a succession of terrorist attacks. On July 18, 2016, an Afghan asylum seeker stabbed five people on a train near Würzburg. Six days later, a Syrian refugee blew himself up outside a music festival in Ansbach, wounding fifteen people. Then, on November 26, a 12-year-old Iraqi-German boy planted a nail bomb at a Christmas market in Ludwigshafen, though it failed to detonate. The hideous climax came on December 19, when a man drove a truck into the crowd at a Christmas market next to the Kaiser Wilhelm Memorial

94   PREY

Church at Breitscheidplatz in Berlin, leaving twelve people dead and fifty-six others injured. The perpetrator was Anis Amri, a 23-year-old Tunisian failed asylum seeker who had sworn allegiance to the Islamic State.

Amri's case illustrates all that was wrong with the management of the 2015–2016 migration crisis. Born in Tataouine, Tunisia, he had fled to Europe in 2011 on a refugee raft to escape imprisonment for stealing a truck. Having come ashore in Sicily, he lied about his age, pretending to be a minor; was involved in a riot at the temporary migrant reception center to which he was sent; and was sentenced to four years in prison, where he appears to have become radicalized by Islamist inmates. He was released in 2015 but, after the Tunisian authorities refused to accept his repatriation, he made his way to Germany, where he applied for asylum in April 2016. In his time in Germany he used at least fourteen different aliases and posed variously as a citizen of Syria, Egypt, or Lebanon. Strongly suspecting him of planning a terrorist attack and knowing him to be involved in drug dealing, the Federal Criminal Police Office recommended that he be deported, but the state government of North Rhine–Westphalia declined to act, and the Tunisian government initially denied that Amri was its citizen. The State Criminal Police Office of Berlin had also failed to keep Amri under observation in the period before the attack.

WAS 2015–2016 A BLIP?

Angela Merkel's "We can manage that" slogan was overwhelmed by the scale of immigration Germany saw in the years after the summer of 2015. In just three years, the country took in a quarter of all the asylum seekers it had received since it had started collecting data in 1953.[4] But what happened next? How many asylum seekers were granted asylum? How many were denied it and deported? How many stayed regardless of the decision?

As we have already seen with the migration and crime statistics, these are highly politicized questions that have been made hard to answer. European states have done a reasonably good job of collecting and publishing the numbers of asylum applications they have received, but these figures do not tell the whole story.

Despite the decline in illegal entries and asylum applications after the peak years of 2015 and 2016, I believe it is premature for Europe to assume that its migration crisis is over.[5] Asylum applications exceeded half a million in 2018, double the average level between 2009 and 2013, which was around 250,000 per year.[6] I see few reasons why it would revert to that lower level for long and many reasons why it could rise higher. The countries sending asylum seekers are not likely to resolve their political conflicts and economic problems any time soon. In 2019, the Fragile States Index ranked Yemen, Somalia, South Sudan, Syria, and Congo as the world's least stable states. The authors warned that the conditions that had led to the Arab Spring in Algeria, Tunisia, and Morocco had resurfaced. In Libya alone, between 700,000 and 1.5 million migrants were said to be "waiting for their turn to cross to Europe" in 2018.[7] According to the UN High Commissioner for Refugees, in 2018 there were 3.7 million refugees in Turkey, 1.4 million in Pakistan, 1.2 million in Uganda, and 1.1 million in Sudan.

The demographics in the developing world are also set to increase the pressure on Europe. UN projections for the main asylum-seeker sender countries to Europe predict high population growth rates over the next thirty years. The United Nations predicts that the populations of Afghanistan, Syria, Iraq, and Nigeria will double by 2050 and that of Somalia will triple.[8] Though the majority of people who leave their countries of birth will, as in the past, stay within their own continent, there are many millions who would come to the West if they thought they could get here.[9] Until recently, most sub-Saharan Africans were too poor to make it to the West.[10] Since 2000, a newly mobile class has emerged with cell phones that connect them not only to the diaspora but also to online sources of information that make a better life no longer seem so remote. Remittances sent from relatives already in the West are being used to buy airline tickets that are getting ever cheaper and, of course, to pay human traffickers. Improved transport infrastructure in Africa is also helping swell the ranks of migrants.

A Gallup World Poll found that remarkably high numbers of people in sub-Saharan Africa (31 percent), the Middle East, and North Africa (22 percent) would move to another country if they had the opportunity.[11] The implied total of potential migrants is 700 million worldwide, a figure that dwarfs Europe's recent influx of a few million. Another survey found that 75 percent of Nigerians and Ghanaians would move if they had the means and the opportunity.[12] Poor economic prospects are also the main reason for Albanians and Iranians wanting to come to Europe, although in Iran religious intolerance is a motivator, as it is in Pakistan.[13] In Eritrea, people flee a repressive dictatorship.[14] In Syria, Iraq, and Afghanistan, ongoing conflict, political instability, and religious tensions encourage citizens to leave.[15]

The human cost of this great *Völkerwanderung* is shockingly high. More than 10,000 migrants, intent on making it to Europe, drowned in the Mediterranean between 2015 and 2017.[16] Others risk their lives stowing away in trucks or crossing the Alps on foot in freezing temperatures.[17] Europe should not underestimate just how much these people want to make it there. And the demand is not dying down, even though the numbers admitted are being reduced.[18] As the Iranian-Swedish economist Tino Sanandaji put it, "There is extreme push and extreme pull all the time. If you were in Iran in 1981, almost everyone would have moved to Sweden if they could. It was just so hard to do that few made it. The entry point is what matters, not the pressure pushing against it; that pressure has not and will not change. It's the size of the hole to squeeze through that matters."[19] In 2015, that hole was suddenly expanded. Shrinking it back to its original size may be beyond the powers of Europe's leaders.

Even without continued immigration, Pew Research expects Europe's Muslim population to rise to 7.4 percent by 2050 because Muslim women tend to have more children than other Europeans. According to Pew, if Europe resumes a moderate level of in-migration—assuming that there are no new spikes at "crisis" levels—the Muslim share of the population will either double to 11 percent or triple to 14 percent by 2050.

THE TROUBLEMAKERS

Already governments have learned that migrants whose asylum applications have been refused are more likely to commit crimes, especially robbery and violent crime.[20] The Austrian police put the turning point at four hundred days: at that point, rejected asylum seekers tend to begin causing problems.[21]

Not all migrants are troublemakers, of course. The mayor of Tübingen, Boris Palmer, estimated that around 10 percent of the migrants allocated to his city by Germany's federal government have been problematic. "They are not grateful and respectful toward German society," he told me by phone from his office in June 2018. The city government first noticed it had a problem when young migrant men began frequenting parks and train stations selling drugs.

"That's how some migrants got their start as career criminals, moving on to more serious incidents, especially violent and sexual assaults. We see the most problems with those with no right to stay in Germany. They don't have much to lose so take higher risks and commit more serious crimes."[22] If the ratio in Tübingen is extrapolated to the rest of western Europe, somewhere between 200,000 and 300,000 actual or potential criminals may have been let into the continent since 2015.

Most Europeans assume that applying for asylum or any form of residency requires an applicant to abide by the laws and customs of the new society. If nothing else, the prospect of being kicked out of a country that you have expended significant resources and effort to get to should be a deterrent to breaking the law. In most European countries, this is indeed what is supposed to happen. In Germany, a foreign criminal who receives a three-year prison sentence must be deported. A one-year sentence is enough to deport foreigners convicted of sexual offenses. For asylum seekers, any one-year sentence will strip them of their refugee status.[23] In Sweden, too, foreigners given a one-year sentence can be deported.

The question is how far those rules are enforced. It is no longer a surprise to me that there are no data available on how many foreign criminals are deported from Germany.[24] Similar rules apply in Denmark, but an investigation by the Danish prosecutor general found seven cases between 2012 and 2017 in which prosecutors had failed to request that convicted foreign rapists be deported.[25] Sweden's deportation law is another that is honored mainly in the breach.

In June 2018, a Somali asylum seeker who had been given temporary protection in Sweden raped a woman he attacked as she lay asleep in her bed. He was convicted in Linköping District Court and sentenced to one year and ten months in prison, to be

followed by expulsion from Sweden. On appeal the ruling was upheld, but he appealed again, and in April 2019, Sweden's Supreme
Court overturned the deportation order. The court had no doubt
that the man had committed the crime, as the evidence (including DNA) was certain. His recent history, the court admitted,
included convictions for drug possession, driving offenses, and
causing bodily harm. However, the court felt that his crime was
not severe enough to outweigh the ties he had built during the
eight years that he had lived in Sweden. The judgment makes for
strange reading:

> Although there are signs of shortcomings in his social adapta-
> tion in Sweden, partly through his previous crime, and partly
> because he, a few months before arrest, resigned his previous
> employment and housing without securing other employ-
> ment or other own accommodation. The investigation does
> not, however, support the fact that he has an asocial way of life
> or criminal values.[26]

Two months previously, the same court had appeared to set a
precedent. It had ruled against three asylum seekers convicted of
crimes: a Palestinian from Libya convicted of serious robbery, another Palestinian guilty of petrol-bombing cars outside a synagogue,
and a Syrian guilty of rape. They were deported. But the Somali
rapist stayed.

THE DEPORTATION FICTION

Setting aside the issue of whether or not a migrant should be deported for committing a crime, let us ask simply whether or not

those ordered to be repatriated actually were. Like so many aspects of European immigration, the extent to which deportation orders are carried out is hard to ascertain. Here is what we do know. Europe's border agency, Frontex, reports that it has increased its deportation activities in recent years. It was involved in returning 3,500 people in 2015, 5,000 in 2016, and 10,000 in 2017. However, the return of rejected asylum seekers is usually the responsibility of national governments rather than Frontex.[27] So how well do they perform? In Germany in 2018, there were 236,000 people who had been ordered to leave, more than 50,000 of whom had no form of "toleration permit," but fewer than 24,000 were deported.[28] Another 31,100 attempted deportations were canceled by German authorities.[29] In Sweden, around one-third of repatriations go ahead. In the first quarter of 2018, 3,000 people were due to be expelled, but the National Border Police could find only 1,000 of them to remove.[30]

David Wood, the UK Border Agency's former director general of immigration enforcement, has described the comparably lax enforcement of deportation in the United Kingdom.[31] He reported that around half of all asylum applications, including appeals, are approved, but only a third of failed applicants go home. Between 2010 and 2016, according to Wood, 51,154 failed asylum seekers stayed on for at least a few more years. The number of forced removals from the United Kingdom has in fact fallen from 15,000 per year in the mid-2000s to just 2,541 in 2017.

In total, according to Eurostat, 718,000 non-EU citizens were refused entry into the EU-27 in 2019, the highest number of any year for which data are available (since 2008). Compared to 2018, 10 percent more non-EU citizens were found to be illegally present in the EU-27 in 2019. Yet the total number of non-EU citizens returned to locations outside the EU-27 in 2019 was 142,000, 2 percent fewer than in 2018.[32]

EUROPE'S NO-RETURN POLICY

The reasons why deportations are not happening are mixed. In many cases, the rejected asylum seeker simply goes into hiding, as was the case with the 2,000 illegal migrants the Swedish border police could not find in 2018. It does not help that municipal councils such as Malmö's provide financial aid for rejected applicants, which is against the express instructions of Sweden's prime minister.[33] In other cases, deportations are impeded for administrative reasons. If someone does not have a passport or other legal documentation, the bureaucrats and the lawyers declare that it is impossible to send him back to his country of origin. This helps explain why an estimated 240,000 migrants in Europe do not have any documentation.[34] Even if individuals due for deportation have their papers, the authorities can do little if the destination country refuses to take them back.[35] Giving evidence to a Home Affairs Select Committee in 2019, a spokesperson for the UK National Crime Agency said that illegal migrants were not worried about being caught "because, rightly or wrongly, they don't fear being returned. And that is, I think, something that is a significant player in the issue here. . . . In the minds of facilitators [people smugglers] and in the minds of those people willing to take the journey, there is a very low risk that they will be returned."[36]

Another major hurdle is the complex laws and international conventions that European countries have signed. According to the international asylum system, no matter what the circumstances, a person cannot be deported back to a country where his or her life will be in danger. Considering the places that Europe's asylum seekers come from—countries such as Syria, Afghanistan, and Iraq, where all people's lives are to some extent in danger—that is a prohibitively broad policy. Even asylum seekers suspected of terrorist activities in their host country sometimes cannot be deported for this reason. This was the case for the Tunisian Anis Amri, who drove a truck through Berlin's Christmas market in 2016, and the Palestinian Ahmad Alhaw, who went on a stabbing spree in Hamburg in 2017.[37] Neither could be deported because their lives would have been in danger in their native countries.

As well as international conventions, bilateral relations between migrant sender and recipient countries can be a constraint. If there is no cooperation between the two, the host country cannot force the migrant back inside the sender's borders. Individual countries, or the European Union as a whole, initiate repatriation deals with sender countries. One such deal was made with Bangladesh, from which the European Union estimates 200,000 of its illegal migrants come (not including those in the United Kingdom). The European Union offered Bangladesh €12.5 million to accept 500 of its illegals per year.[38] However, of the 200 Bangladeshis whom Germany identified for repatriation, only 67 were sent back; 38 refused to leave, while others could not be located. The Bangladeshi program is a bargain compared to the repatriation deal the United Nations and European Union set up with fourteen African countries in 2015.[39] The European Union has allocated €3.8 billion to help repatriate African migrants in Europe and Libya.[40] In all, 50,150 migrants were repatriated between May 2017 and November 2018, mainly from Libya to Niger, Mali, Mauritania, and Djibouti. We do not know how many were sent home from Europe.[41]

HUMAN ROADBLOCKS

Even when all the formal conditions to deport a failed asylum seeker have been met, another obstacle can get in the way: well-meaning citizens. Let me give an example. Mustafa Panshiri, the Afghani Swede we shall later encounter as a proponent of new integration methods for migrants, described to me an encounter he had had with an asylum seeker in Sweden. Morteza was an Afghani living as an unaccompanied minor with a host family. He had lodged his asylum application with Mustafa at the police station two years before. Even then, Mustafa and his colleagues had suspected that he was not a child. "He had wrinkles on his face and was losing his hair," said Mustafa. "He looked to be at least thirty-five years old . . . but the old couple he lived with called him their 'dear child.'" Morteza's asylum application had been rejected by Swedish authorities three times, but the host couple spoke openly about helping him to live there illegally. The Swedish government went on to give Morteza another chance with temporary protection and residence permits in Sweden.

Other obstructionists are less subtle in their approach but equally misguided. In August 2018, a Somali refugee, Yaqub Ahmed, was escorted onto a Turkish Airlines flight at London's Heathrow Airport to be repatriated to Somalia. He didn't get very far. The pilot refused to take off when passengers loudly protested his deportation. "Take him off the plane!" they chanted—which was exactly what the security personnel did.[42] What the passengers did not know was that Ahmed was being deported as part of his conviction for gang-raping a 16-year-old girl with three of his friends. Before his abortive deportation, he had served four years of a nine-year prison sentence. Shortly after his release, one of his fellow rapists traveled to Syria to fight for the Islamic State.

In Sweden, protests against individual deportations are less spontaneous. In April 2018, a hundred pro-refugee activists formed a human blockade against the deportation of twenty-seven Afghan failed asylum seekers in Kållered.[43] Activists staged a 1960s-style "sit-in" on the road, locking arms and chanting as they blocked a bus carrying the Afghans out of an asylum-seeker center. In the end, five or six were deported that day and another fourteen removed under cover of night later in the week. But nine of the Afghans managed to escape the facility. One of the protesters, a blond-haired, blue-eyed Swede, blogged about her motivations for the protest. She worried that the migrants had been traumatized a second time by "bureaucratic attacks" by the Swedish Migration Agency during their asylum process.[44]

Migrants themselves have also protested against enforcement of the law. In May 2018, police who had been sent to deport a Gambian migrant from an asylum-seeker center in Donauwörth, Bavaria, had to send for reinforcements when other migrants at the center began rioting against his removal, throwing bottles and chairs at police and pouring hot water on them from above. Soon after, 150 West Africans continued the protest at a train station, leading to 32 arrests.[45] In a separate incident the following month, police had to abort the deportation of a 23-year-old Togolese man from an asylum-seeker center in Ellwangen, Baden-Württemberg, when 200 migrants surrounded their vehicle, demanding that the man be released within two minutes. Fearing a violent escalation, police freed him. He has since gone underground.[46]

PUSHING NEWCOMERS UNDERGROUND

Just how many failed asylum seekers are living in Europe? As you might now expect, there are no straight answers to be had. The figures reported by Eurostat count only those illegal immigrants who have come into contact with immigration authorities, not those who have gone into hiding underground. In fact, no country in the border-free Schengen Area has worked out how to measure its levels of illegal migration or the numbers of individuals living in hiding within its territory.

The Schengen Area's open borders, combined with migrants' double-dipping by lodging asylum claims in multiple countries, make it next to impossible for governments to know where those migrants denied asylum have gone. Rainer Münz, the European Commission's special adviser on migration and demography, said in 2019, "We have no clear view what happens to people who are arriving, who are asking for asylum, who don't have a successful claim. These people somehow disappear in our statistics."[47] In Germany, in theory, migrants in this situation have six months to leave voluntarily or face deportation. But that is not what happens. Germany's Federal Ministry of the Interior, Building and Community says that there are currently 240,000 failed asylum seekers in the country who are required to leave. However, it has given 182,169 of them permission to stay on under a special category of *Duldung*, or "tolerance."[48]

Sweden's Migration Agency estimates that 10,000 asylum seekers a year disappear underground to avoid deportation. A report by an Oversight Committee of France's National Assembly estimated there were between 150,000 and 400,000 illegal migrants living in just one Parisian suburb, Seine-Saint-Denis, in 2018. However, a former French minister of the interior, Gérard Collomb, had suggested in 2017 that there were only 300,000 illegal migrants in France overall.[49] Widely varying estimates such as these suggest that European governments have simply lost control of their immigration systems.

When policy makers are struggling with a problem, they often throw money at it. Both the German and British governments offer financial incentives for failed asylum applicants to return home. Germany offers €1,200 to individual migrants who leave during the asylum process and €800 to those who have already been rejected, and in some cases an additional €3,000 for "reintegration support" to cover furniture, renovations, and rental costs. The incentives have not proved particularly attractive, however, with only 29,587 voluntarily leaving Germany in 2017, down from 54,006 in 2016.[50] The United Kingdom has also had little success in encouraging failed asylum seekers to return home, despite offering to pay for their flights plus £2,000 each for their trouble.[51] For some, taking the money and going home makes sense.[52] For most, however, these bribes to leave are worth much less than what it has cost them—not only in money but in effort—to gain access to Europe.[53]

Living in limbo is not fun. The scenes I saw in asylum-seeker centers in Holland in the 1990s and 2000s were grim. Some people had been there for up to ten years, unable to work and living off modest pocket money while waiting for a decision about their asylum cases. They were at an impasse with the Dutch migration authority. They could neither prove that they were escaping persecution nor be returned under international law. Families lived in small caravans, rather than in containers as many do now. Usually they had a living room and two small bedrooms, plus a bathroom if they were lucky; kitchen facilities were communal. Asylum centers were fenced in, with security guards patrolling the gate. When I was in one such center in Lunteren, we had a curfew and had to be inside our caravans by 11:00 p.m. The conditions are not much better in asylum-seeker accommodation in Europe today, and in most cases they are much worse. White containers are stacked on top of each other like Lego bricks. Some have stairs to their entry, and all those I have seen have windows. The interiors are sparsely furnished. Their exteriors are fenced off, though some have children's swings and bicycles outside.

In the "no-man's-land" between the Hungarian and Serbian borders at Tompa, the Hungarian government has erected a container camp to house asylum seekers. Surrounded by barbed-wire fences, the containers have air-conditioning units but are otherwise spartan. The area outside is strewn with garbage, and stray dogs wander around hungrily. It is said that three hundred asylum seekers can live there. It is a sign of how desperately people want to get into Europe that anyone would endure such conditions.

Outside Europe's official asylum system but inside the continent are thousands, perhaps hundreds of thousands, of failed asylum seekers. They have gone underground and dispersed into the immigrant enclaves of western Europe. For some, such as those in Calais or in Millénaire in northeast Paris, that means camping illegally outdoors in tents and makeshift shelters. French police attempted to clear out such camps thirty-four times between 2015 and 2018, but the migrants persist.[54] Being locked out of open society is not as impossible as it sounds. Even without government-issued identification, illegal migrants can still access housing, money, jobs, and protection, all provided by the gangs and clans that run Europe's parallel societies.[55] Life in the underground often means a life of crime or abuse. Illegal migrants too often find themselves exposed to drugs, violence, crime, and prostitution.[56] Berlin's criminal police report that organized crime groups recruit young refugees for the most menial jobs, such as selling drugs on the street or in the subway.[57] Even so, life as an "illegal" in Berlin is still better than life in Mogadishu.

Chapter 8

THE BROKEN WINDOWS
OF LIBERAL JUSTICE

Arnold Mengelkoch is a Berlin integration officer. In an interview in 2018, he explained that newly arrived asylum seekers are confident that they will be released quickly after arrest. For them, an overloaded and underresourced justice system poses no threat.[1] I have seen this again and again in the course of researching this book: if a man harasses a woman and gets away with it, he may try groping the next one who walks past him or follow another down the street, and if he gets away with that he may go further still, because it is highly unlikely that his actions will make it to court, let alone subject him to prison or deportation.

With the European governments having lost control of the asylum system, it falls on the police and social services to manage the fallout. Local police and courts in particular have found themselves unprepared. The problem begins early on. Migrant men who commit misdemeanors may get a warning or receive a suspended sentence or probation for a first-time offense. They are given the benefit of the doubt, especially as new arrivals to Europe. However, this often means that they walk out of the courtroom feeling emboldened that they can get away with breaking the law and go on to do worse. Flying in the face of the "broken windows" policing strategy that transformed New York in the 1990s, the European authorities are failing to punish initial infractions, even when they are quite serious. And so the problematic behavior escalates.

Criminological research has shown that rapists tend to be repeat offenders. According to some studies, the majority of rapists admit to having committed repeated rapes.[2] This is not news to criminal justice experts. Yet too often first-time sex offenders are let off lightly by the European judiciary.

In any case, the idea of spending a spell in a northern European prison is not much of a threat for a young man who may have survived much worse conditions in his homeland. Former Swedish policeman Mustafa Panshiri met many young men in immigrant enclaves who laughed at the prospect of serving a sentence in a Swedish jail.

> They would say, "You could go to Swedish prison and just do bodybuilding." Well, that is true. It's not like prison in Afghanistan or prison in Somalia. They know that there's television there, you can play cards, you can play pool. So it's not something that is so intimidating.

When I asked him what the young men think would be a deterrent, he replied:

> They see prison as a second chance because they are still in Sweden. I've met young men in prison for rape, and they are not being deported. The only thing that really scares them is being deported. And this is not just what I am saying; this is what these young men are telling me.[3]

By now, for the reasons given in the previous chapter, I suspect that these young men have learned that deportation isn't really a credible threat, either.

THE POLICE APPEAR WEAK

In the eyes of young men arriving from Syria, Iraq, Afghanistan, and other war-torn and authoritarian societies, it is not just prison that looks soft in western Europe; the police look weak as well.

What is lost on many in the debate about integration is that the individual's relationship with government is vastly different in the undemocratic societies the immigrants are fleeing. In Somalia, for example, people avoid interactions with government officials like the plague. When you see a government representative in uniform, you assume that he is both corrupt and violent. People do not take their problems to the authorities as citizens do in Europe. If they agitate or criticize the government, they can end up in prison or dead. In such countries everyone has a story of a relative or friend who has "disappeared" at the hands of the authorities.

For a new arrival, being stopped by a European policeman or policewoman is a disconcertingly tame experience. A caution followed by a letter with a warning is no big deal to someone who in his home country would expect to be beaten or immediately thrown into prison. The vice chair of Germany's police union complained in 2018 that migrants have no respect for German police because the consequences of crime are so much harsher in their home countries. A warning or even a suspended sentence is seen as a green light to continue with bad behavior.[4]

Mustafa Panshiri told the story of "a guy, Barsheen in Gothenburg, who was a second-generation migrant from Syria":

> He is a successful man with a restaurant, he pays his taxes and is a good guy, but he is being blackmailed by criminals in his city. He says the police cannot help, and he's very stressed out. He told me, "Listen. Politicians must realize that we who come to Sweden from Syria and Iraq, we are used to guys like

Saddam Hussein and Bashar al-Assad. We are used to dictatorship. Somebody has to watch us [immigrants]. In Sweden, there's
too much freedom. We cannot handle so much freedom."[5]

Mustafa asked, "How do you handle that? Of course, we cannot
have a Saddam Hussein, of course, we cannot have a dictatorship,
we are a democracy, but what do you do with people who are used to
that kind of lifestyle?" I have heard the same point echoed by other
successfully integrated migrants working with new arrivals in Germany. Those who have known life only under a dictatorship "cannot
just flip a switch to become active participants in German democracy overnight."[6]

In some ways, the young men I am writing about are correct in
their perception that European police are soft. Police brought up
in countries such as Sweden, Austria, and Denmark—where it has
been illegal to spank a child since the 1970s—are unused to being
punched in the face during a routine traffic inspection. I have come
across numerous police reports in recent years about police confronted with this new reality. Often during mundane, low-level police work, officers ask a driver to present his identification for a minor
traffic offense. Rather than hand it over, the driver calls his friends,
and soon the police are surrounded by five, ten, or more men, hostile to their enforcing even the most basic laws. Some police call for
backup, but others back down. One such case was reported by two
police officers, one of them female, in Essen in Germany. While ar-
resting a 17-year-old "southerner," they were attacked by five of his
friends. The two officers defended themselves with pepper spray and
batons, but they were both injured. When they eventually got the
boy to the police station, his father and brother arrived and threatened to mobilize the whole family to attack the police if he wasn't
released. They, too, were arrested.[7]

In 2016, Germany's Federal Criminal Police Office reported an increase in attacks against German police since the previous year.[8] Last year the magazine *Der Spiegel* interviewed police officers, prosecutors, and other authorities about their experiences with crime involving migrants. Here is what four of the police officers had to say:

> I drive patrol cars in Tempelhof district [in Berlin]. . . . People are becoming more and more aggressive. Some time ago I was seriously injured in a mission. We wanted to end a fight at a circumcision party. Then a man hit me over the head with two chairs. My cervical spine suffered badly; I was on sick leave for half a year.

> Recently, colleagues wanted to write up several cars that had parked on the bicycle lane. The owners sat opposite each other in a hookah bar. In no time, eggs flew out of the bar; a group of fifteen to twenty men surrounded the colleagues. Both retreated into their patrol car and got reinforcements; I also joined. We needed two police dogs to calm things down.

> What bothers me is the increasing political correctness that I experience. Once a woman came forward, indicating a sexual assault on the stairs to the subway station. When I asked her what the color of the suspect's skin was, she just said, "You should not ask that kind of thing, it does not matter." I was stunned.

> Migrants are causing us special problems. On the street, I deal with them 60 to 70 percent of the time. Many people from the Muslim culture do not accept women in uniform,

do not even talk to them. They often do not take us seriously because we do not use physical force. But that conflicts with our understanding of the law.[9]

Hostility among men from Muslim societies toward female police officers is common. One female German police officer, Tania Kambouri, wrote about this in the German police union journal in 2015. Like Mustafa Panshiri, Kambouri is a successfully integrated second-generation migrant raised by her Turkish parents in Germany. She acknowledged that native-born Germans such as football hooligans and left-wing radicals can cause problems, too, but it is mostly men with Muslim backgrounds who give police trouble in routine interactions. When Kambouri spoke up about her experiences, other German police wrote to the journal in support of her. They had experienced the same thing but were afraid to discuss it publicly for fear of being called Nazis.[10] "I do have to compromise sometimes," she said in 2016. "Once at a spot check, I wanted to test a suspect for drugs or alcohol, and he said, 'Don't look me in the eyes,' because some of these men won't let a woman do that. So I let my colleague take over to prevent any escalation. If I had kept at it, the suspect would probably have resisted, and we don't want to get hurt for some minor offense."[11]

In Swedish immigrant enclaves, police report an increase in crimes involving lethal weapons.[12] For example, grenades left over from the Balkan conflict are used by suburban gangs. "This is a different criminality that is tougher and rawer. It is not what we would call ordinary Swedish crime. This is a different animal," said Peter Springare, a Swedish policeman.[13] He was promptly investigated by Swedish police prosecutors for "inciting racial hatred" when in frustration he mentioned that crimes he was investigating had been committed by immigrants from the Muslim world. Yet an official report by Police Sweden stated in 2017 that as well as facing physical assaults in poorly integrated migrant enclaves, police were being personally threatened both at work and off duty. The practice is so systematic that criminal groups select one police officer on a given day as their target for harassment and threats.[14]

In France, the police report an increasing number of suicides in their ranks. One of a number of reasons for the deaths is the increased need for underresourced officers to work long hours in the face of sometimes murderous antagonism. In 2018, one of the directors of the French riot police spoke of "a new type of aggression [that has] appeared in recent years, clearly intended to cause physical harm to the police, even to kill."[15] Yet police officers are discouraged from openly discussing the problems they face at work. Whistle-blowers such as Springare and Kambouri are accused of stirring up racism and anti-migrant sentiment when they speak out.

POLICE ARE ILL EQUIPPED TO DEAL WITH THE PROBLEM

The vast majority of police I worked with as a politician and translator were committed to tackling the problem of sexual violence. In most cases, their ineffectiveness was caused by decisions made higher up the chain of command. Police find themselves caught in a bind as demand for their services increases but insufficient resources hold them back. A Police Sweden report on crime-ridden immigrant enclaves clearly stated that "there is no institutional capacity to handle the problems when the number of people is so big."[16] The police are therefore forced to choose between dealing with crimes involving lethal weapons and investigating sexual assaults on women.[17] It comes as no surprise that women's safety is not their top priority.

Police in Germany have also been frustrated by the tactics of gangs of molesters. Young men hunt in groups for women who look vulnerable. They know that working in a pack makes it harder for police, witnesses, and victims to pinpoint who the guilty party is. I have heard it said, half-jokingly, by a young Moroccan man that "all brown men look the same to white people." Out of a gang of five men committing a sexual assault, who is responsible for initiating the attack, holding down the victim, cheering on the offenders, or serving as a lookout to warn them of interruption?

Having lived in the United States for the past decade, my view of criminal sentencing may be distorted when I look at Europe. In the United States, many criminals are given absurdly long sentences, often for less serious crimes. Many criminologists question how far locking people up works at all when petty criminals generally become more hard-bitten or politically radicalized in prison. But if incarceration does not work, what will? If we accept that serving a prison sentence is the appropriate punishment for an act of sexual violence, why are European judges and prosecutors reticent, or at best inconsistent, in imposing prison sentences on migrants who commit such acts? I suspect that some of their judgments are tinged with compassion for the perpetrator rather than for his victim.

I have seen this before in the context of honor violence. For many years, those who engaged in honor violence against their sisters, cousins, or other female relatives were sentenced leniently by European courts unfamiliar with the honor/shame complex that is so prevalent in Muslim societies. Judges who felt uncertain about how to deal with cases of domestic abuse committed by men with foreign backgrounds sometimes showed too much leniency to abusive husbands. The same pattern can be observed in the context of sexual assaults perpetrated by migrants in Europe.

JUDICIAL LENIENCY

I have kept a running list of the explanations offered by European judges for acquitting or leniently sentencing the migrants who come before them for sex offenses. The most common are that the offender was drunk and therefore had diminished responsibility or that the victim could not prove that it was not consensual sex. But some judges make allowances for migrant sex offenders' lack of understanding of Western women's sexual self-determination. "I believe Mrs. G.'s every word," said a Berlin judge in 2017.[18] Mrs. G. had refused the advances of the defendant, so he threw her onto a bed, wedged her head and shoulders between two metal struts, and raped her for four hours while she screamed "Stop!" and scratched him. At some point she gave up struggling. The assault was so vicious that she could not walk properly for two weeks. The court had no doubt that the victim had been raped. Nevertheless, the judge wondered if the 23-year-old Turkish defendant might have thought it was consensual. In court the plaintiff was asked if in Turkish culture the assault she had experienced might just be considered wild sex. In typical fashion, the defendant claimed that it had been consensual, adding that he would never rape a woman because he, too, had a mother and sister. The judge acquitted him.

We have already encountered the case of Firas M., the man who hit Marie Laguerre in the face with an ashtray after she told him to stop harassing her as she walked in the 19th Arrondissement of Paris. That was caught on video and made news headlines. When Firas M. was brought to court in 2018, it emerged that he had been born in Tunisia but had lived in France since the age of 8 and was now homeless with psychiatric problems. The prosecution dropped the charge of sexual harassment, even though Laguerre told the court he had made comments to her and noises such as "hisses [and] dirty licks in a humiliating and provocative way." The only charge that stuck was assault with a weapon, and for that he was sentenced to one year in prison, of which six months were suspended in lieu of probation, despite his long list of previous convictions.[19]

Another such case in France was that of a 28-year-old Moroccan, Mustafa Elmotalkil, an asylum seeker whose applications had previously been rejected in Germany and the Netherlands.[20] Drunk at a grocery store in Croisilles in 2018, he rubbed himself against an 11-year-old girl. "He smiled like [she] was prey," said a witness. The court heard that he had been involved in a case two years earlier in the Netherlands for groping a woman and masturbating in front of her but had not been charged. In France, he was convicted for sexually abusing a minor and received a six-month prison sentence and a listing on the registry of sex offenders. Elmotalkil was not in the courtroom to hear the verdict as he had been so aggressive that the judge had ordered him out.

Another child sex offender had his sentence reduced on appeal by the Austrian Supreme Court. Iraqi migrant Amir A. was given a two-year reduction of his sentence from six years in prison to four because he had no prior convictions and the court considered his offense a "one-time incident."[21] That "one-time incident" was the rape of a 10-year-old boy at a Vienna swimming pool. Amir A. grabbed the child in a changing room, locked him into a toilet cubicle, and raped him. After he was let out, the boy reported the assault, and police arrested Amir A. as he jumped off the diving board. Amir A. told the court that he had traveled to Austria in 2015 via the Balkan route as an economic migrant (he did not claim to be a persecuted refugee). He explained that his actions had been the result of a "sexual emergency" because he had "had no sex for four months."*

---

* This case and its appeal in the Supreme Court were reported not only by Austrian news media but also by RT, Breitbart, and British tabloids such as the *Daily Express*. The Russian president, Vladimir Putin, even commented on it. However, there is no evidence that the case did not happen or that the boy was not raped.

YOUNG OFFENDERS GO UNDER THE RADAR

In many European jurisdictions the juvenile justice system censors the identities of minors. Court cases with underage defendants are closed, and the only information made publicly available is selected and distributed by the courts. This means that few cases see the light of day.

When minors commit any crime, there is a strong case for leniency in sentencing. But that is one reason why some migrants claim to be younger than they really are. In addition to receiving more generous government benefits and support than are given to adult migrants, minors in the criminal justice system can expect softer punishments—hence the phenomenon of "beard children" in Sweden. When they come before the courts, grown men with beards and body hair often claim to be unaccompanied underage asylum seekers. Previously, they were tested by doctors to confirm their age. Such tests included X-rays of hands, knees, or jaws and in some cases inspection of genitals. However, refugee advocates and medical ethics bodies protested that those age tests violated migrants' bodily integrity.[22] Calls to reinstate such tests were made in Germany during the trial of an Afghan refugee, Abdul D., who was convicted of raping and murdering 15-year-old Mia V. in Kandel in southwestern Germany in 2018. Contrary to claims by a witness, Abdul D. claimed that he himself was 15, so he was tried in the juvenile system, where the maximum sentence for any crime is ten years. He was found guilty and sentenced to eight years and six months in prison. In October 2019, he was found dead in his prison cell, having hanged himself.[23]

Farther north, on the outskirts of Hanover, 24-year-old Vivien K. went to her local supermarket on a Saturday evening in March 2018. There she told two boys—one aged 13, the other 14—to stop fighting and have more respect for older people around them in the store.

The boys called over their big brother, 17-year-old Abdullah. All three boys were asylum seekers from Syria. After shouting and insulting Vivien K., Abdullah punched her, drew a knife, and stabbed her multiple times in the torso. Vivien K. fought for her life in the hospital. On waking from a coma, she found that she had several broken ribs and parts of her pancreas and her spleen had been removed. Abdullah A. and his 14-year-old brother Mohamad A. were given reduced sentences because of their age, while the youngest boy was not tried at all. Abdullah A. received five years of youth punishment for attempted manslaughter and dangerous bodily injury; Mohamad received two weeks' detention and ten hours of social training. During his hearing, Abdullah A. explained that in his culture stabbing like this was justified if the family honor had been insulted.[24] He did not understand why he should go to prison and accused the court of trying to destroy his life.[25] Indeed, he described himself as "a model refugee." In September 2018, his victim was still on painkillers and had a forty-centimeter scar on her stomach but insists, "The nationality of the perpetrator plays absolutely no role for me."[26]

The Swedish justice system is especially lenient toward juvenile criminals. One perpetrator convicted of sexually assaulting underage girls at Sweden's "We Are Sthlm" festival in 2015 was a 15-year-old Somali boy.[27] His victim told the court that he had grabbed her legs and bottom and tried to put his hand into her pants. When her friend had intervened, he had punched her in the face. The boy was convicted and sentenced to do twenty-five hours of youth service and pay SEK 10,600 ($1,100) in damages to the girls. Another immigrant, 16-year-old Ahmed, was convicted of sexually harassing three 14-year-old girls at a Malmö school in 2017. He was sentenced to do fifty hours of community service and pay damages. Just two weeks after his conviction, he was back at the same school and raped another underage girl.

Even gang rapists can expect a light sentence if they are under-age. Thirteen of the forty-three gang rapists uncovered by a Swedish newspaper in 2016–2017 were younger than 18 years. Some received youth and community service sentences rather than jail time. Among all forty-three offenders, including the adults convicted, the average punishment was only three years.[28]

FAILURE TO ENFORCE THE RULE OF LAW

As we have seen, the mass sexual assault of women in Cologne on New Year's Eve in 2015 would never have occurred had the police enforced the rule of law. Formal investigation into the failures of po-lice and metropolitan government that night found that there had been too few officers deployed to control the attackers.[29] The police did not intervene when groups of drunk men began behaving aggres-sively, nor did they request backup when the situation escalated.[30] Instead women who complained were ignored or rebuffed by police. When women escaped the crowd and ran to police for help they were ignored or told they could do nothing to help. One of the women, Alice Schwarzer, described how she and her friend had managed to get away and run toward two nearby policemen. But their assailants had run after them.

> Both police saw us and also clearly these perpetrators [in pur-suit]. We told the police we needed help and tried to describe everything in a rush. One policeman did not let us finish; the other turned towards the banks of the Rhine and acted as if he had something important to look at. We were told that we should calm down, it certainly was not that bad. They could only advise us not to go into the crowd; they would not. My

friend yelled at the officer that it was brutal in there. He admonished us to speak decently with him. More women arrived, and we were all in agreement. Both police either did not want to or were not allowed to do anything about it. It would certainly have been easy for them to immediately arrest one of the perpetrators behind us. The officials did not do that. . . . They did not take us seriously.[31]

Years later, the women sexually assaulted in Cologne still have not seen justice. As we have seen, there were just three convictions for sexual assault, out of forty-three cases brought by prosecutors. More than two-thirds of the charges (828) were not investigated at all because the perpetrators could not be identified. Out of the 290 charges for which police did identify a suspect, more than half were dropped for other reasons. The first sexual assault charge from that night that made it to court was dismissed in May 2016. An Algerian, Farouk B., and his younger brother were accused of being in a group of ten men who had surrounded and groped women, as well as stole their cell phones. The brothers had been in trouble with the Cologne police earlier for breaking into a car. During the hearing their victims, Karin P. and Cordula M., could not confidently identify them, even though Karin P.'s phone was found in Farouk's possessions at the asylum-seeker center where he was residing. The charge of sexual assault was dropped. The men were convicted only of theft and receiving stolen goods and were let off with six months' probation.[32] Three other perpetrators received suspended sentences: 21-year-old Iraqi Hussein A. and 26-year-old Algerian Hassan T., both new arrivals in Cologne, as well as a 19-year-old Afghani from Hamburg.[33] The only convictions for sex crimes depended on the fact that the perpetrators had taken selfies of themselves and their victims.

THE CONSEQUENCE IS DISTRUST

In surveys, Europeans have long considered respecting their country's laws and institutions the most important aspect of national identity. It outranks speaking the language and even being born in the country.[34] In Sweden, however, only 55 percent of the population now say they have confidence in the police and the criminal justice system, a downward trend that began in 2015.[35]

When crimes are too lightly punished and perpetrators have little fear of retribution, the result is a downward spiral. As more and more people experience or hear about crimes of the sort described above, not only does hostility toward immigrants increase but trust in social institutions erodes. This surely is a troubling trend for Europe's governing elites. Yet, as we shall see in the next chapter, they would rather deceive themselves than confront reality.

Chapter 9

THE PLAYBOOK OF DENIAL

In 1969 the Swiss-American psychiatrist Elisabeth Kübler-Ross published *On Death and Dying,* which introduced to the world the now-famous five stages of grief in terminal illness: denial, anger, bargaining, depression, and acceptance. I sometimes think that Europe is stuck in stage one. It is not only judges who make excuses for criminal behavior by young migrant men; politicians, mayors, bureaucrats, journalists, academics, community spokespeople, and refugee advocates all offer a variety of rationalizations and in some cases downright denials.

When psychologists work with people in the grip of denial, they often begin by asking them to examine the false stories they tell themselves and recognize them as excuses. A psychologist looking into Europe's collective head today would see not a single story of denial but clusters of stories. I have identified eight of these narratives of denial.

1. THE BRUSH-OFF

When responding to an accusation of offense that has been committed by an immigrant, the most immediate response by members of the establishment tends to be "the brush-off." For example, a Danish inspector of police commented on nine sexual assaults of young women by asylum seekers at a festival as follows: "The characteristics of the offences are all very different, so one must not conclude that all the abuses were committed by boys from the asylum centre."[1] In 2018, the Swedish minister for employment and integration insisted that the numbers of reported rapes and sexual harassment cases were "going down and going down and going down"[2]—whereas, as we saw in chapter 3, the opposite is the case. Similarly, following the Cologne New Year's Eve sexual assaults, commentators insisted that "refugees committed no more offenses than did the native population," another blatant falsehood.[3]

Niklas Långström, a professor at the Swedish National Board of Forensic Medicine (Rättsmedicinalverket), has argued that figures such as "93 percent foreign-born or first-generation migrant offenders . . . do not indicate any causal relationship."[4] And Jerzy Sarnecki, a professor of criminology at Stockholm University, has explained away the overrepresentation of migrants in the crime statistics by arguing that migrants "are discriminated against in different ways by the judicial system, and it cannot be excluded that the police are more likely to investigate the crimes" that migrants commit.[5] One study has indeed indicated that victims who are attacked by a perpetrator who cannot speak their language are twice as likely to report the incident to police and so foreigners show up in the data more often.[6] But it is also true that the degree of violence inflicted and the presence of a weapon predict the likelihood of victims to report.[7] Migrants might be more likely to be reported because their sex crimes are more violent.

For some Germans, public fears about sexual crimes by migrants are atavistic in nature. Wolfgang Benz, professor emeritus at the Technical University of Berlin, has argued that the arrival of the refugees has "reactivated" an image that has long existed in the minds of Germans—one of a country occupied by foreign forces behaving like barbarians. "Today, the horde that is invading us is no longer the Russians but the refugees, and the rapes, as in every past war, are part of the conduct of war," said Benz.[8] In other words, the contemporary crisis is a kind of figment of the imagination based on German historical memory.

We have already seen how researchers sought to disprove the connection between the increase in migration and the increase in sex crime by largely omitting from their study data after 2015. But there is more than one spurious way to say "Nothing to see here."

2. MISDIRECTION

A second category of denial is misdirection and false comparisons. Like a magician distracting an audience, commentators conjure up a smoke screen by universalizing the problem of sexual violence. It is not immigrants who disproportionately rape women, they say, because "all men are rapists" and "every third woman experiences physical, sexual, psychological and economic violence."[9] "The media beat-up was huge about the women's safety, exaggerated completely," I was told by a senior Austrian bureaucrat. "We had a murder and some cases [of rape] three times in Vienna, although of course it happens everywhere."[10] "This kind of harassment and violence has been going on for a long time in every country," said Gudrun Schyman, a Swedish politician and spokeswoman for the Feminist Initiative. "The common factor is men."[11]

3. THE SEMANTIC MUDDLE

One widespread form of denial is to manipulate language in a process I call "the semantic muddle." Suspects in police reports and media coverage are described as "southerners," "men with dark skin," or people with "poor German" language skills, deliberately omitting their migration status.

The semantic muddle often leads to absurdity. One study I came across proposed separating out concerns about immigrants in public debate from concerns about asylum seekers. Germany's "non-word of the year" in 2018 was *Anti-Abschiebe-Industrie* ("anti-deportation industry"), which refers to refugee advocates who support rejected asylum seekers staying on in Germany. The word was condemned for being "defamatory and discrediting."[12]

In some parts of Europe, the semantic muddle is officially imposed by media regulators. In mid-2018, the head of the German Cultural Council called for political talk shows that portrayed refugees negatively to be axed until they can "come up with more suitable contents with regards to social cohesion in our society."[13] A code of media ethics enforced by the German Press Council was modified in 2017, requiring publications to omit all religious, ethnic, and other background information about criminals that is not "absolutely necessary to understand the reported event." The new code reminded journalists "that such references could foment prejudices against minorities."[14] The editors of the Bavarian newspaper *Süddeutsche Zeitung* explained that such information should be disclosed only in "exceptional offenses such as terrorist attacks or capital crimes, or for crimes committed by a larger group (such as on New Year's Eve 2015 in Cologne). There is also a public interest in the search for a wanted man or if the biography of a suspected person is relevant to the offense. We decide on a case-by-case basis and are fundamentally reluctant to avoid bias against minorities."[15] This is a far cry from the first edition of *Süddeutsche Zeitung*, published just five months after the capitulation of the Nazis in 1945, when the editors stated, "For the first time since the collapse of the brown rule of terror, a newspaper run by Germans is published in Munich. It is limited by the political necessities of our days, but it is not bound by censorship nor gagged by constraints of conscience."[16]

The media's preference for redacting cultural and migration information from crime reports has generated suspicion among readers. When I asked a senior German journalist whether he thought immigrants' culture had something to do with their attitude to women, the reply I received was "That is a question above my pay grade. It's very interesting, because we had that debate after Cologne. I'm sorry, I'll shut that down here." For journalists in Europe today, reporting the facts can jeopardize their careers.

4. BOGUS RESEARCH AND COMMENTARY

Another tactic in the playbook of denial is the manufacture of statistics, studies, and surveys to debunk the reality on the ground. Attitudinal studies are the most common. These can be designed in such a way as to reflect the preferred conclusions of researchers. For example, in 2017, one study concluded that "Attitudes to immigration in France, as in most European countries, are highly stable and are in fact becoming slightly more favourable."[17] In reality, numerous surveys on attitudes toward migrants find that less educated, older, and more conservative Europeans hold more negative views of migrants.[18]

5. DISMISSAL OF HONEST ACADEMICS AS BIGOTS

As well as producing bogus research, some establishment academics reject evidence that does not support their prejudices. For decades, anthropologists have observed gender relationships in the Arab world, finding the same results time and again. But they are now dismissed as bigots for publishing "orientalist fantasies that . . . non-Western and particularly Muslim cultures are more patriarchal than Western ones."[19] I spoke to the respected Dutch sociologist Ruud Koopmans about this in Berlin in 2019. As he told me:

> We have the research on attitudes toward women, it is clear that Muslim immigrants have very conservative values about women. It's an established fact, not a research question anymore. . . . In Germany there is a strong idea that there is no connection between Islam and gender inequality, terrorism, anti-Semitism—the line is that the answer has nothing to do with Islam, or religion, and if it does, then who are we to say, "Yes, that is bad," because we're not perfect, either.[20]

False charges of racism are the easiest way to enforce denial, as the Algerian novelist Kamel Daoud discovered. After he published an article in *Le Monde* on the cultural component he had detected in the sexual violence on New Year's Eve in Cologne, he was pilloried. Soon afterward, he announced his retirement from writing in newspapers, preferring to confine himself to writing fiction.[21] The economist Thilo Sarrazin was denounced by German elites and removed from his position on the executive board of the Bundesbank following the publication of his book *Deutschland schafft sich ab* ("Germany Does Away with Itself") in 2010.[22] Likewise, the German author Uwe Tellkamp was dropped by his publisher in 2018 after criticizing the country's open-door migration policy and warning of a "moral dictatorship" in Germany.[23]

The Egyptian-born, German-based writer and broadcaster Hamed Abdel-Samad, the author of the 2009 memoir *Mein Abschied vom*

Himmel ("My Departure from Heaven"), explained that because of their country's history, Germans are easily blackmailed:

> Books like mine receive accusations of Islamophobia and hurt feelings. When defenders of Islamism come out asking whether "you want to do to us what you did with the Jews?" everyone shuts up. I'm not a racist, and I know what I'm talking about, so I can't be morally blackmailed like most Germans. For me the consequence of the Holocaust is never again to shut up or give up freedoms, to never shut up about wrong developments in society. That doesn't mean platitudes like "No more wars" or always being kind to immigrants. It means not accepting any lack of freedom and not importing the terrible problems we left behind in Egypt.[24]

6. APPEALS TO COMPASSION AND PLATITUDES

Another form of denial is to appeal to compassion at the expense of reason or caution. Virtue-signaling politicians implore citizens to fulfill their moral duty to rescue migrants. Those who dissent are immediately considered immoral, inhumane, and racist. In 2014, Swedish prime minister Fredrik Reinfeldt appealed "to the Swedish people to open their hearts to refugees." In September 2016, the mayors of New York, Paris, and London published a joint article on the refugee crisis in the *New York Times* that pledged to "continue to pursue an inclusive approach to [refugee] resettlement in order to combat the growing tide of xenophobic language around the globe. Such language will lead only to the increased marginalization of our immigrant communities, and without making us any safer."[25]

7. BAD ADVICE AND BOGUS SOLUTIONS

Another category of denial is the poor advice and bogus solutions authorities offer in response to sexual assault or harassment. This often takes the form of veiled or outright blaming of the victim. Following the mass sexual assaults on New Year's Eve 2015, the mayor of Cologne, Henriette Reker, suggested that women who were afraid of being assaulted should keep themselves "an arm's length" from strangers.[26] Police have also advised women to wear comfortable shoes rather than high heels on a night out so they can run if they need to. Rather than taking responsibility and implementing measures to ensure women's safety, officials use this form of denial to place the onus on women to protect themselves from predatory men.

Another iteration of "bad advice" is an excuse that takes the form of "Yes, but . . ." Politicians and community leaders obliged to condemn sexual violence agree that the behavior of predatory men is wrong: yes, but it is never the right time to deal with it. For example, Aiman Mazyek, the president of the Central Council of Muslims in Germany (Zentralrat der Muslime in Deutschland, or ZMD), said in 2016, "We have seen it again and again how women were abused, mistreated and discriminated against. But this subject never got the attention that was required before" and "It would be fatal to do it now in connection with refugees. We need to talk about it. We need the discussion. But please let's not do it at the expense of refugees."[27] Another striking "Yes, but . . ." was given by Sisi Eibye, the manager of an asylum center in Denmark. Boys from her center had sexually assaulted teenage girls at a summer festival. When police asked her how many boys from her center had been in the area, she did not know. She agreed that the boys' behavior had been "totally unacceptable" and added, "We have no sanctions, and all we can do is report it to the police if the boys are gone more than a day. We can not lock them up."[28]

8. FEAR OF BIGOTRY AND BACKLASH

Arguably the most powerful way to maintain a taboo on the cultural aspects of sexual violence is to claim that talking about the facts will fan the flames of racism, empower populists, and further divide society. This excuse has repeatedly been used by police, politicians, social workers, media, and many other members of the establishment across Europe. To avoid being perceived as xenophobic or to avoid giving ground to actual xenophobes in political debate, these authorities would rather cover up the problem and leave victims at risk. In the words of Södermalm police chief Peter Ågren, "Sometimes we do not dare to say how things really are because we believe it will play into the hands of the Sweden Democrats"—an anti-immigration party in Sweden, previously a fringe element but now a significant political force.[29]

THE PLAYBOOK OF DENIAL

Some people wonder why so many establishment institutions persist in their denial of the problem. They often assume it is out of naiveté. I think this is too charitable. What other motives might they have? Self-interest is one.

Take the case of the left-wing political parties that, having seen their traditional white working-class voter base erode over the decades, turned to immigrants as a new source of votes. To earn the political goodwill of this "ersatz proletariat," left-wing parties brush off issues such as sexual violence and gender discrimination in immigrant communities. Once upon a time these parties stood for the emancipation of women, for gay rights and equality. Now they are in bed with Islamists who seek exemptions from these core values on religious grounds. This political partnership is now operative to varying degrees in France, Belgium, Sweden, Germany, the Netherlands, and the United Kingdom. In Stockholm's notorious immigrant enclaves of Rinkeby and Tensta, for example, Social Democrats campaign vigorously, giving out free food and playing Arabic music.

True, not all of this is cynical electoral calculation. Radical socialists in Germany identified the migrant crisis as an opportunity to "deal a blow to capitalism" and enthusiastically adopted refugee rights as an instrument in their "project of universal liberation."[30] Indeed, some have embraced the idea of open borders as an almost revolutionary project.

THE WINNERS AND LOSERS

The consequence of living in a state of denial is that almost everyone loses. Governments that feared populist parties would benefit if they openly discussed the problem have found that this is exactly what happens when they shut down debate. Populists across Europe have prospered precisely because they alone have been willing to violate the taboo. Center-left parties that have embraced the idea that growing numbers of Muslim immigrants are the new proletariat have lost the trust of their traditional voters. In elections across Europe, as we shall see, they have paid the price for their opportunism at the ballot box.

At all levels, then, trust between citizens and governing institutions has been eroded. Citizens can see that the authorities have lost control of the borders and, in some cities, of the streets. The apparent breakdown in the rule of law adds to the trust deficit. The consequence is division and fragmentation.

Perhaps nowhere are the corrosive consequences of denial more obvious than in the modern feminist movement.

Chapter 10

THE FEMINIST PREDICAMENT

As I learned at university in the Netherlands in the 1990s, personal autonomy and security had not simply been bestowed on Western women; they had fought for their rights over centuries. And they had achieved more freedom for women than I had ever seen. For me, coming from Africa to Europe was more than a geographic journey. I had sped forward in time from a fundamentally tribal society ruled by violence and religious dogma, in which individuals were subordinate to the collective and public institutions were to be distrusted, to a modern society in which the individual has equal rights regardless of gender or other innate attributes.

At the time, it looked as if the liberties that Western women enjoyed would trickle down to newly arrived immigrants and then spread out to the rest of the world. Naively, I assumed that we were on the right side of history. Back then, no one would have predicted that Europe would begin to accept the attitudes of cultures that deliberately limit women's rights. Having seen firsthand how quickly history can fast-forward, I am keenly aware that it can just as rapidly rewind.

The successes achieved by the women's movement throughout modern history have hinged on women's presenting a unified voice. First-wave feminists pushed for voting rights and access to education, property rights, and political representation. Second-wave feminists achieved greater access to Western labor markets for women and pushed for reproductive rights and effective contraception and against the ostracization of single mothers. These feminists dragged sexual and domestic violence out from the shadows to become issues of public policy. Rape within marriage was criminalized, and victim-blaming attitudes toward sexual assault and harassment were excoriated.

A question I have often asked myself is why there has not been a feminist outcry about the increase in sexual violence against women that I have described in previous chapters. Surely, women's safety in public places should be a core issue for those who seek to uphold women's rights.

The omission is especially surprising as women have, as we have seen, never been more politically powerful. All over the Western world today, and especially in western Europe, a growing number of women can credibly aspire to hold the highest positions of political and economic power. At first sight, we are living through a triumph of feminism. Or are we? For the irony is that, even as individual women in the West hold the offices of prime minister and president, managing director and chief executive officer, women's rights at the grassroots are under increasing pressure from imported notions of female subordination. Worse, many of today's female leaders in the West are doing little or nothing to stop this turning back of the clock on gender equality.

Outside the West, women are killed, raped, enslaved, beaten, confined, and debased. Female fetuses are aborted and baby girls abandoned. Girls are denied education or have their genitals cut and sewn. Girls and young women are forced into marriage with men they hardly know. In the 1990s, the Dutch feminist Cisca Dresselhuys asked, "How is it that we overlooked those women?" Western feminists had been so focused on themselves they had ignored what was happening to other women in societies where they are seen only as sexual objects, mothers, and caregivers. Meanwhile, the concept of universal women's rights yielded ground to the new ideals of multiculturalism and intersectionality. Women in Islamic societies who demanded equal rights were told that those were Western values. Western feminists came to believe that imposing their values on the Muslim world was a form of neocolonialism.

FEMINIST MISSION DRIFT

In historical terms, the liberal feminist movement has been short lived. For two hundred years, women pushed to have autonomy and equality with men. But since the turn of the century, the women's movement has stepped away from this goal. The feminist mission has drifted, and women's rights have been trumped by issues of racism, religion, and intersectionality. Liberal feminists today care more about the question of Palestinian statehood than the mistreatment of Palestinian women at the hands of their fathers and husbands. In the battle of the vices, sexism has been trumped by racism.

Feminism has also become deeply politicized, with women on the left claiming it exclusively for themselves. Conservatives and moderates are shut down as "right wing" if they talk about women's issues. Women's studies departments in universities are teaching the next generation of feminists that the only just cause is a relentless attack on the white man. Liberal feminists excuse immigrant men of crimes against women because the perpetrators are victims of racism and colonialism. Take the response of Tina Rosenberg, a founding member of Sweden's feminist party and a "gender scholar" at Stockholm University, to the increase in sexual harassment by migrant men in Sweden in 2016: "It is very dangerous to racialize sexual harassment. There is a long post-colonial history of the white patriarchy trying to rescue the brown women from the brown men. . . . We should talk about all the harassment against women. We should object and pro-test, but we should not make the distinction about people from another ethnic background that they are more violent than we are . . . because otherwise we find ourselves in a place of saying: 'I'm not a racist, but . . .'"[1]

One woman who is unafraid to confront the issue is Sofie Peeters. Speaking in Belgium in 2018, she said:

> I think it's very unracist to confront people with their behav-ior regardless of their culture. Some guys who harassed me said, "You're a racist because you don't want to talk to me." That's not the case. It's not that I don't want to talk to you be-cause you're Moroccan, I don't want to talk to you because you're acting like an asshole. You call me names, you follow me around, and it's irritating. I have Moroccan friends, it's not a race issue for me. These guys use "racism" like a protective shield and think they can do whatever they want and get away with it. And then it becomes a bigger problem.[2]

When Sofie's film *Femme de la Rue* was released in 2012, she was applauded for showing daily sexism and street harassment in a way that allowed people to really understand the gravity of it. But she was also criticized for showing men from a multicultural background harassing women. But as she explained, "It was just my experience, and I filmed it. When you walk past ten guys with a multicultural background on the street, one of them might give you a remark. So you could say that it is just a minority. But when you pass a hundred guys and ten of them harass you, it scales up."[3]

POLARIZATION AMONG FEMINISTS

There is a paradox at the heart of contemporary Western feminism. Ideological feminists insist on grandiose goals such as "ending the patriarchy." Yet campaigns against men-only clubs or for female representation on corporate boards are elitist concerns far removed from the daily existence of the average woman. If we think back to the sociologist Abraham Maslow's hierarchy of human needs, the issues Western feminists prioritize today are in the realm of self-actualization: enhancing conditions at work, having access to state-sponsored child care, joining all-male associations, balancing housework duties with male partners, and gaining prestige. This is not to say that we should forgo laudable goals such as smashing the glass ceiling. But the freedom for all women to live free from violence should come first.

I do not want to mock feminists today, but I do want them to wake up. They have come to take for granted the more foundational needs such as basic safety in public. To me it looks as though they are busy fixing a leak in the roof of a house while the basement is collapsing into a sinkhole.

Female students on university campuses seem to inhabit a parallel universe. Protected by "safe spaces" from the threat of "microaggressions," female law students ask not to be taught about rape cases as they are too upsetting and might "trigger" them. But every now and then the real world breaks in. In October 2017, academics and students at Goethe University in Frankfurt protested against a speech titled "Police Work in an Immigrant Society" by the head of Germany's police union. Fearing a backlash by students, the university authorities canceled the speech. Ironically, that same month, four women were victims of attempted sexual assaults at the university. In each case the attacker was described as 1.65 meters (five feet, five inches) tall, of North African appearance, and speaking German with a thick accent. In a dignified response, the police union chief said, "I am anything but happy that the university has been given this reality check."[4]

THE LIMITS OF #METOO

The #MeToo movement crystallized and accelerated a major shift in attitudes toward sexual harassment. Journalists and whistle-blowers encouraged other women to name and shame the men who had sexually harassed them at work. The movement spread rapidly from North America to western Europe—#BalanceTonPorc ("Squeal on your pig") being the catchphrase in France. Dozens of serial offenders lost their jobs and reputations; a few faced prosecution.

#MeToo has crossed an ocean. Yet it appears unable to cross a cultural barrier. The victims of migrant gangs are largely ignored, the claims by women that migrant men are harassing them are dismissed, despite the fact that the number of victims of harassment—to say nothing of more serious crimes such as rape—is far greater in Europe than, say, in Hollywood or on Wall Street.

As I have argued in this chapter and the last, part of the problem is that feminists feel uncomfortable discussing offenses by brown men. Denial that the offenses occur is a preferable option. Yet there is more at work here than just willful ignorance. I believe that many Western feminists genuinely do not understand the deep-seated cultural antagonism of men from the Muslim world to the very notion of equal rights for women. It is to this cultural clash that I now turn.

PART III

Clashing Civilizations, Revisited

Chapter 11

THE MODESTY DOCTRINE

Now that we have established that there is indeed a relationship between increased immigration and higher levels of sexual violence in Europe, the next step is to understand that relationship in the way that Europe's elites have conspicuously failed to do.

Why would men who have traveled thousands of miles for a better life behave this way toward women in their new country? The naive answer is human biology. It is a well-established fact that young men brimming with testosterone are designed by evolution to want to have a lot of sex.

But culture and civilization exist in large measure to restrain such primitive impulses. The more important point is that migrants' attitudes to women are shaped by their circumstances and experiences in their countries of their origin.

An important part of the story is, of course, the influence of Islam on relations between the sexes. But closely related, as I shall show, is the role of a practice that almost certainly predates the rise of Islam, namely polygamy. Cultures that tolerate or encourage polygamy tend to also impose extreme modesty on women and exclude them from public life. Polygamous cultures, because of the way they turn women into a rare commodity, often produce violent and misogynistic outcomes. A large number of recent migrants to Europe come from such cultures.

BOYS WILL BE BOYS

The most plausible counterargument—that culture does not matter—is simply that young men are the population cohort that is most likely to commit sex crimes and the asylum-seeker population has a much higher proportion of young men than the typical European society does.[1] In Germany in 2017, for example, two-thirds of asylum seekers were male.[2] Across Europe in 2015, there were 2.6 male migrants for every female; in Italy the ratio was seven to one, and in Sweden it was ten to one. By 2017, the overall ratio in Europe had dropped to 2.1 males for every female asylum seeker, but in Italy it was still five to one.[3]

In 2016, the political scientist Valerie Hudson sounded a warning that societies with disproportionate numbers of young, unmarried men are less stable and more violent, especially toward women. She questioned why Europe would gamble its enviable record on gender equality by bringing in large numbers of unfettered young men.[4] Decades of academic research have linked unbalanced sex ratios with violent crime.[5]

Hudson calculated that by the end of 2015, there were 123 16- and 17-year-old boys in Sweden for every 100 girls that age.[6] Such demographic bulges of young men, she cautioned, tend to erode the social barriers that create a peaceful society. In response, the Swedish media savaged Hudson.

Why were there so many more male migrants? The German journalist Maria von Welser went in search of the missing refugee women and found most of them stuck in refugee camps in the Middle East. Even though they wished to join their male relatives in Europe, money for travel was tight and families had sent the "strongest" ahead—that is, the young men. Underpinning the decisions of displaced families is the idea that women, especially women traveling alone, "would risk—as they see it—more than just their lives: they risk their honor."[7]

In the same way, Dominic Kudlacek of the Criminological Research Institute of Lower Saxony (KFN) says that age and sex rather than culture are the key. The migrants, he argues, are overwhelmingly young and male, a demographic responsible for the lion's share of crimes in nearly every human society. In 2014, for example, German men between the ages of 14 and 30 made up 9 percent of the population but were responsible for half of all the country's violent crimes. Among new arrivals to Germany, men aged 16 to 30 made up 27 percent of all asylum seekers who came in 2015. "It is because of the demographics," argued Kudlacek in 2018. "Whether they're asylum seekers or EU migrants, they are younger than the average population and mostly male. Young men commit more crimes in every society."[8] He also noted that the majority of migrant-perpetrated violent crimes were against fellow migrants. Their situation—crammed into squalid camps or trapped in bureaucratic limbo while their asylum applications await processing—helped explain their propensity to commit acts of violence.

Martin Rettenberger, the director of the German Centre for Criminology (Kriminologische Zentralstelle, or KrimZ), makes a similar argument. Although conceding that the wave of post-2014 immigrants tends to come from societies that tend to not punish sexual offenses, he concludes that "Arabs or Africans are not intrinsically more likely to commit assaults than Europeans." He attributes the rise in migrant-linked crime in Germany to the migrants' poverty, their lack of access to employment, and trauma due to their long treks to Germany.[9]

Yet the authors of the meticulously researched Zurich report on violence in Lower Saxony took a quite different view. They presented an ambitious framework for understanding the increase of violent crime in Germany at a time of rising migration, distinguishing carefully among "proximal" factors (personal origin, economic circumstances, family circumstances, parental upbringing, school history, substance consumption, friend networks, and leisure behavior) and "distal" factors (class, religious, ethnic, age, and political affiliation, plus macrosocial barriers such as restrictive employment opportunities, poverty, social norms, and discrimination).

Though acknowledging the significance of the age and gender composition of the migrants, as well as the hardships they have faced in getting to Germany and the frustrations of their new lives, Christian Pfeiffer, Dirk Baier, and Sören Kliem added an important cultural variable:

> Most of the refugees come from Muslim countries that are characterized by male dominance. Representative surveys conducted by the KFN have shown that young male immigrants from such cultures have internalized so-called violence-legitimizing masculinity norms to a far greater extent than Germans of the same age or young men born in Germany who come from these countries. These masculinity norms are captured by statements such as "The man is the head of the family and may enforce if necessary by force" or "A man who is not ready to defend himself against insults by force is a weakling." Acceptance of such a "macho culture" has proved to be a significant factor in promoting violence in many studies conducted by the KFN.[10]

As Camille Paglia wrote in 1990, "Rape is the sexual expression of the will-to-power, which nature plants in all of us and which civilization rose to contain. Therefore the rapist is a man with too little socialization rather than too much."[11] The issue, however, is what kind of civilization and what kind of socialization the rapist has experienced.

SOCIAL CONTROL IN MUSLIM-MAJORITY COUNTRIES

In those parts of the Middle East, North Africa, and South Asia where society is stable and order is intact, individuals are subject to quite stringent social control. Men and women, boys and girls have their places in that order, which is often rigidly enforced. In wealthier, more cosmopolitan neighborhoods, there is less social control than in rural areas, but behavior is still policed by the family, religious groups, schools, and the surrounding community.

Another general point about these societies is that men are perceived to be strong and women weak. Men are expected to protect women and children by providing for them and, if necessary, fighting for them. Women are expected to nurture their children and submit unconditionally to their husbands. Sex is understood as a necessity to procreate within the context of marriage. An important element of maintaining social order in these societies is keeping male sexual desire, which is seen as a powerful force, locked within the bounds of marriage. The biggest dread in these societies is *fitna*, which is chaos or the breakdown of social order. Male sexuality is seen as one of the key threats to that social order.

To manage male sexuality, men are permitted to have more than one wife. Polygamy is encouraged as a matter of necessity to cushion this chaotic force. But marrying more than one wife comes with a burden. Not all men can meet the religious rule that a husband should treat all his wives equitably. A more cultural, rather than religious, phenomenon is that fathers will wed their daughters to the highest bidder. Since poverty is one of the biggest problems in these societies, this leaves lots of men with the prospect of not being able to marry one wife, let alone more than one. Needless to say, sex outside marriage is proscribed. Women who engage in it are irreparably tarnished. The consequence of all this is a great deal of sexual frustration.

At the core of this set of norms is the idea that women are commodities, valued primarily for their capacity to transmit genetic material to the next generation. Women are invested in and valued not for themselves but for the price their virginity can attract in the marriage market. This explains why a girl's virginity is viewed as capital, as something valuable to be guarded, whereas a boy's virginity is insignificant. It starts early on. Boy babies are favored in most parts of the world, but especially in the non-Western societies I am talking about. Young boys are given more freedom to play outside, and girls are forced to take on domestic chores. When the boys become sexually assertive, they are hardly discouraged, while girls are compelled to remain chaste. From the moment she begins menstruating in these societies, a girl becomes an object of arousal for men. Formally, pubescent boys are discouraged from exploring their sexuality, but in practice a blind eye is turned to their exploits. A Muslim girl is taught to protect her virginity as an expression of loyalty to her creator and to her family and future husband.

Many religions share such ideas about male and female sexuality, to be sure. A number of conservative Jewish communities and Christian denominations have comparable views of the innate inferiority of women to men. But because Islam fuses rather than separates politics and religion, the inferiority of women is enshrined in holy law in the Muslim world. Moreover, although polygamy is illegal in the West with few exceptions (some splinter sects of Mormons defy the law), Muslim men can cite the Quran to justify taking up to four wives at a time.[12]

At the personal level, being a second, third, or fourth wife is a miserable existence. I have written about this in the case of my own family. The feminist psychologist Phyllis Chesler and others have made similar observations. But the social consequences of polygamy—to be precise, polygyny—affect more than the quality of life of the women in such households.

The American social scientist Dan Seligson argues that polygamy gives rise to more violent and less prosperous societies. Using the McDermott Polygyny Scale to divide the world's countries into polygamous and nonpolygamous societies, Seligson and the economic historian Anne McCants have demonstrated the deleterious effects of polygamy upon social trust, family formation, and economic development. In polygamous societies, "families transfer wealth to the bride's family, women marry young and men marry old, fertility rates are high, women are sequestered like commodities, person-to-person trust is low, making institutional trust very low," they argued. Where marriageable women are regarded as commodities, the upper strata of wealthy and powerful men monopolizes the most desirable mates. Since accumulating wealth and status takes time and work for most men, the norm of polygamy pushes up the age of marriage for males, drives down the age of marriage for females, removes incentives for female educational and economic attainment, and increases the fertility rate. The surplus of unmarried males scrambling for an artificially reduced pool of marriageable females spurs the growth of crime and violence. The dual need to protect one's assets and wives prompts the claustration of women into large extended households revolving around a single high-status male.[13] Today, the vast majority of places where polygamy is legal are Muslim-majority countries situated in Africa and Asia. By contrast, ever since ancient Greece and Rome went down the very different route to monogamy, the Western world has prohibited both polygyny and polyandry.[14]

Seligson is a middle-aged, liberal Jewish scholar with curly gray hair and an unassuming attitude. He is a physicist and computer nerd who is applying the tools of science and technology to a complex cultural issue. Speaking to me in California, he explained his approach:

> The commodification and objectification of women begins with polygamy. When one man takes two wives, he leaves another man without one. This creates scarcity, and we humans hoard resources when they are scarce. Men do not trust each other with their wives, so they sequester this rare commodity behind walls and veils and restrict their movement. Those without the scarce resource, typically young men, then have to maraud for it, leading to civil unrest and belligerence. And efforts to control those behaviors lead to authoritarianism and the corruption and poverty it begets.

In typical Silicon Valley style, Dan spoke quickly, taking me through pages of complex calculations on his laptop.

> I have run tens of thousands of models combining parameters to identify the sources of violence against women in societies over time. What I am tracking is the accumulation of cultural effects that indicate attitudes toward women on average. These attitudes go back well before monotheism; they predate even tribal culture. Islam is simply not there. Neither is colonialism. It's polygamy, the marriage law, that produces distrust and patriarchal violence toward women. And the historical legacy of polygamy can be tracked down [through] the generations. It raises the social temperature, creating a hostile, angry culture.[15]

THE MODESTY DOCTRINE   149

If Dan is right, the West is opening its doors to high numbers of people who carry with them a whole syndrome of problems inherited from polygamy. Sexual harassment is one of them. The groping of women in the street is not just sexual behavior; it is proprietary behavior.

RELIGIOUSLY ENFORCED MISOGYNY: THE MODESTY DOCTRINE

In Muslim societies where the social order is intact, women are (subconsciously) divided into categories. These divisions are conventions, some of which are codified while others are not. For instance, on a Muslim marriage certificate a woman is required to confirm that she is a virgin. The crucial distinction is between modest women and immodest women. All modest women avoid being out alone after dark, but, most important, a modest woman is expected to dress modestly. What does this entail? It requires covering all parts of your body that might arouse a man: your hair, arms, shoulders, and legs. As a Muslim woman, before you leave the house, you debate whether to wear a simple head scarf or the full burka. Short-sleeved clothing is not sufficient to meet the modesty threshold.

Within the category of modest women, there are four subsections: virgins, married women, divorced women, and widows. A virgin is a young girl living in her father's home, waiting to be married off. She is expected to stay at home, to leave the house only with good reason and then only in the company of other family members. Most certainly, she is expected to return to the house before dark. She is being groomed to be a wife and expected to do housekeeping, to learn to cook and how to dress. If she shines in these skills from the time of her first period, she is eligible to be married. Once a modest virgin is married, she is expected to maintain these same norms and behaviors in the home of her husband, where she moves into the second category of modest women, married women. The third sub-category is divorced women. If a marriage breaks down, a woman returns to her father's house or to that of another male guardian. There she is expected to continue to uphold the same norms and to help in the running of the household and the rearing of children. Divorced women still do not go out at night, and they protect their reputation in the hope of making another marriage. The final category of modest women is that of widows. Often a brother of the deceased husband will take the widow as his second, third, or fourth wife, and the same norms and behavior will be enforced. These older women, regardless of their status, tend to be the enforcers of the social norms on the next generation of women: the virgins and newly married. All older women, whether they are divorced or widowed or not, are expected to uphold and perpetuate the modesty doctrine.

The most important aspect of these social norms is that all categories of modest women are considered protected. The trade-off they make is upholding the modesty doctrine in return for protection from their menfolk. Any man in these societies who behaves inappropriately toward these women, by leering at, groping, or harassing them, knows there will be consequences. The men in the woman's family will gather together and plot their revenge, usually by violent means. This violence is directed not only against the man considered to be the transgressor but also against his family and extended family, for example with retaliatory rapes.

In these societies there is another overarching category of women: the immodest. If a woman breaks the rules or is perceived to have broken the rules, her family's protection will be withdrawn. Whether she is a virgin, married, divorced, or widowed, if she works outside the house, if she moves around freely in public without a chaperone, if she ignores the modesty dress code, she is deemed immodest. A woman who has no male relatives to protect her is, by default, also considered immodest. Women with this unprotected status are seen as fair game by other men. They can be leered at, harassed, groped, or sexually assaulted because the perpetrators have no consequences to fear, whether because there is no one to retaliate on her behalf or because the woman is simply thought to be "asking for it." The Algerian author Kamel Daoud rightly described this system as creating "sexual misery" for both men and women throughout the Islamic world.

More than any other major religion, Islam formalizes the subordination of women. Islamic religious law, as codified by the "official" schools of Sunni Islamic law (the Hanbali, Shafi'i, Hanafi, and Maliki schools), insists on male guardianship over women. In Islam, "any woman must have a 'guardian,' *wali*; her closest male relative if she is unmarried, her husband if she is not."[16] This remnant of seventh-century Arab culture—which has spread through Islam to the other parts of the world that are now Muslim majority—has never been revised in official schools of Islamic law.[17] Imams and other Islamic religious leaders today continue to chastise women for disobeying the modesty doctrine. They cite passages in the Quran to assign girls a position in the family that requires them to be docile, to depend on male relatives for money, and to submit to their husband's dominion over their bodies. Marriage is typically arranged, and there is often an exchange of money in the process. Under the religious rule of Islam, it is still common today that a woman's rights are essentially sold to a man she may not even know.

Religious teachings from the twelfth century, still cited in mosques today, distinguish some women as virtuous and chaste by nature and others as licentious. Western women as far back as the Crusades are described by Muslim historians as immodest whores who "glowed with ardor for carnal intercourse . . . offering themselves for sin. . . . They were all licentious harlots . . . appearing proudly in public, ardent and inflamed, tinted and painted, desirable and appetizing . . . blue-eyed and gray-eyed, broken down little fools . . . abandoning all decency and shame."[18]

"Your wives are as a tilth unto you, so approach your tilth when or how you wish" (Quran 2:223) and "When the man invites his wife to his bed she should satisfy him even if she were on the camel's saddle" (Sahihul-Jami'). It was passages like these that ISIS used to justify the buying, selling, and raping of Yazidi women in Iraq. The women were not sexually enslaved because of their ethnicity but rather treated as the Quran ordains non-Muslim women should be treated.

Under Islamic law, such as governs Saudi Arabia, Iran, and parts of Nigeria, the civil rights of women are radically circumscribed. The threat of violent punishment in the form of whipping and stoning makes the prospect of sexual freedom all but impossible for women. If raped, a woman in a territory governed by sharia law has to bring four witnesses to substantiate her accusation.[19] As one expert on Islamic law has pointed out, "a worst-case scenario would be if a hostile Sharia judge decided that without witnesses there is neither proof of violence nor that the accused man was involved, so there is no *zina** for him while the woman's accusation must be considered admission of sexual relations with an unspecified man, and as such punishable."[20] In some cases, the pregnancy of an unmarried woman is considered proof of her "fornication" when in fact the woman was raped. Victims are blamed for sexual assault and face ostracism. Reporting rape to the police can make a victim's plight worse if the perpetrator's family seeks vengeance.[21]

When sexual violence occurs in holy places, victims are encour-

---

*   The twelfth-century scholar Ibn Rushd defined *zina* as "any copulation [between a man and a woman] without a valid marriage contract, a suspected matrimonial relationship, or lawful concubinage" (Ruth Miller, *The Limits of Bodily Integrity*, 74–75).

aged to cover it up to protect the sanctity of religion. Just like systemic child sexual abuse in the Catholic Church, victims of sexual violence in Mecca are told to keep quiet so as not to tarnish their religion. Mona Eltahawy was groped by a policeman and a fellow pilgrim as a young girl while praying at the hajj in Mecca. She did not tell anyone out of shame and later wrote, "Even now when I do talk of being groped during hajj, I get accused of making it up or told that I'm maligning Islam."[22] Riazat Butt had the same experience in 2001, when she was sexually assaulted three times while praying near the holy Kaaba stone during the hajj. "Being sexually assaulted," she wrote, "is . . . an almost occupational hazard for the female pilgrim."[23] In the words of Phyllis Chesler, "You might say there are horrible things that happen to Muslim women in Muslim countries, and that's true. But the Muslim woman expects it, she's used to it; it's terrible, but it is something she already knows about. That is not the case with the foreign or Western wife in a Muslim country."[24]

THE ISLAMIC WORLD'S MISOGYNY IS NOT UNIQUE, BUT IT IS SEVERE

This framework has yet another layer of complexity. In societies where the social order has broken down due to civil war or famine, drought or economic collapse, the moral order protecting even modest women is dismantled. After social breakdown, the men and women who had passed on the norms beforehand, the moral enforcers, either are weakened or are no longer in the picture, for example, the men conscripted into militias like those in Eritrea. The disruption in these societies has lasted for decades. The civil war in Somalia has been going on since 1991, and many children born into that context grow up witnessing Hobbesian anarchy. Fighting in

Afghanistan has been going on even longer, since the 1970s. Though their descent into violence has been more recent, Iraq and Syria are not a great deal better. The main places asylum seekers are fleeing from are failed states with broken social orders.

The failure of secular states in these countries helps explain the resurgence of Islam as a political as well as spiritual force. Islamism has become the "go-to" haven for those seeking order amid such chaos. Sharia courts have been established in these countries, filling the void of social control. After the savagery of dictatorship and civil war, the promise of divine law is understandably welcomed by a population hungry for order and stability. When the Islamists come to town, they therefore reestablish order again with their own savagery. For example, the immodest woman is no longer considered simply immodest; she is an adulterous sinner who must be flogged and stoned.

To be sure, this kind of thing is not unique to Muslim societies. In all kinds of countries around the world, as we have seen, women lead the lives of second-class citizens. Lesotho in southern Africa is not a Muslim society, yet rapists there can walk free because it is accepted that men can treat women as they please. Nevertheless, nowhere is the law more skewed against women than in countries that impose sharia.

In Dubai and Sudan, for example, sharia courts sentence women to prison for enticing men to rape them.[25] Rapists can avoid prosecution in Algeria, Bahrain, Iraq, Kuwait, Libya, Palestine, and Syria if they marry their victims. Three years after Morocco abolished its "marry your rapist" law in 2014, the majority of Moroccan men and 48 percent of Moroccan women still believed that a raped woman should marry her attacker.[26]

Likewise, sexual harassment in public places is not prohibited or prevented in much of the Middle East and North Africa.[27] Mona Eltahawy has written eloquently on the "epidemic" levels of sexual harassment in the Arab world.[28] She noted that women are blamed in cases of groping and assaults for being "in the wrong place at the wrong time, wearing the wrong thing." She described daily life for women in Egypt, where 99.3 percent report being sexually harassed in the streets and 62 percent of men admit to doing it:

> Before leaving her home, every woman I know braces herself for the obstacle course of offensive words, groping hands, and worse that awaits her in the streets she takes to school, university, and work.[29]

A survey of British tourists who visited Egypt found that all the women, especially those with blond hair and blue eyes, received "unwanted male attention ranging from staring, gesturing and touching to verbal and sexual assault." Like their local sisters, those women modified their dress or avoided walking in the streets to dodge harassment.[30] A UN survey of more than four thousand men in Morocco, Egypt, Palestine, and Lebanon found that between one-third and two-thirds admitted to having carried out street-based sexual harassment.[31] The vast majority said that they had done it for fun and had targeted women who were dressed provocatively. But covering up does not prevent harassment or assault in those cultures. The sociologist Marnia Lazreg described the farcical nature of the "gentlemen's agreement" that women will not be harassed if they wear the veil.[32] In 2017, an Egyptian lawyer was prosecuted for declaring on television that "when a girl walks about like that [dressed immodestly], it is a patriotic duty to sexually harass her and a national duty to rape her."[33]

WHERE WOMEN ARE NOT A FEATURE OF PUBLIC LIFE

I am not sure which came first: confining women to the home or sexually harassing them in public places. The latter certainly reinforces the former. Even the threat of harm will frighten some women back into the home. Public places such as streets, coffee stands, and tea shops are the domain of men. As the keepers of women, men have public-facing jobs in shops, in offices, driving taxis. A woman's domain is the private sphere, and she is immediately at risk if she steps out without a male relative, unless she is in all-female company.

Though some restrictions on women's freedom have recently been eased under the influence of Crown Prince Mohammad bin Salman, Saudi Arabia is renowned for taking gender segregation to the extreme with single-sex wedding celebrations, women-only shopping malls, and men-only concerts. In Lebanon, women-only beaches are popular, and in mosques the world over women sit in a separate room or at the back.[34] This divide along gender lines has even been replicated in refugee camps. Women left behind by their male relatives, many of whom are in Europe, huddle inside tents and containers, avoiding public areas such as washrooms for fear of being sexually assaulted.[35] The German journalist Maria von Welser, who visited refugee camps across the Middle East in 2015, noted that most of the women she encountered were afraid for their safety without male relatives to protect them.[36] The Office of the United Nations High Commissioner for Human Rights (OHCHR) reported in 2018 that almost all female refugees passing through Libya experienced some form of sexual assault.[37]

It is the combination of all these complex factors—the modesty doctrine, the breakdown in social order, Islamist orthodoxy, and an upbringing in some of the world's most misogynistic societies—that shapes the attitudes of so many of the young men migrating from

Muslim-majority countries to Europe. Whether or not these men are accepted as legitimate asylum seekers or migrate illegally, their attitude to women is unlikely to coincide with the notions of gender equality that have come to dominate in western Europe.

LET'S (NOT) TALK ABOUT SEX

In the West, where relations between the sexes have become more equal since the 1960s, male predatory behavior is criminalized rather than lionized. Second-wave feminists have worked hard to challenge patriarchal attitudes and sexist behavior. They have argued that gender inequalities are socialized in children from an early age and that rape is a product of social context and conditioning.[38] "Rapists are created, not born" has become the accepted wisdom.[39] But when it comes to migrants and minorities, pointing to cultural explanations for their behavior toward women is taboo. This seems contradictory. Indeed, when you consider how Muslim men are educated about sex—or not—it makes no sense at all.

Compared to liberal societies, sexual education is sadly lacking in Muslim societies. Rather than boys and girls being educated about their bodies, relationships, and sex, they are taught to repress themselves. Boys are not taught that a woman's views about sex or relationships are important. Instead they are taught to abstain from all sexual contact and masturbation outside marriage; within it, on the other hand, anything goes.[40] In Western countries, Muslim parents object to their children being exposed to frank discussions about sex at school. They fear that talking about it implicitly encourages their children to transgress the rigid principle of no sex outside marriage. In Toronto in 2018, Muslim parents withdrew their children from public schools to avoid sex education classes. One family profiled in a local newspaper reenrolled their sons in public school once they had successfully lobbied for sex education to be removed from the curriculum. But they sent their daughter to a private Islamic school.[41] Similarly, in Saltley in the United Kingdom, parents withdrew their children from school in protest against a sex education curriculum that discussed homosexuality.[42] An angry mother said, "It's inappropriate, totally wrong. Children are being told it's OK to be gay yet 98 percent of children at this school are Muslim. It's a Muslim community."[43]

Straitlaced websites encouraging abstinence compete with online pornography for teenagers' attention. The advice offered to young Muslims by online communities makes for pitiful reading. Teenage boys post questions to Ummah.com, seeking guidance on managing the conflict between their hormonal urges and their religion. Some are worried about evil spirits ("night jinns") giving them wet dreams; others fret about masturbating or looking at "uncovered" women wearing shorts in the streets ("My hormones can't handle all the women in public"). The advice they receive from "senior" forum members is always the same: pray more to Allah and fast.[44] Kamel Daoud described these repressive contradictions as "unbearable tensions" that can swiftly descend "into absurdity and hysteria"[45]—or, as we have seen, into sexual misconduct and violence.

THE RAPE GAME

The extreme, yet perhaps inevitable, expression of all these beliefs and behaviors—polygamy, religiously sanctioned bigotry, unchecked sexual harassment, a lack of sex education, repressed sexual urges, and the honor/shame dichotomy—is *taharrush gamea*, "the rape game" in Arabic. Gang rape is considered a particularly reprehensible crime in the West, but in the Arab world, where speaking about sexual violence elicits more suffering than support, the rape game takes place openly.

US television audiences were shocked by CBS journalist Lara Logan's ordeal while reporting on protests in Cairo's Tahrir Square in 2011. In her own words, this is what Lara went through:

> We were filming in the square—myself and my team of four men, a producer, cameraman, security person, and local fixer. We had been filming and doing interviews surrounded by the massive crowds for some time when the battery went down on my cameraman, Richard Butler's, camera. He knelt down to change the battery and we stood around him, surrounded by the crowd who were excited but calm and happy. The last person I had interviewed had just said, "Thank you Mark Zuckerberg, thank you Google, thank you Facebook—this is your revolution."
>
> As we stood with the crowd and Richard was changing his battery, our young Egyptian fixer turned to me in a panic, his face totally white with panic and fear and he said, "We have to go now, NOW—RUN!" So we started to run and managed to get ahead of much of the crowd. I was running with him and our team security person, Ray.
>
> It was confusing because I thought the men/boys running with us were trying to help and they were telling me to slow down and wait and I could feel people's hands between my legs and grabbing my crotch violently and I was worried about the team. It was just me and Ray and our Egyptian fixer at this point. We seemed to get far from the mass of people but there were still many men around us who were saying they were helping but I began to realize they were slowing me down and also grabbing me and then the mass of the crowd had caught up to us and began to tear at my body and my clothes and stick their hands inside my shirt and my pants. I was stripped

naked, my clothing was shredded and [I was] violently raped with sticks, flag poles, hands—at a certain point I lost track. I recall Ray telling me they were beating us with sticks and stealing our passports and so on, but I was so consumed with trying to fight the sexual assault and gang rape that it barely registered. I could feel my bra strap tear and give way and the air on my skin and their nails as they tried to tear my breast from my body. My limbs were distended as they tore my body in different directions as the mob seethed.

I was with Ray for at least twenty minutes and he kept telling me to hold on to him and to stay on my feet. But eventually I lost hold of him and that was what may have saved me because he forced the Egyptian soldiers to beat a path through the mob and carry me away. The last time I went down there were too many men on top of me to stand and I was dragged into a part of the square where crowds of women and children blocked the path of the mob and young men jumped up to stand between them and me and the mob. By the end I was beaten and gang raped and sodomized to the point where I was near death and had lost my ability to breathe freely from the crush of the mob and the physical pressure on my lungs.

What I failed to understand—that I learned from that paper—is that this is a form of social control in Egypt. That women do not want to go out without men if they know this could happen to them. That African women going to work every day in Egypt experience some level of this harassment. That women of course bear the burden because the government uses this to remind them to cover themselves.[46]

The practice is well known but rarely discussed throughout North Africa. Accounts of *taharrush gamea* have been recorded in Algeria and Tunisia since the 1960s.[47]

In 2006, Egyptian bloggers witnessed hundreds of men thronging the streets to celebrate the end of Ramadan, harassing women with or without hijabs, ripping off their clothes, encircling them, and trying to assault them.[48] Girls ran for cover in nearby restaurants, taxis, and cinemas. As protests continued in Tahrir Square in 2012, mob attacks against women became more organized. Men formed concentric rings around individual women, stripping and raping them.[49] Some Egyptian women spoke out, taking their accounts and video evidence of sexual assaults to police, but little headway was made until laws against sexual harassment were introduced in 2014.[50]

The rape game crossed the Mediterranean in December 2015. During New Year's Eve celebrations in Cologne, as we have seen, more than a thousand young men formed rings around individual women, sexually assaulting them.[51] When the victims identified the perpetrators as looking "foreign," "North African," and "Arab," they were pilloried as racists on social media.[52] The local feminist and magazine editor Alice Schwarzer's dogged reporting established that the young men had coordinated and planned the attacks that night "to the detriment of the Kufar [infidels]."[53] Schwarzer was vindicated twelve months later, when Cologne police chief Jürgen Mathies confirmed that the attacks had been intentionally coordinated to intimidate the German population.[54]

As I will explain in more detail in the following chapter, I am skeptical about the claim that a minority of immigrant men use sexual violence to lash out at host societies because they feel disenfranchised. Such men behave the same way in their own communities, as well as in the refugee camps and smuggling routes on their way to Europe. If Egyptian men harass Egyptian women in the streets of Cairo and then come to Germany and do the same thing to German women in the streets of Cologne, it is not because they feel inferior or oppressed; it is because they think they can get away with it, just as they did back home.

Chapter 12

CULTURE CLASH

As an immigrant and former asylum seeker of Somali origin, I am for immigration. I have no objection to people packing up their possessions and leaving their homes to try to improve their circumstances. I completely understand why they would wish to do so because I did it myself. My concern is with the attitudes some bring with them, with the behaviors that these attitudes generate in a minority of migrants, and with the seeming inability of Western countries to understand how to cope with the resulting problems. In fact, the West is failing migrants by refusing to prepare young men for the culture clash they will experience and then by refusing to hold them accountable for their lack of self-control.

I am aware of the fact that I am generalizing. The reality is, of course, more complex than even a book can convey. There are huge differences between people living in cities and those living in rural areas. There are differences among individuals in the amount of importance they attach to faith and tribal constraints. It is not my intention to dismiss all immigrants as incapable of adapting to their new surroundings. There are many who, once they come to the West, find it easy to reconcile their tribal or religious heritage with life in a hypermodern society, or, like me, gladly jettison their cultural inheritance in favor of Western norms. But there is a problem with the attitudes and behaviors that some immigrants bring with them. These things might have been a source of survival or even wealth in their country of origin, but in the West they lead to conflict and stunt immigrants' opportunities.

In this age of identity politics, intersectionality, and manufactured offense, it is unfashionable to criticize anyone's culture, unless it is that of white heterosexual men. But one of those men, Samuel Huntington, deserves credit for seeing clearly—and early—the nature of the challenge we face. In his 1993 essay "The Clash of Civilizations?" he said that culture would be the most important distinction between peoples in the post–Cold War world.[1] Though his thesis has repeatedly been attacked, I believe he was right. The debate about immigration is really about the integration of non-Western minorities into Western societies, and that is a debate, inevitably, about conflicting values.

IMPORTING VALUES

It would seem almost self-evident that people bring their attitudes and values with them when they migrate, even if they are open-minded about the society they are arriving in. But in today's debate about immigration, that is a controversial statement. The "transfer of norms" literature focuses on the export of democratic attitudes from the West to the "global South." Describing a boomerang effect, these studies track migrants coming to liberal democracies, absorbing some democratic political norms, and then introducing those new norms to their country of origin when they return home.[2] This is good news for all concerned, but what I find fascinating is that the studies are not replicated in reverse. If returning migrants export democratic values from the West, why don't they also import non-democratic values when they first arrive in the West? Or are we to pretend that they are value-free blank slates when they arrive?

A study tracking the boomerang effect in Jordan found that Jordanian women were more likely to internalize gender discrimination if a member of their family had at some point lived in an even more conservative Arab society, "suggesting a transfer of negative norms from highly discriminatory destinations."[3] If it can happen to Jordanian women, surely it can happen to German women as well. Yet academics are loath to acknowledge this kind of finding today. In the 1990s, there was a consensus that gender attitudes learned early on in the country of origin "continue[d] to exert an influence on migrants' attitudes long after migration."[4] That view is now taboo.

Of all the ideas migrants bring with them, it is their attitude toward women that interests me the most. Migrants are a diverse bunch, as I have said. Those who have been well educated and may already speak other languages generally find it easier to settle and establish themselves in the West. Those with deeply traditional views, who will not shake a woman's hand or interact with a female teacher or policewoman, are the ones who pose a problem. Coming from Afghanistan does not mean that a young man will treat all women poorly, but having grown up in a society where women are institutionally inferior must surely influence his views. Those may change with exposure to other customs over time, but we must try to understand how he thinks when he arrives in the West.

Analysts working with World Values Survey data have mapped the variations in global cultural values for us.[5] The blobs in the map group countries according to their majority beliefs and attitudes.[6] Diametrically opposed to each other are Protestant Europe, top right, with the most secular-rational and self-expressive values, and the African-Islamic world, bottom left, with the most traditional and survival-oriented values.

The distance between these two sets of values is vast. The authors pointed out that "emancipative values," in the "self-expression" cate-

Figure 1: World Values

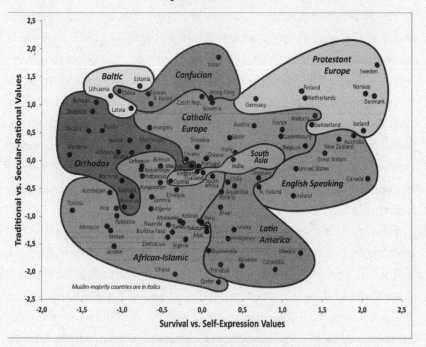

Source:"Inglehart-Welzel Cultural Map, World Values Survey Wave 6 (2010–2014),"
http://www.worldvaluessurvey.org/WVSContents.jsp.

gory on the right, are the most important factor in advancing women's empowerment. They wrote that for less educated Muslims, "the social dominance of Islam and individual identification as Muslim both weaken emancipative values." This tends to support the commonsense position that migrants can import as well as export values and that the two sets of values that are coming into contact are the most dissimilar of all, with one set being distinctly hostile to women's rights.

The bulk of asylum seekers who have entered the European Union in recent years have come from countries in the bottom left quadrant. As we saw in chapter 2, their principal countries of origin are Muslim majority: Syria, Iraq, Afghanistan, Eritrea, Iran, Nigeria, Pakistan, Bangladesh, Somalia, and Albania.[7] Not all migrants coming from those countries are Muslim, and no doubt a proportion of the Muslims are not strictly observant. But compared to north-western Europeans, they are five times as likely to think religion is important and twice as likely to say men are justified in beating their wives.[8] Most immigrants from those places have not gone through the process of individualization, rationalization, and secularization that European societies have over many generations. The societies they come from still institutionalize the inferior status of women in the ways described in the previous chapter. These are places where women are not a feature of public life and their right to sexual self-determination is disregarded.

Hundreds of thousands of young men who have grown up in parts of the world where these attitudes toward women are dominant have arrived in Europe in the space of a few years. We can assume that a proportion of them are open-minded and keen to adapt to life in the West, but some still hold on to their cultural attitudes, maybe even more tightly than they did at home. When surveys of migrants' attitudes toward women are published, they are inevitably controversial.

YOUNG IMMIGRANTS ARE TOTALLY UNPREPARED FOR A SEXUALLY LIBERATED CULTURE

Seen through the eyes of a young man fresh from the Arab world, the streets of Amsterdam, London, or Brussels must appear filled with temptation. Girls walking past in skinny jeans and high heels, their hair flowing in a fog of perfume: we should not be surprised that young men who have never been taught how to have an equal relationship with a woman react the wrong way. Billboards on buildings and buses show scantily clad women selling anything from jeans to holidays. Curvaceous singers twerk for the camera in music videos. Sex sells. In Cologne, a model advertising a low-cut bra gazes dreamily at the Grand Mosque across the street. To a new arrival the ad must seem as incongruous as the intergalactic architecture of the mosque itself. The Belgian filmmaker Sofie Peeters described the cognitive dissonance as "creating an explosion" for the young men in her film: "When very conservative views get in contact with naked, semipornographic images of women, the guys become confused and freak out."[9] For some of them, that means overstepping boundaries that no one ever told them were there.

Girls like me were taught never to draw attention to ourselves, but in the West women deliberately draw attention to their bodies. They work out in gyms, select outfits to highlight their best physical features, and constantly refer to their bodies. I've come to realize that Western women don't do this for men; they do it for themselves. They grow up watching advertisements on television with slogans such as L'Oréal's "Because I'm worth it." Men from the cultures I am describing in this book see Western women doing their hair and makeup, but the first thought that enters their mind is not that they are doing it because they are "worth it"; they have been taught that women who emphasize their bodies in this way are asking for it. This stereotype about white women is confirmed by the Hollywood films and pornography they have nearly all consumed before arriving in Europe.

THE ENCOUNTER

I wanted to know if the nongovernmental volunteers and social workers—those looking to help young asylum seekers—have seen this culture clash in action. I asked some of those working with them what the young men think about women in the West. Pastor Cai

Berger, who works with both new arrivals and second-generation immigrants in Sweden, told me, "Some guys have asked me, 'I want to meet someone, how do I do that here?' I've spoken with many of these men about how we view women in Sweden, and when they are given a straight answer, they often say 'Oh' and begin modifying their position. They're not stupid."[10]

However, others have no intention of changing their views to accommodate the cultural norms in their new country. Efgani Dönmez is a Turkish migrant to Austria. Before being elected to the Austrian government, he ran shelters for underage asylum seekers. "The way Austrians live," he told me, "the idea that women have equal rights and can make their own decisions is an irritating factor for some of these guys. They've learned it a different way and grown up with a taboo on sexuality. When they arrive here and see women dressing as they do on the streets, they feel sexually attracted to them. It creates a lot of conflict."[11]

This conflict can have dire consequences. The psychologist Mia Jörgensen, who works at a treatment facility for underage sex offenders in Sweden, says that coming from a culture where sex is taboo is considered "a risk factor" for sex offenders.[12]

Mustafa Panshiri is an Afghan-Swedish former policeman who has done more than most to grapple with the potential cultural confrontation for new arrivals. Casually dressed in jeans and a hoodie, he shares photos and quotes from many of the young migrants he meets on social media. One of the stories that affected him most was that of a 15-year-old boy he met with at Linköping police station. In tears, the boy relayed his journey from Afghanistan through Iran, Turkey, Germany, and Denmark to Sweden. Traveling with hundreds of others, he lost his mother and brother, and he asked Mustafa if he would ever see his mother again. After encountering so many young migrants like that boy from his homeland, struggling to bridge the centuries-wide cultural gap between Sweden and Afghanistan, Mustafa quit his job with the police. He now travels around Sweden, talking with young migrants to help them adjust.

When I interviewed him in 2018, Mustafa told me that most new arrivals are serious about adapting to a Swedish way of life. He told me they get "pissed off" when their countrymen harass women in Sweden. They want to enjoy swimming pools and concerts in Sweden but can't when a minority generates so much distrust in the community. "When I first started this," he recalled, "I called up refugee camps and communities in Sweden, and at the beginning they said what was important was that these guys had somewhere to sleep and eat. 'We don't have time for integration.' That set off an alarm for me. I knew they needed this information right away, especially young men here without their parents and without role models."

Unlike most Swedes, Mustafa is frank about the problem. I am certain that this is because he knows what life is like in Afghanistan, having fled from there with his family as a child. In his words:

> If we just take Afghanistan, it has been one of the worst places for a woman to live in recent decades. So of course, someone coming from Afghanistan to Sweden will have ideas and values that are not going to work here. We have been seeing that in the form of sexual harassment for the last few years. But there are those who come here as secular and democratic as Swedes; they respect women, and they want to be a part of Swedish society.

I wanted to know if the young men he speaks to know much about sex and relationships. "Some are informed," he told me, "but others aren't. I've had fifteen- and sixteen-year-olds asking what a condom is and what do you use it for. What they really need is more information."[13] By late 2017, the Swedish government agreed with Mustafa and produced a website with advice for those working with asylum seekers on how to discuss sexuality and consent with them.[14]

Perhaps not entirely wisely, some people decided to teach the young men about Western women in a different way. I have come across anecdotal accounts of asylum-seeker advocates and volunteers, typically middle-aged women, taking young migrant men as boyfriends. Unaccompanied minors of indeterminate age, known in the vernacular as "beard children," are no doubt exotic and attractive to those women. (In one tragic case, a 70-year-old Swedish woman, an asylum activist and member of the local Green Party, was murdered by her Afghan lover.)[15] When I spoke with the Egyptian-German political scientist Hamed Abdel-Samad about this phenomenon, he told me he had heard similar reports in Germany: "Asylum workers told me that no single female refugee helper left the asylum home still single. It's not benign. The men see these women as easy to manipulate, and it confirms their idea that all German women are looking for someone like him to satisfy her."[16]

CULTURE AS AN EXCUSE

The occasional cultural confrontation can serve a greater good by forcing a society to restate the values it believes in. But the question is, which values should prevail? Too often in the West nowadays, minority values are privileged over liberal values such as women's rights. But a culture that says it is acceptable to harass women in certain circumstances—that it is in fact a God-given right—is fundamentally incompatible with the principle of gender equality.

When pressed about the role of "cultural defenses" in judicial decision making, Western legal scholars tend to deny that they are used in court. Yet culture is sometimes used as an excuse to get some perpetrators off the hook. On the coast of Normandy, in La Manche, a Bangladeshi refugee received a suspended sentence for raping a 15-year-old girl.[17] It was his second offense, as he had previously been charged with molesting an 18-year-old. The prosecutor referred to the defendant's "predatory behavior" and said he "considers French women whores" (*putes*),[18] but court experts said he had been "deeply influenced by the culture of his country, where women are relegated to the status of sexual object." During the hearing, a police person had to stand between the defendant and his interpreter, as he shamelessly tried to grope her thighs. Nonetheless, he was put back onto the streets by the court.

British member of Parliament Jess Phillips says that such culture defenses belittle men: "All men can control themselves, they just need to be taught to manage their urges."[19] Phillips makes it very clear that she does not agree with the view that sexual violence is increasing due to immigration from Muslim majority countries. "I saw no evidence while working in rape crisis that any heritage group of victims or perpetrators was overrepresented." Writing about sexual assaults by Afghan migrants in Europe, the political scientist Cheryl Benard has pointed out that sexual assaults against women in their 70s, mothers pushing baby carriages, and underage girls do not fit the idea that offenders are conforming to the norms of the countries where they were born. Benard suggests instead that young migrants simply select targets that look like easy prey. I agree with her. On the night of the mass groping incident in Cologne, the temperature was barely above freezing, 4 degrees Celsius. It was winter, so partygoers were bundled up in thick coats, scarves, gloves, and hats. The argument that seeing scantily clad female bodies had sent the men wild simply does not stand up.

VICTIM BLAMING

At the core of the culture defense is the idea that women are to blame for enticing men to harass or assault them. Victim blaming is not unique to the Muslim world, needless to say; it was a widely accepted justification for male sexual violence in the West until quite recently. One American journalist publicly blamed Lara Logan for her rape in Cairo, saying "Earth to liberated women: When you display legs, thighs or cleavage, some liberated men will see it as a sign that you feel good about yourself and your sexuality. But most men will see it as a sign you want to get laid."[20] In recent studies of convicted rapists' motivations in the United States, the majority blamed their victims or thought their sexual entitlement took precedence over their victims' wishes.[21] This is the "classic rapist defense" according to former UK Crown prosecutor Nazir Afzal. In the case of the grooming gangs in the north of England, who sexually exploited and abused young girls (see chapter 15), he told me:

> The main perpetrator, Shabir Ahmed, said that Western society has trained these girls for him. In his view we allow immodesty, and he balks at the freedoms we give girls. He said that's what made the girls lesser individuals and therefore ripe for him to pluck.[22]

In reading through pages of court proceedings, arrest reports, and eyewitness accounts, I have come across a plethora of excuses for attacks on women. The most common are that the perpetrator was drunk or on drugs and therefore unable to remember what had actually happened. Mistaking the victim's age in sexual assaults of minors also comes up quite often. Some perpetrators blamed the rejection of their asylum applications; others said that they had been framed by racist police. Post-traumatic stress disorder is regularly cited. Some attribute their actions to the supernatural, blaming the Devil for their behavior. Ignorance of the law is another common excuse, best articulated by one Egyptian immigrant who was prosecuted for sexually assaulting thirteen women on the Berlin subway. He told the court, "In Egypt this happens frequently, it isn't penalised. I'm not well versed in law. There were no police in my village. Nobody told me that this was wrong here."[23] Victim blaming makes regular appearances in court proceedings: "She would certainly have sex because she had drunk too much." Some excuses verge on the ridiculous, such as "sexual emergencies" and the difficulty perpetrators have had in finding a girlfriend. Defenders of Tariq Ramadan, the Swiss Islamist scholar accused of sexually assaulting two women, have resorted to claiming that the allegations are a "Zionist conspiracy" or an "Islamophobic effort" to discredit him.[24]

RELIGIOUS JUSTIFICATIONS FOR CRIMES AGAINST WOMEN

It was not so long ago that Christian priests advised battered and raped wives to return to their abusive partners. It has taken roughly four decades for this to change. The same shift has not taken place in Muslim communities, however, including many in the West. Rather than condemn the actions of perpetrators of sexual violence, imams and religious authorities defend them. Their default response is to blame the female victim for provoking an attack. Writing under a pseudonym about her ordeal, one of the survivors of the grooming gang rapes in Rotherham said she had been the victim of "religiously sanctioned sexual violence." "They made it clear that because I was a non-Muslim, and not a virgin, and because I didn't dress 'modestly,' that they believed I deserved to be 'punished.'"[25] That punishment included more than a hundred rapes by perpetrators, some of whom quoted the Quran while beating her.

Speaking about the conviction of Lebanese-Australian men for gang rape in 2006, Australia's most senior Muslim cleric echoed the words of my grandmother in Somalia: "If you take out uncovered meat and place it outside on the street, or in the garden or in the park, or in the backyard without a cover, and the cats come and eat it . . . whose fault is it, the cats or the uncovered meat? The uncovered meat is the problem. . . . If she [the victim] was in her room, in her home, in her hijab, no problem would have occurred."[26] A similar attitude was expressed by the president of the Islamic Sharia Council in Great Britain, who claimed in 2015 that there was no such thing as rape in marriage, and the Danish cleric who said in 2004 that "Women who don't wear headscarves are in many ways themselves to blame if they are raped."[27] A Danish Muslim youth organization (Muslimsk Ungdom i Danmark) invited that same cleric to speak to young Muslims in Copenhagen just days after the Cologne New Year's Eve incident.

VICTIMHOOD IS NO EXCUSE

At the core of any discussion about culture is the relationship between the group and the individual. It took me a while to understand this after I came to the West. In liberal societies the individual, whether male or female, is recognized as a decision maker responsible for his or her behavior. All liberal institutions are predicated on this idea: from signing a contract to voting in an election, in every instance responsibility is located at the individual level. In the Muslim world, by contrast, it is the group that is responsible. Whether it is the family, the clan, or the whole *ummah* (community), the group makes decisions on behalf of individuals. Because the individual is inextricably linked to the group, condemnation of the individual is considered vilification of the group. If the group does not recognize an individual's actions as criminal, for example in the case of sexual assault, then the group feels unjustly targeted and victimized by the state. This victimhood complex is important to understand.

A study by the Netherlands Institute for Social Research (Sociaal en Cultureel Planbureau, or SCP) found that two-thirds of Muslims felt they had suffered discrimination in one year alone.[28] Compared with other minorities, including LGBTQ people and the disabled, their perceptions of negative attitudes and unequal treatment were among the highest. In Belgium, it is Moroccan men and Muslim women with higher education who self-report the most discrimination.[29]

Refugee advocates often argue that asylum seekers "have experienced psychological trauma as a result of fleeing civil war and conflict in their home countries."[30] But wounds of psychological harm appear to be a heritable condition.[31] In Parisian banlieues, the French-born children of immigrants say they feel victimized and resentful.[32] Researchers studying second-generation immigrant criminals in the United Kingdom find that "ethnic minority offenders have higher rates of post-traumatic stress."[33] Even when individual Muslims commit crimes, their communities seek to deflect responsibility by focusing instead on Islamophobia and the fear of a backlash if community members are held to account.[34] They invoke fears that "the Holocaust will be repeated," claiming that "the next time there are gas chambers in Europe, there is no doubt concerning who'll be inside them."[35] As Camille Paglia pointed out, giving special protections to some groups by legislating against "hate crimes" and "hate speech" has "unfortunately created segregated zones of new privilege."[36]

RESENTMENT OF HOST SOCIETIES

The flip side of the victim mentality is that many Muslims believe that they are superior. As both a spiritual and political doctrine, Islam presents itself as a way of life superior to all others. Even if the West offers greater economic and personal freedom to Muslim migrants, its moral system is seen as inferior. En route from Muslim-majority countries, many migrants are forewarned by friends and family to "take care when entering a morally degraded society."[37] And when they arrive, it looks that way. Westerners dole out welfare, food, clothes, health care, and accommodation to anyone arriving, yet leave their women unprotected on the streets. Then new immigrants discover that they have arrived at the very bottom of a social hierarchy. They find themselves in jobs they consider beneath them or get stuck in refugee shelters with nothing to do.

Adding to the sense of humiliation are the expectations of family members left behind. Many young men are sent away with the goal of establishing a more prosperous future for their families. Assets have been sold, savings accounts emptied, and money borrowed to pay smugglers to get them to Europe. But the hopes of a new life are often dashed when they arrive—that is, if they arrive. When a Nigerian migrant whose family had funded his journey by selling their land was turned back by the Libyan coast guard, he told journalists, "I don't want to go back to my village, because if I hear people saying: 'This is the guy who got nowhere,' I'd probably kill them."[38]

Others who do make it find themselves embarrassed by their reduced status in the West. Their feelings of disappointment and humiliation are projected onto the host society. Some become so resentful that they lash out, attacking women, police, or even librarians as symbols of Western society.[39] In the 1990s, the historian Bernard Lewis explained "the rage of the traditional Muslim" as a reaction to losing supremacy over territory, over women, over economic power.[40] This is not a fashionable analysis, but it seems to me that there is much truth in it. And it is not only new arrivals who are resentful about their lives in the West; many children and grandchildren of migrants feel a deep ambivalence about the societies they are born into.

Even the most successful migrants struggle to feel fully part of the social fabric in Europe. And of course there is prejudice against newcomers—prejudice that, as we shall see, is becoming an increasingly explicit part of European politics. But these difficulties cannot be used to justify or downplay the kinds of behavior I have been discussing. Indeed, the widespread reluctance to speak frankly on the issues I am addressing in this book is one of the key reasons for the rise of the far Right. It is also one of the reasons why the social integration of immigrants has proved to be so difficult to achieve in Europe.

Chapter 13

WHY INTEGRATION HAS NOT HAPPENED

The arrival in Europe of large numbers of Muslim immigrants, Bernard Lewis wrote in 1990, would have "immense consequences for the future both of Europe and of Islam."[1] At the time, European policy makers thought that immigrants from Muslim countries represented more of an economic opportunity than a social challenge. We continue to hear this assumption even today. In 2016, the mayors of New York, Paris, and London asserted, "Refugees and other foreign-born residents bring needed skills and enhance the vitality and growth of local economies."[2] Others dismiss the difficulties of assimilation. "Most people quickly adapt their behaviors to their new social environment," argued Martin Rettenberger, the director of the German Centre for Criminology, in 2018. "Social values and norms that were once internalized can still be changed. Arabs or Africans are not intrinsically more likely to commit assaults than Europeans."[3]

Another assumption was that the inherent superiority of secular, democratic pluralism would be so attractive that newcomers would soon embrace it. The question of competing values would take care of itself as migrants established themselves in their workplaces and their children went to local schools.

But that was not what happened. For a significant number of migrants from Muslim countries, as we shall see, the values have not rubbed off. The cause comes down to religious, rather than ethnic, differences, as religiously enforced attitudes about women inhibit employability for migrants and compel them to form parallel societies where antisocial behaviors such as honor violence and forced marriage reinforce separate systems of law. All of this combines to lessen the chances that immigrants will successfully integrate into the surrounding liberal culture.

Commentators tell Europeans to be patient. According to the journalist Doug Saunders, cultural integration takes around seventy-five years, whereas Holland's first guest workers from Morocco have lived there for only around fifty years and Great Britain's Pakistanis and Bangladeshis for barely seventy years.[4] But for more than fifteen years I have argued that having patience is not a viable strategy. This is true now more than ever as over ten thousand migrants arrive in Europe each month—and as at least some of the children and grandchildren of first-generation immigrants turn toward the Islamic values of their family's country of origin.

By the late 1990s, some European governments acknowledged that they had a problem with failed assimilation or integration, but they still believed it was a problem with an economic solution: if new arrivals could be brought into the labor market quickly, they would not become a drain on the public purse.[5] But that approach has been overwhelmed by the sheer number of migrants arriving since the outbreak of the Arab revolutions in 2011. Since then, the challenges of integration have become undeniable.

THE ADAPTATION DEFICIT

Over the last fifteen years, I have watched, read, and participated in the debates over immigration. I have also observed the realities on the ground. Based on Europe's experience of Muslim immigration, I would say that there are four paths that immigrants can take.

First, let us acknowledge that integration has not wholly failed. Many Muslim immigrants have adapted over time by adopting the core values of liberal Europe. These "adapters" use the freedoms they find in Europe to learn, to educate themselves and their children, to find gainful employment, to start businesses, to vote, and to take part in politics and thrive in many ways. I think of myself in the Netherlands in the 1990s as one of the adapters.

The second category I call the "menaces." These are mostly young men who become a danger in their own homes and outside in public. Some drop out of school, some commit crimes big and small, and many spend periods of their lives in prison. Alcohol and drugs fuel their misbehavior, and most are unemployable. They tend to be neither religious nor attached to anything resembling a moral framework. These are the migrants who take full advantage of the welfare state's generous provisions, including the lawyers paid for by the state to assist them when they are charged with stealing, vandalism, sexual assault, or worse. Just one example is furnished by the members of Arab and Kurdish organized crime families who came to Germany in the 1980s. In an interview in 2018, the young mayor of the Berlin suburb of Neukölln, Martin Hikel, said, "We have literally ignored these people for 30 years and now we have a huge problem on our hands."[6]

Then there are the "fanatics," those who came to Europe as religious zealots. The fanatics use the freedoms of the countries that gave them sanctuary to spread an intolerant, fundamentalist version of Islam. If integration is measured by such variables as language proficiency, employment, and knowledge of how the host country's system works, the fanatics may check off all of these indicators. For the fundamentalists speak the local language and are well acquainted with the law, institutions, and culture of the land. The problem is that they reject them as un-Islamic. They seek to work within the system to destroy it and replace it with an alternative: sharia. They may use violent means, including threats, intimidation, blackmail, peer pressure, or worse, to achieve their politico-religious objective. Or they may confine themselves to "peaceful" tools of persuasion in the form of *dawa*, the ideological infrastructure of political Islam.

Finally, there are the "coasters": men and women with little or no formal education who thankfully accept the various welfare benefits to which they are entitled, live off them, and invite their families from abroad to come and join them. They see no reason to work because the jobs available to them are of the menial, repetitive sort that pay only slightly more than the benefits they can claim. They attend prayers at their local mosque but also enroll their kids in the local school.

Coasters are not criminal; on the contrary, they become skilled at following the host state's bureaucratic rules. But when enough of them live in close proximity to one another, they can create ghettoes— or, more politely, "parallel societies"—in which the way of life in their country of origin is replicated in the West. It is in these neighborhoods that the children of coasters become menaces—or find their way to the fanatics.

These four categories are not rigidly separate. A coaster's children can become adapters; some menaces clean up their acts; some fanatics get disillusioned with the pursuit of religious utopia. It also goes the other way: menaces can turn into fanatics, often as a result of exposure to Islamism in prison, as we have seen with some of the perpetrators of the Paris and Brussels terror attacks in 2015 and 2016. The children of coasters can become menaces, to the horror of their parents.

If European elites are honest with themselves, they will concede that not insignificant numbers of immigrant Muslims *before* the "migrant crisis" fell into one or another of the last three categories: menace, fanatic, or coaster. The adapters are there, but they are a minority, particularly when it comes to the attitudes of Muslim immigrants toward women.

WHAT IS HOLDING BACK MUSLIM INTEGRATION?

More than twenty years ago, my Hoover Institution colleague Thomas Sowell surveyed the history of migration throughout the centuries.[7] He found that the speed with which immigrants integrated depended on "whether they perceive[d] the surrounding culture as desirable or undesirable."[8] The Italians, Irish, Jews, and Chinese who arrived in the United States in the nineteenth and early twentieth centuries once seemed as "alien" as Muslim immigrants in Europe today. They lived in crowded accommodation, did not speak English, married within their own communities, and gravitated to cultural ghettoes. Like a large proportion of today's migrants, many were unskilled young men, sent out by their families to make a new start. For instance, Italian migrants to the United States in the early twentieth century were 90 percent male, and Chinese immigrants' male-to-female ratios were even higher in the decades before the 1882 Exclusion Act, which began the process of restricting immigration from China.[9] There were problems, of course, and many contemporary nativists insisted that those groups could never be integrated, leading to the first restrictions of immigration into the United States as early as 1882. Some immigrants took to crime (the most notorious example is the Italian Mafia), but the majority worked hard in legal occupations, sent money home, and sought integration and upward social mobility for their children.[10] Italian and

Chinese immigrants were known for doing the hard, dirty, dangerous, and poorly paid work that locals avoided.[11] Those who did not
succeed, or who found the conditions unbearable, returned home.
By the middle of the twentieth century, Italian Americans and Irish
Americans were more or less fully integrated into American society.
Without repudiating their cultural heritage, they had adopted the
core values of the host society. Why has this not—or at least not
yet—been the case for Muslims in Europe?

"Islamophobia" cannot be the explanation. Earlier batches of
migrants faced far worse hostility from host societies. Chinese
migrants in the nineteenth century were thought of as the "yellow
peril" and faced "sweeping discrimination and sporadic mob violence," followed by an immigration ban.[12] Jewish migrants to the
United States were also exposed to anti-Semitism and discrimination; those who settled in central and western Europe ended up suffering the worst genocide in history. Yet despite the Holocaust, Jews
have enjoyed exceptional economic, social, and cultural success in
the Western world. Their experience of terrible mistreatment tells
us that discrimination cannot be the force holding back Muslim integration.

It is common among academics and integration experts to blame
poor language skills, low education, or past trauma for the adaptation deficit of Muslim immigrants. But the history of Vietnamese integration in Western countries undermines such arguments. In the
1970s and 1980s, many Vietnamese refugees fled war, communism,
and poverty. They arrived in the West with poor education, few language skills, and little money. Some relied on welfare when starting
out, but within a couple of decades they were thoroughly integrated.
Many retain their customs, language, and religious beliefs, but their
children do as well in school as natives do and sometimes better.[13] In
Australia in the 1980s and 1990s, Vietnamese immigrants living in

segregated communities in outer-city suburbs formed ethnic gangs, dealt in drugs, and plotted the country's only political assassination. But today the Vietnamese are scarcely mentioned in the country's immigration debates.

I am not the first to have made this comparison. The Egyptian-born, German-based writer and broadcaster Hamed Abdel-Samad suggests that unlike migrants arriving in Germany from Turkey around the same time, the Vietnamese did not put up "moral and social walls" between their children and the locals.[14] In his latest book on the crisis of the Islamic world, the Dutch sociologist Ruud Koopmans compared the integration outcomes for two other groups of migrants: Christian and Muslim Lebanese refugees who fled civil war for Australia in the 1970s.[15] Their reasons for leaving Lebanon were identical, and their circumstances when they arrived in Australia were the same. On each variable that Koopmans tested—education levels, participation in the labor market, and income—Muslim Lebanese underperformed relative to their Christian compatriots. He repeated the analysis in the United Kingdom. Again, three groups of people—Indians, Pakistanis, and Bangladeshis—had migrated to the same place for essentially the same reasons. They had faced the same starting conditions in the United Kingdom. Measuring the same three variables, Koopmans found that the Hindus and Sikhs either outperformed or were on a par with the native population, but Muslims, especially Muslim women, performed less well.

Koopmans suggested that the problems observed in the Muslim diaspora are a microcosm of the problems playing out in the countries they came from. Across the Muslim world there is a lack of democracy, poor protection of human rights, and political instability. But all that was true of Vietnam and Lebanon in the 1970s and 1980s. To my mind, a more plausible explanation for the apparent adaption deficit is the attitude of Muslim migrants toward women.

All cultures seem to feature some form of misogyny. Women the world over are held in lower esteem than men. Indian and Sikh cultures force their girls to marry, the Chinese still practice selective abortion of girls, and Italians notoriously sexualize women. But Islamic societies, as we have seen, do not merely devalue women; they treat them as commodities.[16]

AN ETHNIC PENALTY OR A RELIGIOUS ONE?

The sociologist Ernest Gellner once said that Islam is hard for the West to digest. He has been proved correct by more recent empirical studies that suggest that Islam has a regressive impact on migrant integration. A report by Great Britain's Social Mobility Commission referred to an "ethnic penalty," the origin of which can be traced back to the patriarchal gender relations in Muslim families. In my view this is more a religious penalty than an ethnic one.

Of all the forces holding back immigrants who grew up Muslim, Islam is the biggest precisely because it enshrines the subordination of women. I saw this time and again when translating for women in domestic violence shelters in the Netherlands. Social workers and doctors tried to help them find their way to independence. But often the women rejected that help. They would say, "I am able to stand up to my husband or my father, but I cannot stand up to God. If I defy him, I will burn in Hell when I die."

Unlike Judaism and Christianity, Islam incorporates a political philosophy along with its spiritual aspects, and this is passed on through the activity known as *dawa*.[17] More than proselytizing, *dawa* is the means by which Islamism, or political Islam, is transmitted to Muslims. The *dawa* process sees Islamists running schools and madrassas, proselytizing in mosques. Their work systematically instills into the hearts and minds of young people from outside Europe, or whose parents hailed from outside Europe, a rejection of the freedoms and the equalities that are supposed to be the continent's core values—particularly the equality of the sexes. *Dawa* encourages young Muslims to take a strict interpretation of Islam as their moral guide. They are encouraged to adhere to the modesty doctrine, to implore female family members to wear the veil, and to think of women as good or bad, modest or immodest.

Though it is not the focus of this book, the susceptibility of Muslim migrants to Europe and their children to radical Islamism is striking. The authors of the seminal study of violence in Lower Saxony, who rightly emphasized the role of culture in explaining the propensity of migrants to commit sex crimes, also argued that extremism—not only Islamic but also left-wing and right-wing extremism—was playing a part in the increase in violent crime in Germany because these ideologies gave young people an "increased affinity" toward acting violently upon extremist beliefs. They clearly defined "Islamic fundamentalism," including "Islamist, Salafist or jihadist extremism," as a threat not only to the postwar German liberal-democratic constitutional order in the abstract but also to individual lives.[18]

But it should also be noted that in the eyes of its leaders, the Islamist movement has long been regarded as a solution to the problem of bad behavior—including sexual depravity—by young people. In the eyes of the proponents of *dawa* and jihad, they are part of the solution, not part of the problem.

On the other hand, radical Islam also gives men religious authority to control the women in their lives and license to abuse women

Table 14: Islamic Fundamentalist Attitudes in Germany: Evidence from a Survey of 500
Self-identified Muslim School Pupils in Lower Saxony, 2016

Propositions	Share in Agreement (%) (Male/Female)	Number
The Quran is the only true book of faith; the rules contained therein must be exactly followed.	69.6 (69.0/70.3)	290
Islam is the only true religion; all other religions are of lesser worth.	36.6 (35.0/37.6)	281
I can envision fighting for Islam and risking my life.	29.9 (27.1/32.6)	284
Islamic sharia laws, for example the harsh punishment of adultery or homosexuality, are much better than German laws.	27.4 (32.2/22.5)	284
Muslims are oppressed across the entire world; therefore they must defend themselves with force.	19.8 (24.0/15.2)	295
It is the duty of each Muslim to fight the infidel and to spread Islam to the entire world.	18.6 (16.9/20.1)	293
Measures against the enemies of Islam must proceed fiercely.	17.7 (19.3/15.7)	286
It is just, that the Muslims in the Near East attempt to found an Islamic State (IS) through war.	8.0 (9.7/6.7)	277
It is permissible for Muslims to achieve their goals through terrorist attacks.	3.8 (4.8/2.9)	286
I find sermons and videos in which Muslims are called to violence against the infidel good.	2.4 (1.4/3.6)	283

Source: Extracted from Christian Pfeiffer, Dirk Baier, and Sören Kliem, *Zur Entwicklung der Gewalt in Deutschland Schwerpunkte: Jugendliche und Flüchtlinge als Täter und Opfer*, Institut für Delinquenz und Kriminalprävention, Zürcher Hochschule für Angewandte Wissenschaften, January 2018, https://www.bmfsfj.de/bmfsfj/service/publikationen/zur-entwicklung-der -gewalt-in-deutschland-/121148, Table 10.

they deem immodest. To glimpse *dawa* at work, you need only browse YouTube and social media, which are awash with "brothers" extolling modesty, shaking their fists when they talk about girls walking the streets alone and without veils.[19]

Dawa works to counter the effects of secular education and socialization. In surveys comparing the attitudes of the children of migrant parents, it is only Muslims who do not develop more egalitarian views about women as they grow up in the West.[20] In the United Kingdom, only slightly fewer second-generation Muslims approve of polygamy than do their parents born overseas.[21] In the Netherlands, almost 20 percent of young Muslims follow a more fundamental interpretation of Islam than their parents do.[22] This is *dawa* in action.

Dawa is happening not only in Muslim communities but also in Western prisons. Believing that religious education will benefit prisoners, the authorities mistakenly give agents of *dawa* access to Muslim prisoners. Like wolves in sheep's clothing, they claim to be religious community representatives, all the while harboring links to terrorist organizations such as the Muslim Brotherhood, ISIS, and Hizb ut-Tahrir. Omar El-Hussein was a petty criminal who was radicalized in a Danish prison. Upon being released in 2015, he procured weapons and shot at attendees of a free-speech event and in a synagogue. Another criminal radicalized in prison was Benjamin Herman, who was given forty-eight hours' leave by the Belgian corrections authority and promptly shot three dead in a Liège school.

Many community organizations that advise Western governments about their integration policies are in fact purveyors of *dawa*. Their approach to Islam is often more fundamentalist than the communities their lobbying impacts. They seek dispensation for removing Muslim pupils from sex education classes or permitting girls to wear head scarves to school. This further entrenches the segregation of those communities from the rest of liberal society. The Austrian politician Efgani Dönmez, himself a Turkish immigrant, observed the irony of this situation: "We have more than four hundred Turkish associations and community groups in Austria, for less than three hundred thousand Turks and Kurds, half of whom hold Austrian citizenship. These groups are organized around religion, politics, and culture. Even though this group has lived in Austria for the longest time and has the most cultural representation in the civic space, regardless which study one looks at, they come in at the bottom for integration. They have the most community organizations and the worst outcomes in education, crime, and the labor market. Of course there is a correlation here."[23]

In research carried out by the European Foundation for Democracy in 2018, refugees and government and civil society actors were interviewed about integration procedures in Austria, Belgium, Denmark, France, Germany, the Netherlands, and Sweden. In every country, the interviewees reported that refugees were being discouraged from integrating into their host society and indoctrinated with "radical ideologies." Refugees reported higher levels of religious fundamentalism in asylum-seeker accommodation than in the countries they were fleeing. They also reported Islamist organizations trying to act as intermediaries in their interactions with government agencies. In Sweden, for example, fundamentalist organizations were being funded by the government to provide material needs and preschool education for refugee children, with little oversight. LGBTQ asylum seekers reported being harassed and women verbally abused for not wearing a veil. One quote from the report is particularly telling:

We also heard that some women refugees feared their own menfolk in Europe when they did not wear the hijab and behaved more like Western women—in fact, they feared repercussions from their own community more than they did acts of racism or anti-Muslim sentiments.[24]

The founder of the Ibn Rushd–Goethe Mosque in Berlin, Seyran Ateş, told me that some new arrivals opt for her liberal mosque over traditional mosques run by Turks and Egyptians. "They come to us and say, 'We went to a few mosques here, and they were much too conservative and fundamentalist. They concentrate on politics rather than religion, and we are not comfortable with that. We are happy that you are here.'"[25] It is paradoxical that in the name of freedom of religion, governments permit Islamist organizations to hamper the integration of communities and especially of new arrivals. Dönmez described it as "trying to put out the fire with a flamethrower."[26]

MUSLIMS' EXCEPTIONALISM INHIBITS THEIR EMPLOYABILITY

Regressive religiosity also impacts Muslims' employability. As young men become observant, they avoid employment that seems un-Islamic. They refuse to work in places where alcohol is sold or where men and women mingle, and they especially refuse to work for a female boss. This helps explain the higher unemployment rates in Muslim communities. The UK Social Mobility Commission found that only 19.8 percent of adult British Muslims had a full-time job in 2017.[27] Discrimination is generally thought to be the cause, but I believe this is wrong. As a politician in the Netherlands working on integration, I met with employers across the country to find out why they would hire Indian, Vietnamese, black, and white employees but not Muslims. Their reasons were compelling. They had tried hiring Moroccan men, they told me, but had found them unemployable. They did not show up on time, they were aggressive and rude to female colleagues, and, when they were eventually let go, they would make threats or litigate, sometimes both.

I write here about men because it is men who are expected to work in Muslim households. Study after study restates the fact that migrant women born outside the European Union are more often unemployed than both other women and migrant men.[28] In Great Britain, 69 percent of Muslim women were "economically inactive" in 2004.[29] In Holland, Turkish and Moroccan women were 40 percent less likely to work than were Dutch women and migrants from non-Muslim countries.[30] Across Europe, more than half of all female refugees are unemployed.[31] Consequently, their families tend to be poorer than those with two working parents, and their poverty is passed on to the next generation.[32]

Language and education are cited as barriers to their success in European labor markets. This is especially the case for Europe's refugee women, who are twice as likely as refugee men to have had no formal schooling at all.[33] Compared to other categories of migrants and native women, they have fewer work and language skills, cutting them off from social and employment opportunities.[34] More than a fifth of British Muslim women struggle to speak English.[35] This is true of refugee women in other Western countries as well. In Australia, twice as many refugee women as men (16 percent versus 7 percent) speak no English three years after arriving.[36] Great Britain sees similar figures among Muslim women, more than a fifth of whom struggle to speak English.[37]

Solving the language and educational disadvantages of migrant women may seem simple. There are whole government departments and an industry of training organizations dedicated to improving literacy. But neither public nor private providers are prepared to grapple with the cultural attitudes holding Muslim women back. For one thing, they are married younger and bear more children than others. Refugee women are often pregnant the year after they arrive.[38] In Muslim families, women are discouraged from working outside the home in case their honor may be jeopardized. Even when they wish to work, husbands with traditional views veto their career aspirations.[39] In a survey by Germany's Federal Office for Migration and Refugees (BAMF), 70 percent of asylum-seeker men said it would be a problem if their wife earned more than they did.[40]

PARALLEL SOCIETIES PUSH AGAINST INTEGRATION

Aggravating Europe's integration failures is the emergence of "parallel societies." These are the geographic manifestations of a cultural segregation of immigrants and their children within Western societies. In these neighborhoods, entire apartment buildings, streets, and schools are populated by migrants of certain ethnicities. Children in these neighborhoods may grow up not speaking the language of the host society until they go to school, and in their local school they will find few students from outside their community. They will grow up in a cultural cocoon watching TV and movies from overseas, and vacations—if they have them—will be spent in their parents' country of origin. They will go to the local mosque. When their parents decide it is time, they will be pushed into an arranged marriage, often with a distant cousin sourced from their country of origin, using a marriage certificate to enable the cousin to immigrate. Marrying outside their ethnic or religious community is proscribed. This cultural isolation creates what has been called in one UK report a "first generation in every generation."[41]

In 2017, the Swedish police reported that the number of "especially vulnerable areas" (code for parallel societies) in Sweden had risen from fifteen to twenty-three in recent years.[42] In Stockholm's Rinkeby (or "Little Mogadishu"), young men accost those who are white, asking why they are in their neighborhood, while in some Copenhagen neighborhoods, "being too Danish" is a slur.[43] In parts of the United Kingdom, one encounters similar attitudes: "Manningham belongs to Muslims. We don't want whites. We rule Bradford. We are going to get you out."[44]

Yet it would be a mistake to think of parallel societies as dominated by loutish youths. In the course of my research in Sweden, Belgium, France, and the United Kingdom, I was told again and again about well-adjusted, employed Muslim men who work among Europeans during the day in hospitals, restaurants, and taxis but whose journey home is not just to a nearby neighborhood but in effect to their country of origin. "I feel like I'm at home in Tensta, it's like Baghdad," said one. "Everyone speaks Arabic, so why should I learn Swedish?" asked another.[45] "When I go to Malmö and Gothenburg it doesn't feel like I'm in Sweden, it feels like a Middle Eastern or African community," said a third.[46] "When I drive home in the Midlands," a fourth man observed, "I leave this country. At home we only speak Arabic, eat Arabic food, watch Arabic TV and radio, I raise my family Arabic."[47] And "When I'm outside in my taxi, I am in Belgium. But when I go back home, I am in my home country."[48]

Brussels is an interesting example. At one end of the city is Matonge, a traditionally Congolese and now quite mixed neighborhood in the gentrified Ixelles district. Cars squeeze through its narrow, winding cobbled streets, somehow avoiding pedestrians and never colliding. Many of the ornate Art Nouveau buildings have seen better days but retain a lived-in charm compared to the standoffish bureaucratic buildings nearby. African men in cotton shirts and trousers talk in their own language as they walk past hair-braiding salons and shops selling beads and jewelry. Young and old, black and white sit side by side in cafés chatting or reading books. Assita Kanko is a Belgian member of the European Parliament who was born in Burkina Faso. I asked her what is it that makes integration successful in areas like this. She said that it's about town planning, architecture, and design. "Local governments have to embed integration into their design of physical spaces. Housing developments and services like shopping centers and transport hubs must be designed to create opportunities for socially integrating people. Designers have to make sure people living there bump into each other, so they can cross paths and interact. But more generally, our laws and values must be respected or there can be no integration. So law enforcement and education are very important. Tradition and religion can never be above our laws and values. Learning the Belgian languages is a way to success and emancipation. One must adapt and grab opportunities."[49]

Superficially, the Brussels quartier of Brabant looks much the same as Ixelles, though the buildings seem dirtier and there is detritus along the canals. This area is home to a parallel society; across the canal are heavily Muslim Laeken and the notorious slum suburb of Molenbeek. Here young men of African origin play soccer in the park, but no women are to be seen aside from the occasional woman draped in a black hijab from head to toe, pushing a baby carriage. The cafés are full of men with Middle Eastern backgrounds, but they are not joined by their women. The gender segregation is unmistakable.

THE CONSEQUENCES OF PARALLEL SOCIETIES

Some multiculturalists may argue that such cultural segregation is harmless. But parallel-society neighborhoods produce disappointing social outcomes. Their schools perform poorly, and children drop out early.

From kindergarten, children attend schools with few pupils outside their ethnic and religious groups. In the United Kingdom, for example, 60 percent of ethnic-minority students attend schools in which most pupils are minorities.[50] And this is true of public schools before taking into account the rigid segregation of Islamic schools. Moreover, children in such effectively segregated schools are sometimes not taught the same curriculum as their counterparts in the majority population. A survey of Dutch high school teachers found that one in nine avoided talking about "sensitive" topics such as homosexuality, terrorism, and slavery, so as not to provoke their students.[51] Standards of discipline are often low. One Malmö school was closed in 2015 when social tensions among its ethnic student population reached such a level that teachers could not guarantee students' safety.[52]

Not surprisingly, unemployment and poverty are rife in parallel societies. Drugs, crime, violence, and antisocial behavior are all features of life in such ghettoes. In 2017, the Swedish police defined parallel societies as alternative social orders run by criminals and religious leaders, which threatened democracy and the rule of law.[53] Following riots in Bradford in the United Kingdom in 2001 and in Paris's eastern banlieues in 2005, official reports admitted that segregated societies were a breeding ground for male aggression.[54]

PARALLEL SOCIETIES ARE ATTRACTIVE DESTINATIONS

The tendency for people to cluster with those who are most like them—what network scientists call homophily—is a powerful human instinct. The comforts of having a common language and cuisine and understanding the way things are done are very attractive. It is hard negotiating a new culture. Interactions with locals are awkward if you do not know what is expected of you. I, too, experienced the terrible loneliness—the gnawing sense of being permanently misunderstood—when I first arrived in the Netherlands. And I can understand what a relief it is for new migrants to band together with those who understand them rather than to feel detached and isolated.

There is, however, a downside to birds of a feather flocking together. As the Oxford University economist Paul Collier has argued, when the size of an immigrant community increases, its members' interaction with the native population diminishes, and integration, or "absorption," as he calls it, slows down.[55]

The gravitational pull of parallel societies is a threat to the successful integration of Europe's recently arrived asylum seekers. Even when asylum seekers have been distributed across regions, as they have been in Germany, they soon head toward communities where people they know from home already live. "We moved to Salzgitter because there are already many Arab and Turkish migrants here, we have friends here. The people here are nice. We can attend mosques here," one Syrian refugee told the *Wall Street Journal*.[56] But Salzgitter is a town in which 91 percent of asylum seekers were living on welfare in 2017. As one charity worker put it, "We don't have the jobs that these people could take."[57]

For some politicians, mentioning parallel societies is controversial in itself. Some avoid the use of phrases such as "ghettoes" and "no-go zones" and tie themselves in knots to try to explain the problem away. A frequently quoted study by Germany's Bertelsmann Foundation claimed to disprove the existence of parallel societies in Germany, Switzerland, Austria, France, and the United Kingdom. The study blamed discrimination and labor market constraints for the poor education and employment outcomes among Muslims. Presenting its findings triumphantly, the authors claimed that "78 per cent of Muslims in Germany report frequent or very frequent contact with non-Muslims in their leisure time."[58] But that means that 22 percent of Muslims in Germany do not. Of the 4.4 million to 4.7 million Muslims currently living in Germany, that equates to 1 million Muslims not maintaining social contact with the rest of society. True, just 4 percent of respondents, or around 176,000 German Muslims, do not feel "connected with Germany." In Austria, however, the proportion is higher—13 percent—and in the United Kingdom, it is 11 percent—around 330,000 people.

ARE WOMEN THE KEY TO INTEGRATION?

It has become a truism that "women are the key to integration." I agree. Migrant women who are educated and working tend to have children who succeed at school and go on to thrive. But only very gradually has the deplorable position of Muslim women been noticed in the West. If they looked, Westerners would see women being bossed about by their menfolk. They would see brothers imposing curfews on sisters. They would see wives walking three feet behind their husbands. They would see women peeking out from behind drawn curtains, waiting for permission from a male guardian to go out the front door. Occasionally they would read about a teenage girl being pulled out of school to marry a stranger from her country of origin—or about little girls as young as 4 and 5 being flown abroad to have their clitorises cut and their genitals sewn. But at that point, in my experience, Western observers quickly look away.

It is Muslim women who have the most to gain by integrating in the West, and their husbands and fathers know this. Muslim girls see the freedom and opportunities of their Western counterparts, but when they try to enjoy the same, they are pulled back. Indeed, the process of migration itself causes some men from honor cultures to crack down more severely in the European diaspora than in their country of origin.[59] They forbid their girls to date and have boyfriends or even boys who are friends. They fear rumors and gossip that might tarnish their family's honor. Girls are discouraged from swimming, going to concerts, and participating in leisure activities where boys are present. They are not permitted to wear makeup and Western clothes. A 2016 survey of 1,100 young people aged between 12 and 18 years in Stockholm suburbs found that 56 percent of girls were not allowed to take part in recreational activities with boys.[60]

For many young Muslim women, that means leading a double life: changing into Western clothes after leaving home and changing back before returning there. But maintaining a secret life has become much harder in the era of mobile phones and in neighborhoods where immigrant numbers have risen sharply. "Honor police" can now text message each other reports about girls in their community. Girls in Copenhagen report being afraid of taxi drivers spotting them and reporting back to their families. One man in a Danish housing estate used security camera footage to track the whereabouts of a girl in his community, promptly telling her parents when she had sneaked out.[61] In Sweden, a third of girls surveyed in Stockholm's suburbs are subject to intense social control.[62] In Manchester in the United Kingdom, youth workers report increasing numbers of boys controlling girls, constantly phoning to keep tabs on them and demanding photographic proof of their whereabouts.[63] These are not just overzealous big brothers. A tenet of Islam is commanding right and forbidding wrong. A good Muslim takes it upon himself to inculcate Islamic values into those he comes across. This has given rise to an informal religious police in Europe's parallel societies, forcing girls to cover up and stay inside.

The cost can be high for young women who insist on their independence to study, work, or have a boyfriend. Girls who behave in "too Western" a manner are categorized as immodest and become targets for forced marriage or kidnapping and removal to the family's country of origin. Even if they manage to avoid violent retribution at the hands of male family members, they may still be treated like pariahs. For many young women, the fear of social exclusion is enough of a deterrent. But the ultimate sanction is so-called honor violence.

MEN USE VIOLENCE AS A MEANS OF CONTROL

Honor violence is a set of enforcement measures used to uphold the modesty doctrine. Girls and women who step out of line face injury and even murder at the hands of relatives if they drift too far toward emancipation. So-called honor killing is meant to remove a stain on a family's honor caused by real or alleged sexual misconduct. In Western countries, the victims of honor violence also include Sikh, Hindu, and Kurdish women, but most appear to be Muslim.

The practice is difficult to measure, but there are some statistics. In the United Kingdom, eighteen honor killings and eleven attempted honor killings were recorded between 2010 and 2014. In Germany, researchers at the Max Planck Institute identified twenty honor killings "in the strict sense" between 1996 and 2005. German researchers also found that despite stringent sentencing guidelines in cases involving "honor" as a motive, German court punishments were often mild in these cases. In Canada, a 2010 report prepared for the Department of Justice found "there were at least a dozen killings that appear to have been committed in the name of 'honor' in the decade between 1999 and 2009." In the United States, there were nine publicly documented "honor" killings between 2000 and 2011, with most of the victims Muslims. But a study by my organization, the AHA Foundation, and John Jay College estimated that between twenty-three and twenty-seven honor killings take place in the United States each year.[64]

Quite rightly, honor violence has been described as organized crime.[65] Families and communities conspire to entrap girls who are deemed to have violated their moral code and punish them. Think of your local police station receiving an emergency call. A murder has been committed at a certain address; the murderer is armed. The police rush to the scene, prepared for a dangerous confrontation. Instead, a stoical family greets police, with one of their own dead on the floor in a pool of blood; the killer is hovering over the victim; the killer is often a teenager, because of the leniency shown toward sentencing minors in European legal systems. It is a crime scene, yet there is almost nothing to investigate. There, right in front of you, are the victim, the murder weapon, the murderer ready to confess, and all the witnesses you will ever need to call. Case closed.

If you have served such communities long enough, you know that the witnesses are in fact accomplices and orchestrators of the honor killing, but proving the complicity of the family—a requirement for securing justice for the woman who was killed in the name of honor or deterring future murderers—is nearly impossible. Detective Chris Boughey, who successfully investigated the honor killing of Noor Almaleki in Arizona, said, "In the Almaleki case, I learned very quickly that we would receive no assistance from the family. In fact, we received out-and-out defiance and resistance."[66] Attempts to prove the complicity of family members are usually met with accusations of bigotry.

Honor killings are the most extreme form of honor violence, but there are many gradations of this. In the Netherlands, for example, there were approximately five hundred reported cases of honor violence in 2013, but "only" seventeen of those cases culminated in a killing. The other hundreds of cases involved various forms of threats, coercion, physical abuse such as beatings, and even rape. Less lethal cases of honor violence can be just as perplexing for police. Take, for example, the 33-year-old mother in Bad Nauheim in Germany who in 2018 called for help, having been beaten by her husband for offending the family honor.[67] It was not only the husband; their 16- and 17-year-old sons had also joined in the assault. When the police arrived, all the family members, mother included, went on the attack. The police called for reinforcements, as did the family. In the end, eight people were injured, five of whom were police.

Many women threatened with honor violence seek refuge in women's shelters. When I worked as a translator in Dutch shelters, I observed the overrepresentation of Muslim women seeking safety there. Dutch researchers found as early as 2003 that 59 percent of women in women's shelters were of non-Dutch origin; many of these women are Muslim. The incidence of honor violence reached such a level in Holland that the authorities considered extending the country's witness protection program to those women. In Denmark in 2017, 41 percent of women in domestic violence shelters were immigrants, rising to 50 percent in 2018.[68] Among all those seeking help in 2017, 14 percent were Syrian, 8 percent Iraqi, and 6 percent Somali.

I shall never forget being called to translate for a woman at Leiden University Medical Center in the Netherlands. The woman's husband had repeatedly kicked her in the belly. She was thirty-seven weeks pregnant with their first child. He had used his shoes and his fists to strike her in the face. In the hospital, her stitches and the swelling on her face were all you could see. There was nothing to translate. The only sounds she could make were moans of pain. In the waiting room, a man who told me he was her father said that bad things were bound to happen if a woman disobeyed her husband.

CONTROLLING WOMEN THROUGH THEIR SEXUALITY

There are other forms of culture-based violence and coercion used to constrain women in immigrant communities. One of these is forced marriage. In 2014 alone, the British government's Forced Marriage Unit gave advice or support related to a possible forced marriage in 1,267 cases, with 79 percent of cases involving female victims. In France, 4 percent of immigrant women aged between 26 and 50—in particular, women from Turkey, Morocco, and Algeria—have undergone a forced marriage. As two-thirds of the forced marriages in question ultimately ended in divorce, most of those surveyed in France were no longer living in their original forced marriage at the time the survey was conducted.

In the United States in 2011, a survey of legal and social service providers found that more than two-fifths (41 percent) of all survey respondents had encountered at least one forced marriage case over the last two years—as many as three thousand cases in total.[69] The experience of one victim, profiled on condition of anonymity by National Public Radio, is illustrative. Lina, a 22-year-old Yemeni American, was taken to Yemen in 2014. Her parents had claimed that her grandmother was gravely ill, but once she was there, Lina's father announced the real reason for the visit: Lina would be getting married to a local man, in spite of her objections. While in Yemen, she "wasn't allowed out of the house longer than ten minutes, and somebody always had their eye on me," Lina said. She emailed the US Embassy, but it was unable to help. Lina went ahead with the wedding after overhearing family friends telling her parents "The cost of a bullet is less than a dollar." "What they meant by that is that my life to these people, it's very, very cheap," she observed. Later, she discovered that three of her close friends had also been forced to marry in Yemen; they had been too ashamed to tell her.[70]

Muslim girls who possess Western citizenship through either naturalization or birth are often viewed as valuable commodities. Families cajole or coerce young women into accepting relatives from the country of origin of their parents in order to give them a residency permit and access to government benefits or the labor market. Conversely, if a Muslim man possesses Western citizenship and a woman travels from abroad to marry him, she may put up with unbearable conditions in the marriage because a divorce could force her to return to her home country.

Another grisly cultural practice designed to control young girls is female genital mutilation (FGM). Estimates are that 200 million women worldwide have undergone FGM; most victims, though not all, are Muslim. As women from areas where FGM is prevalent migrate to the West, the custom is not necessarily left behind. There are "cutting parties" for which a cutter is flown into a Western country such as the United Kingdom to cut up to a dozen girls at a time. Conversely, girls may be flown back to their country of origin to undergo the procedure. Western doctors are increasingly seeing for themselves the consequences of FGM: conservative estimates are that 25,000 women living in Germany have undergone FGM; 53,000 in France; 137,000 in England and Wales. The Centers for Disease Control and Prevention estimates that 513,000 women in the United States are thought either to have undergone FGM or to be at risk of undergoing the procedure based on the prevalence of FGM in their country of origin. A common justification for performing FGM on a young girl is to keep her sexuality in check and thus to keep her "marriageable" for a man who seeks sexual purity in his wife.

Forced marriage and FGM are rarely discussed in public by members of the communities that practice them. But controlling women by keeping them inside and occupied is easily observed. In the Netherlands, Turkish women present at health clinics with vitamin D deficiencies. They are kept in their apartments so much that they are simply not exposed to enough sunlight. Eskild Dahl Pedersen is the head of security at one of Copenhagen's cooperative housing companies. His role includes enforcing the rules of the cooperative, which means intervening when family disputes or behavioral issues transgress Danish law. As an unofficial "integrator in chief," he interacts with the many families in his co-op, most of whom are immigrants from Muslim countries, particularly Palestine and Somalia. He says that young men in the community believe that girls should be in their apartment making food for their husbands and taking care of their children.

They say to me, "Eskild, if you need to control your woman, one child is not enough. Two is a little better, then she is at home taking care of the family, and three is more or less okay. But when she has four, Eskild, four children mean you have total control of where your woman is. She is too busy with four kids to go outside." A mother with four children is certainly not going to make it to work. Unless she has an exceptionally successful husband, she will likely remain on welfare most of her life. Eskild says that often he sees mothers who have four children by the time they are 38 or 39 having an extra one at that point because when their older children reach 18 years of age, they will no longer qualify for child support. "The problem is," he continued, "the mothers were supposed to go to school and get an education so they can get jobs. But with all the children they don't have time and are not forced to go to school. Denmark needs a policy where migrants are all required to finish school. I think of it in the same way as deciding for my own children. They did not decide for themselves whether they wanted to go to school or kindergarten; I decided for them because they needed education."[71]

Chapter 14

THE INTEGRATION INDUSTRY AND ITS FAILURE

Looking at the economic evidence, the prospects for asylum seekers arriving in Europe from Muslim-majority countries are not great. It has been recognized for some time that migrants perform poorly in Europe's labor markets—the unemployment rate for foreign-born workers in continental Europe is typically much higher than for native-born workers—but the realization that refugees, as a subset of all migrants, perform the worst is only just being understood. When it comes to finding work, it takes more than twenty years for asylum seekers and refugees to reach the employment levels of locals in the European Union. Half are employed after the first decade, but unemployment rates are stubbornly high for those coming from Africa and the Middle East.[1] Among the refugees who arrived in the Netherlands in the 1990s, only 55 percent were working fifteen years later.[2] Those who arrived in 2014 have also had lower workforce participation rates than other migrant groups.[3] In Norway, two-thirds of male refugees and one-third of female refugees arriving in 2000 were employed after eight years, but their numbers tended to drop after that peak, with many reverting back to relying on social assistance.[4]

You might have thought that, given this poor record of employing refugees, European governments would have been much more reluctant to welcome several million more. To understand why that was not the case, you need to know that certain elements of society have perverse incentives to keep the crisis of inadequate integration going. I call them the "integration industry."

WHY DO REFUGEES STRUGGLE TO FIND JOBS?

The underwhelming employment rates for refugees are no doubt partly due to their lower levels of education and skills relative to the average in advanced economies such as those in northwestern Europe. Among Norway's refugee cohort in 2000, a third had only primary schooling.[5] And refugees arriving in Europe today are actually less well qualified than refugees in earlier decades.[6] Germany's Federal Employment Agency (Bundesagentur für Arbeit, or BA) reported "lower than expected" education and training rates among the country's 300,000 refugee job seekers in 2016. What BA officials had been hoping for was Syrian doctors and engineers. They soon found that three-quarters of asylum seekers had no job training and more than half were qualified only for menial occupations such as cleaning and maintenance work.[7] Even in terms of language proficiency, refugees tend to underperform. Only 49 percent of refugees living in Europe for ten years have advanced knowledge of the language of their new home, whereas 69 percent of other non-EU migrants there for the same length of time have acquired advanced language skills.[8]

Migrant children have persistently lower education outcomes than locals do. In the European Union, roughly one-quarter drop out of school without qualifications. For the rest, their PISA scores[*]

---

[*] PISA is the OECD's Programme for International Student Assessment, which gauges the performance of 15-year-old students around the world in reading, mathematics, and science.

are 10 to 12 percent lower than those of locals in all areas measured: reading, mathematics, and IT problem solving.[9] That is the case for both first- and second-generation migrant children; for a number of reasons, their poorer performance persists.

Poor education outcomes have long been correlated with high crime rates. In Denmark, the crime rate among male descendants of non-Western immigrants is 145 percent higher than locals', even controlling for higher numbers of young people in that group. The highest crime rates were among men from Lebanese families, followed by Somali, Moroccan, and Syrian families. When it came to violent crime, the male children of non-Western immigrants were three times as likely to be convicted as Danes. Migrants from India and China had *lower* than average crime rates than Danes.[10] The same trend has been observed in the Netherlands, where more than half of Moroccan men, both first and second generation, have been charged with a crime.[11] In the United Kingdom, increasing numbers of Pakistani-British men have become involved in crime since the 2000s.[12] In Sweden's parallel societies, the "criminalization process" begins early, with children as young as 9 committing serious weapon and drug crimes.[13]

Crime rates like these do not surprise me. In the countries where asylum seekers are coming from, violence is often the principal form of conflict resolution. Patriarchal violence is taken for granted in the Muslim world. Children can expect beatings by their parents, especially their fathers, and also by teachers, uncles, older siblings, and stronger children. "Fear is seen as a sign of respect in our countries," says Mustafa Panshiri, who is from Afghanistan. I grew up in a similar culture myself. In Somalia, clans teach their children, both boys and girls, how to be aggressive. When I was 5, my older cousin took me for fighting practice after school. I was encouraged to pick a fight with a classmate, who was encouraged to pick a fight with me. We poked out our tongues at each other, made faces, and called each other names. We were then surrounded by our older relatives, who cheered us on as we went for each other. We kicked, scratched, bit, and wrestled each other until we were covered in bruises and our little dresses were torn. The victor was the child who gave up last or did not cry and run away. The child who ran was doubly a loser, as she would receive a beating from her fighting coach as well.

I do not want to create the impression that all people from Muslim societies are aggressive. They are not. Many are as eager as I was to adopt the Western approach of ceding the monopoly on violence to the state and calling for the law to penalize all other violent acts. But in Europe's parallel societies, violent dispute resolution is normalized. Eskild Dahl Pedersen described this as a particular type of "growing inequality" in Denmark, where native Danes generally live free from violence but those in parallel societies are exposed to it from birth, putting them at a real disadvantage. In Germany, too, a survey of 16,545 male ninth-grade students found that Muslim boys were more likely to be violent than Christian boys.[14] And the more devout they were as Muslims, the higher the likelihood that they would display violent behavior.

Violence is not the only problem. Decades of experience point to entrenched intergenerational welfare dependency among many of Europe's migrants. As immigrant populations have increased, so, too, has their overrepresentation on welfare rolls.[15] The idea of "welfare migration" is of course controversial, but it is surely not coincidental that asylum applications have been highest in the countries with the most generous social assistance programs: Germany, Sweden, Austria, France, and Italy.[16] Econometric research has shown that more generous welfare states attract lower-skilled migrants. The opposite is also true, with higher-skilled migrants viewing a generous welfare state as a deterrent and looking elsewhere.[17]

SET UP TO FAIL

Europe's migration and integration policies are set up to fail. Some still cling to the rosy view that welcoming in millions of asylum seekers will solve the problems created by Europe's aging population. The theory is that "immigrants' tax payments help fund native pensions."[18] However, if it takes twenty years for asylum seekers to find employment at the same rate as native Europeans, the baby boomers who are waiting for migrants to top up their pensions will not live long enough to see it happen.

The ineffectiveness of government integration efforts is an open secret in Europe. Integration is a portfolio hot potato that unlucky ministers would rather avoid. Policies and programs cut across numerous portfolios, including immigration, housing, education, employment, justice, foreign policy, defense, development aid, and health. They also run vertically from metropolitan councils to state, national, and European governments. This makes it hard to implement policy effectively but easy to shift the blame for integration failures from one bureaucratic silo to the next.

As a member of the Dutch Parliament in the early 2000s, I participated in parliamentary hearings examining where the country's integration budget was being spent. Back then, the Netherlands' immigrant population was relatively small, yet it had spent €16 billion on integration, outside of the immigration portfolio, in the previous sixteen years.[19] For all that money spent, the country could not identify a single success story. Much of it had found its way onto the balance sheets of slick consultants, worthy nonprofits, and ethnic community representatives, all promising utopian levels of integration. When their programs were evaluated, we would receive lengthy reports on racism, discrimination, and the invisible hand of prejudice holding people back. I remember telling my colleagues that this was exactly how people talked about voodoo: "Give me your money, and I'll make you feel better." Not much has changed.

THE INTEGRATION INDUSTRY

Pumping billions in public funds into solving a seemingly unsolvable social problem has created a new tier of rent seekers whose failures are self-perpetuating. Governments fear that a lack of integration will cost more in the long run than will investing in integration policies today.[20] But those they employ to integrate immigrants have no real incentive to succeed. From bureaucrats and NGOs to security firms, employment agencies, language schools, legal advisers, interpreters, social workers, psychotherapists, and counselors—from anthropologists to experts on child care and conflict resolution— all would be out of a job if they actually achieved the successful integration of migrants. Some of those involved in this work are altruistic, no doubt, but not all. The Netherlands Court of Audit identified 165 companies offering integration courses with no quality control, leading to a 50 percent *reduction* in the numbers of migrants passing the country's civic integration exam.[21]

During the financial crisis, Germany's leaders strongly resisted pressure from economists to increase public spending and use deficit financing to stimulate the European economy. But the migration crisis of 2015–2016 created a chink in the armor of austerity. Germany's Federal Office for Migration and Refugees (BAMF) saw staff numbers jump from 2,800 in 2015 to 10,000 by the end of 2016.[22] Similar things happened at the local level. The old university town of Tübingen introduced a policy of austerity. The lamps in streetlights were changed only when those on an entire street had gone out. Following the arrival of thousands of migrants, however, local residents

complained of feeling unsafe in poorly lit streets. The local authority promptly agreed to change its approach and replaced defective
lamps as quickly as possible.[23]

Beyond the increased demand they create for basic goods and
services, the newcomers require specialized support to begin their
integration journey. In-house government services provide language
classes, orientation courses, counseling, mentoring, and reams of
publications in multiple languages about the basics of living in Europe.[24] Assuming that his asylum application is approved—which
often involves months if not years of encounters with bureaucrats,
translators, and legal aid services—a newcomer will be settled in
public accommodation and enrolled in language classes. A proportion of language and orientation classes is dedicated to "values," but
not much. One refugee tutor in Munich explained to us that topics
such as "respecting differing opinions" are prescribed by Germany's
migration board but the materials and content are left to the discre-
tion of individual instructors. If the trainer believes that parallel societies are simply a part of modern Germany, as the one I spoke to
did, the discussion of differing opinions is likely to be brief.

Typically, the next step for new migrants is to enroll in education
and skills courses or with employment services, unless of course
they decline to do so and instead opt to remain on welfare. Those
who do wish to work will join work skills, training, and employment
information programs provided by employment services, religious
charities, trade unions, and NGOs. Just one agency, the German
Academic Exchange Service (Deutscher Akademischer Austauschdienst, or DAAD), received an allocation of €100 million from
the German government for refugee education between 2015 and
2019.[25] Among many other programs, the German government rein-
troduced an old work-for-benefits scheme, rolling out a €300 million
"one-euro job" program for 100,000 asylum seekers. The scheme

paid them a nominal $1.20 per hour for basic work such as cleaning and laundry, mostly for government and nonprofit employers.[26] The scheme got off to a lackluster start in 2016, with only 4,392 refugees in "one-euro jobs" by November. The Federal Employment Agency was unperturbed, yet by April 2017, it had scaled down its aspirations and funding to €60 million for 2018. Only 25,000 "one-euro jobs" had been applied for, and, to judge by previous announcements, only half of the applicants would have been accepted. The Federal Ministry of Labor and Social Affairs (Bundesministerium für Arbeit und Soziales, or BAS) cited faster asylum-processing times for the program's weak performance. Where did the rest of the €240 million go? you might well ask. According to the ministry, it went "to increase the budget of administrative costs," including personnel costs, rent, and energy bills.[27]

According to the Dutch Justice and Security National Budget for 2019, of the €1.526 billion dedicated to integration spending in the Netherlands in 2017, the Nidos Foundation—which provides guardianship services for unaccompanied asylum-seeker minors— received €135.6 million (in 2018 it had received €121.6 million).[28] The Dutch Council for Refugees (VluchtelingenWerk Nederland), an asylum-seeker lobbying and advisory NGO, received €10.0 million, and the Council for the Judiciary (Raad voor de Rechtspraak) was given €49.5 million to provide free legal advice to asylum seekers.[29] But the Netherlands' spending on immigration and integration services is tiny compared to those of its neighbors. The German federal government spends around €3 billion per year on integration and another €11 billion to €12 billion on asylum-related expenses, including welfare payments and administrative procedures.[30] In addition, German state governments estimate their spending on asylum seekers to be more than €21 billion per year.[31] In France, immigration and integration services receive around €6 billion per year.[32]

On top of national government spending are European-level funds to cope with immigration and integration. In its current six-year funding round, the European Union allocated €6.6 billion to an Asylum, Migration and Integration Fund (AMIF) and another €7.5 billion to other migration-related spending, including Frontex and internal security. Among the top-five nongovernmental organization recipients of European Commission funding in 2017 were the Danish and Norwegian refugee councils, which received, respectively, €108 million and €94 million.[33] The best that can be hoped is that some of this money will find its way to creating effective solutions. I am not optimistic about that.

WILLKOMMENSKULTUR

None of this analysis on the failure of integration policies and wasted spending is new. It has been a familiar subject of discussion in Europe for decades. The problems of unintegrated migrant communities and their intergenerational welfare dependence were well understood when Angela Merkel made her decision to open the German borders in mid-2015. The US historians Walter Laqueur and Christopher Caldwell and the Dutch professor Paul Scheffer, among others, had published widely read books on the failure of integration in Europe. Numerous government reports and think-tank monographs had appeared on the same topic. The fact that an influx of low-skilled migrants from the Muslim world would cost more than it benefited European economies had been well established before 2015.

When I asked *Die Welt* journalist Robin Alexander why this well-known fact had not been taken into consideration before the German borders were effectively thrown open in the summer of 2015, he explained that "a decision was never taken." Chancellor Merkel had simply refrained from enforcing the borders, and the migrants had poured in. The government, its advisers, the media, and the wider political class had simply not been focused on the likely consequences. "No one was thinking about hundreds of thousands of Arabs coming. That was only debated after it had already happened," Alexander told me.[34]

Until that point Germany's experience of integration had been dealing with reunification of east and west after 1989, as well as eastern European and Russian migrants. Germany's long-established Turkish minority seemed a relatively small problem. In the first phase of the migration crisis sparked by the Arab revolutions and the Syrian civil war, Germany had enthusiastically enforced the Dublin III Regulation, which had insulated it geographically from accepting large numbers of Arab and North African migrants who were likely to apply for entry on the southern edges of the European Union.

I can understand why so many Germans were excited as the first wave of migrants arrived in 2015. Who can forget the images of girls waving signs and teddy bears at train stations as the migrants arrived? Talk of a new German *Willkommenskultur,* or "welcoming culture," reflected a naive euphoria that an opportunity had at last arisen to truly atone for the country's past sins of racial intolerance. The German public had been told by their leader, *"Wir schaffen das"* ("We can manage that"). However, as Chancellor Merkel put it a year later, in September 2016, "I sometimes think this phrase was a little overstated, that too much store was set by it—to the extent that I'd prefer not to repeat it."[35]

The reality was that past experience lent credence to the opposite position: "We can't manage that." If the integration of a much smaller number of refugees in the 1990s had largely failed, how likely was the great *Völkerwanderung* of 2015–2016 to have better results?

Chapter 15

GROOMING GANGS

Nothing better illustrates the failure of previous generations' efforts at integration than the case of the so-called grooming gangs of the United Kingdom. It would be nice to believe—as the integration industry would have us do—that the sex crimes of the latest generation of migrants to Europe are just a passing phase and that over time immigrants' attitudes will adjust to the different status of women in the Western world. The experience of the north of England suggests that this is an illusory hope.

Grooming gangs have been exposed and prosecuted in numerous parts of the United Kingdom, including Rochdale, Telford, Newcastle, Peterborough, Sheffield, Rotherham, Huddersfield, Oxford, and Bristol.[1] A 2014 inquiry exposed the scale of this form of predatory sexual exploitation of young girls. It found that between 1997 and 2013, an estimated 1,400 underage girls had been groomed and sexually exploited by groups of mainly first- and second-generation migrant men.[2]

The perpetrators tended to work in the nighttime economy as taxi drivers and in takeaway food outlets, where they picked up their targets on the streets. They assumed, correctly, that a young girl out late at night without supervision was likely to be uncared for and an easy target to exploit. The girls they selected were considered "vulnerable" by authorities. They came from "chaotic" or "council estate" backgrounds and were cheaply lured by offers of gifts and food, alcohol, drugs, phone cards, and the attention and affection they craved.[3] These "gifts" turned out to be down payments for sex, however. Girls as young as 11 were coerced into having sex with groups of men. Many were drugged and raped. Some were trafficked to other locations to be raped; many were beaten and threatened. Prosecution after prosecution revealed the callous behavior of the perpetrators. In Keighley, West Yorkshire, a 13-year-old girl was repeatedly raped by groups of men, sometimes in an underground car park, where they had spray-painted her name and the word "corner" on the wall.[4] Despite years of systematic sexual abuse of underage girls, few grooming gangs were prosecuted until 2009, and cases continue at the time of writing this book.

A QUESTION OF RACE?

The UK counterextremism organization Quilliam published a report in 2017 examining the backgrounds of the grooming gang perpetrators. Of the 264 perpetrators convicted, 84 percent were "Asian," 8 percent black, 7 percent white, and 3 percent of unknown ethnicity.[5] In Great Britain, it should be noted, "Asian" refers principally to people from South Asia, including India, Pakistan, and Bangladesh, rather than from China or Southeast Asia. The preponderance of British "Asian" perpetrators continued in grooming gang prosecutions subsequent to Quilliam's analysis. Most of the men convicted have Arabic names but were not necessarily from the Arab world, as many had been born in Great Britain to Pakistani migrants. Their Arabic names signified the religious background of their family (just as my name is Ali and my mother's is Aisha; these are not Somali names but Arabic-derived names from the Hadith).

During the investigations into the grooming gangs, some prosecutors and lawyers called for the cultural beliefs and motivations of perpetrators to be better understood.[6] We get an insight into these beliefs from the evidence given in their trials. The 59-year-old ringleader of the Rochdale grooming gang told victims that girls as young as 11 had sex "in my country." In Bristol, another told a victim it was part of "Somali culture and tradition" for girls to have sex with his friends.[7] A Rotherham perpetrator recited the Quran as he beat his victim.[8] Judges in both the Telford and Keighley grooming gang cases noted the lack of remorse of the men convicted. On the stand the men were "contemptuous, disrespectful and arrogant" and viewed their victims as worthless "object[s] that they could sexually misuse and cast aside."[9]

Was it significant that the victims of the grooming gangs were mostly white? Prosecutor Nazir Afzal, who secured the first convictions of grooming gang members, suggested that victims from the Asian community were reticent to come forward because of the shame and dishonor they would bring to their families. But the probability is that there were not many victims from within the Pakistani community. When I spoke to Nazir about those cases in 2018, he explained in his clipped English accent that the perpetrators did not rely on a cultural defense in court but blamed Western society for creating an underclass of vulnerable girls available for them to pick off. "The girls want warmth, food, transport, mind-numbing substances, and love," he explained, "and they think these guys are giving it to them, but they don't know what love is."[10] According to police and prosecutors, the victims were targeted not because they were white but because they were easy prey in the streets at night.[11]

The scope and scale of these crimes were horrific. But for many years they were covered up by the perpetrators' own communities. Ann Cryer was the member of Parliament for Keighley in West Yorkshire during those years. Though she is now in her 80s, her memory of the events is still sharp. She is "absolutely convinced" that the

Asian communities in her constituency knew that sexual exploitation was taking place in the early 2000s. They did not address it because they placed blame on the victims' parents for failing to control their girls. "There was always a silence after speaking about this at public meetings," she recalled when we met, "[then people] saying 'You've got it wrong, you don't understand. It's the fault of parents of the girls.'" One concerned local councilor in Ann's constituency had given the names and addresses of grooming gang members to their local mosque, imploring the religious leaders to intervene. The men at the mosque denied that it had anything to do with them or their community, and the abuse continued. Ann noted the hypocrisy of Muslim elders who sought to influence the parents of girls who, "in their words, 'misbehave,' but when it came to the protection of young white girls from lads who should have known and behaved better, the imams were very forthright in saying 'It's nothing to do with us.'"[12]

Years later, local councilors from the Pakistani community were condemned in the conservative press for dismissing social workers who had exposed the abuse in the interests of "community cohesion."[13] The heads of organizations that were supposed to protect the vulnerable warned that revealing the ethnic backgrounds of perpetrators would "fuel racist attitudes."[14] It was this fear of appearing "racist" that provided cover for the grooming gangs. The few who spoke out were vilified. Ann Cryer was told by other members of Parliament that she was "always giving Asian men a bad rap" by exposing their treatment of women in her community. In 2017, Sarah Champion, another British MP for a constituency afflicted with grooming gangs, was accused of "exacerbating racial tensions" when she stated publicly that the majority of her constituents convicted of child sexual exploitation were Pakistani-British men.[15] Champion said, "I'd rather be called a racist than turn a blind eye to child abuse" and was promptly dumped from her shadow cabinet position.[16]

In Professor Alexis Jay's report on the Rotherham grooming gangs, local government staff described their timidity about exposing the ethnicity of the perpetrators. Some self-censored to avoid appearing racist, while others were directed to remain silent by their managers.[17] It took the journalist Julie Bindel seven years to get her investigations into the issue published. "Editor after editor told me that they were concerned that people would consider it 'Islamophobic' if they were to draw attention to the subject," she said in 2018.[18]

A government review by Dame Louise Casey in 2016 condemned the setting aside of women's rights and the rule of law in favor of political correctness:

> The case of child sexual exploitation in Rotherham was a catastrophic example of authorities turning a blind eye to harm in order to avoid the need to confront a particular community. . . . Destroying evidence of perpetrator ethnicity and shutting down services was preferable to confronting criminals from a minority ethnic community; such was their fear of offending local cultural sensitivities.[19]

In addition to their fear of appearing racially prejudiced, some social workers and police failed to pursue grooming gang cases out of class prejudice.[20] The girls concerned were lower class, so their rights were easier to dismiss. Despite having evidence, police decided against bringing cases to court because they judged the victims to be unreliable witnesses.[21] Ann Cryer explained that the mothers of some of the girls abused gave police not only accounts of what was taking place but also the names, addresses, and even nicknames of perpetrators. Yet the police decided against taking action. They thought the girls would make poor witnesses on the stand and that their time spent bringing a case to court would be wasted.[22]

Appalled by the inaction of the police, Cryer worked with her political colleagues to introduce legal reforms that would allow the mothers to give evidence on their daughters' behalf in court. She recalled:

> Like a flash, within weeks the law relating to the administration of criminal courts in such cases was changed. I could then argue with West Yorkshire police, telling them "I've got these changes made in the law, you do your part and arrest these men and prosecute them." They agreed, and in late 2003 about fifteen of the men were arrested, but only four of them were eventually sent down for about a year for having sex with an underage girl. That's where the prosecutions started. I thought it was wonderful and would stop these men in their tracks, that they'll be terrified of being arrested and sent to prison. I thought I'd won. But then, of course, I started hearing about more of these cases and how widespread it was.[23]

The case of the British grooming gangs also illustrates the persistence of misogynistic attitudes in immigrant Muslim communities. One member of a Newcastle grooming gang told a female ticket inspector, "All white women are only good for one thing—for men like me to fuck and use like trash. That's all women like you are worth."[24] Four men convicted of grooming and raping underage girls in Rochdale in 2012 appealed the court's decision to deport them to Pakistan after they had served their prison sentences. Their lawyers, funded to the tune of £1 million by British taxpayers, took their case to the European Court of Human Rights.[25] The appeal was unsuccessful, but it had the merit of revealing how unapologetic the perpetrators were. One of the four men, Shabir Ahmed, the ringleader of the Rochdale grooming gang, claimed that his conviction had been part of a police conspiracy to scapegoat Muslims. This absence of contrition is a recurrent feature of the grooming gang cases. After sentencing another grooming gang in Bradford, the judge had to clear the courtroom gallery because supporters of the defendants swore and abused female journalists in the courtroom. They claimed that the men were being wrongfully convicted; they were good Muslims being sent to jail for having done nothing wrong.[26]

GROOMING ON THE CONTINENT

Of course, the systematic sexual exploitation of vulnerable girls is not a uniquely British phenomenon. Trafficking and prostitution rings operate worldwide. In the early 2000s, a somewhat similar pattern of behavior was reported in the Netherlands. Rather than "grooming gangs," it was known as the "lover boy" phenomenon. Underclass girls were groomed by young Moroccan men, who gave them the impression that they were their boyfriends, only to find themselves pimped out for sex with groups of men.

In Sweden today, there are signs of similar practices. Groups of migrant men identify vulnerable women and girls and cajole or coerce them into having sex. One such case took place in Fittja, just outside Stockholm, in 2016.[27] A woman living in sheltered accommodation was gang-raped for four hours in a stairwell. She was knocked unconscious, and between eight and ten men raped her while another ten looked on, some filming the crime on their mobile phones. In court some of the perpetrators claimed that the woman had been trading sex for drugs and so the rape was consensual.[28] Five suspects were acquitted and the prosecutor decided not to appeal to a higher court. Police investigating the case suspected that the men had targeted other "socially vulnerable" women in the same way.[29] Yet when I speak to Swedes about the issue, few have heard of the "grooming gangs" in the United Kingdom or the "lover boys" in the Netherlands. Each case is considered in isolation, while their glaring similarities are overlooked.

Inquiries into the UK grooming gangs have blamed the proliferation and persistence of the abuse partly on the siloed nature of the public services. In each town, the authorities were surprised to learn that grooming was happening in their jurisdiction. As Ann Cryer put it, "It seemed odd and unbelievable that in the whole world it was only happening in Keighley, and of course it was unbelievable."[30] Frustrated by the consistent failure of local authorities to learn from the experience of others, prosecutor Nazir Afzal put it like this: "If you look at every serious case review I've ever seen in my life in the last 20 years, it starts off with 'recommendation one: information should have been shared.'"[31]

PART IV

Solutions, Fake and Real

Chapter 16

"FOR YOU WHO ARE MARRIED TO A CHILD"

When grieving people come out of denial, they are supposed to pass through four further stages: anger, bargaining, depression, and finally acceptance. But countries are not individuals, and the appropriate response to a policy problem such as mass immigration and its attendant cultural clashes is not acceptance. Unfortunately, that seems to be the response that many European policy makers and bureaucrats have opted for. In this final part, I want to consider the dangers of accepting the alien values that Muslim men bring with them when they leave their homes for Europe, especially the ways in which they denigrate women. In the final two chapters, I then consider two alternative responses: the one favored by right-wing populists, who would expel illegal immigrants and restrict future Muslim immigration—which I do not think is either right or practicable—and the one I myself prefer, which is to radically reform European states' systems of integrating immigrants.

VICTIM BLAMING BY THE AUTHORITIES

In response to the rising incidence of sexual assaults against women, European governments and bureaucracies are increasingly employing strategies straight from the playbook of the Islamists of my youth.

Rather than policing the behavior of men, their approach favors restricting the freedom of women. The subtext is that women are the problem and they should avoid being in situations where they may be attacked. Whether this response is due to a lack of commitment to an open society, bureaucratic inefficiency, or underfunding, it is a profound setback for women's rights.

In 2015, for example, a high school headmaster in Pocking, near the Bavarian border with Austria, sent letters to parents warning their daughters to modify their dress lest they set off the sexual desires of the Syrian refugees being housed in the school gym. The headmaster, Martin Thalhammer, wrote that "modest clothing should be adhered to, in order to avoid discrepancies. Revealing tops or blouses, short shorts, or miniskirts could lead to misunderstandings."[1] "Discrepancies" and "misunderstandings" are curious terms to describe the sexual harassment of schoolchildren.

Following the sexual assault of a woman exercising in a Leipzig park in September 2017, police advised local women to jog in pairs and "always [to] look back to make sure they are not about to be attacked."[2] Similarly, after a series of violent attacks in Ostersund, Sweden, in March 2016, police warned women not to be outside at night by themselves.[3] In a separate incident in December 2017, following the gang rape and "torture-like abuse" of a 17-year-old girl in Malmö, Swedish police published (but later retracted) advice to women not to go outside alone.[4] (Police commander Mats Attin told the media that he had never seen such a thing in his thirty-five years of police service.) Removing women from public spaces appears to be the default response for authorities who lack the will or the resources to protect them.

Following numerous reports of sexual assaults at another Swedish music festival, Bråvalla, in 2014 and 2015,[5] the next year police handed out armbands bearing the legend "Police cordon, don't grope" (*POLICE AVSPÄRRAT #tafs ainte*).[6] Tino Sanandaji, an

Iranian Kurdish refugee and economist critical of the Swedish government's integration policy, has pointed out the absurdity of police offering women a talisman to ward off potential evil.[7] The magical thinking was clearly a failure, as another four rapes and twenty-three sexual assaults were reported at the festival in 2017.[8] Women voted with their pocketbooks the following year, and Bråvalla was canceled by the organizers due to weak ticket sales.

If talismans do not work, how about segregation of the sexes? In an irony of history, the once discredited notion of segregation—sometimes on the basis of race as well as gender—is making a comeback on the Western left. In August 2018, the Statement Festival was held in Gothenburg.[9] The idea was to create a "safe space" where women could party without fear of harassment. No "cisgender men"—that is, men who were not only designated male at birth but also currently identify themselves as male—were allowed to attend. Similarly, in 2017, Berlin police cordoned off a "Women's Safety Area" at New Year's Eve celebrations near the Brandenburg Gate. A police spokesperson explained, "This is a good opportunity to offer women a place to retreat to if they feel harassed."[10] The irony of such schemes seems to be lost on those who come up with them. For segregation of the sexes is precisely what most Muslim-majority countries practice, albeit to varying degrees. The female-only festival in Sweden ironically coincided with the reforms introduced in Saudi Arabia in 2018, which finally permitted public concerts in the kingdom as long as the sexes did not mix.

THE SUBJECTION OF WOMEN, AGAIN

John Stuart Mill's defense of the rights of women in *The Subjection of Women* (1869)—a work heavily influenced by his late wife, Harriet

Taylor Mill—represents the best impulses of Western civilization. In the space of roughly two hundred years, beginning before Mill in the Enlightenment of the eighteenth century and continuing into our own time, liberalism produced the language, legal systems, and tools that would improve the position of women in the Western countries. It may no longer be fashionable to make such comparisons, but the economic evidence is unequivocal: liberal democratic societies are more peaceful, prosperous, and tolerant than those that permit autocratic rule, as in Russia; one-party rule, as in China; or theocracy, as in Iran. Yet these days, those who advocate the superiority of Western civilization are demonized, especially on university campuses, as racists or white supremacists. Few within the establishment are willing to challenge the politically correct consensus and insist instead on upholding the core classical liberal values.

I fear that European elites have become especially complacent. Young people in Western societies have grown up with the assumption that gender equality is a given. They did not have to fight for basic equality and are often oblivious to its being undermined around them. Even when they are confronted with the erosion of women's rights in the street, they sometimes apologize for criticizing their attackers. In court, victims of sexual assault appearing on the witness stand have to insist that they are not racists. Almost every woman I interviewed in the course of researching this book felt obliged to begin with a caveat: "I'm not against migrants," "I'm from the Left," or "I am not racist."

Once settled arguments about women's emancipation, individual rights, religious freedom, sexual freedom, animal rights, and freedom of speech are up for debate again in Europe. I asked Flemming Rose, the Danish newspaper editor who published the cartoons of the Prophet Mohammed in *Jyllands-Posten* in September 2005, how this rolling back of liberal values had taken place. He described what had happened in his newsroom after he published the cartoons:

In 2006, my paper took the position that there should be no compromise on free speech. Then they started receiving terrorist threats and planned attacks. They soon changed their tune. Management said, "It's no longer about free speech, it's about protecting the newspaper and its staff against a terrorist attack," as if there is no relationship whatsoever between freedom and security. That's how the fear mechanism worked.

Was adapting to this new, constrained environment a deliberate coping mechanism? I wondered. He replied, "People are not very conscious of this; it's happening at a subconscious level. The security concern is just the way life is now . . . it's a normal thing for them. There is this human ability to adapt to any situation in order to survive."

When they start work in the *Jyllands-Posten* newsroom today, young journalists are taken through drills on how to get to safe (i.e., bulletproof) rooms in the event of a terrorist attack. More than a decade after publishing the Mohammed cartoons, Flemming still requires around-the-clock security protection. His bodyguards were hovering nearby as we spoke in a Copenhagen hotel. I asked him how many journalists today were willing to follow in his footsteps or those of Stéphane Charbonnier, the editor of the Paris newspaper *Charlie Hebdo*, who was killed in the newspaper's office on January 7, 2015. He gave a characteristically pragmatic response: "Very few, and I don't blame them, but they need to be aware that freedom always comes at a price. People can have nice principles and values, but most of us have family and kids. We need work to provide for ourselves, and in that process you make compromises when there is a real threat."[11]

Yet if Europe continues down this path, I can foresee a nightmare scenario: European societies will look more like the societies the immigrants have left behind them. The situation in what are now a relatively few urban neighborhoods will become more widespread. More of Sweden will look like the parallel societies of Tensta or Malmö.

There will be multiple "Little Mogadishus." And in response, populist parties will flourish, and some will attract and foster real racists. More native-born citizens will lose faith in the rule of law and take matters into their own hands. Sensing that the police cannot protect them, people may even arm themselves. In this future, I fear that women may lose many of the gains they have made in my lifetime. Just as freedom and autonomy for women receded with the implementation of sharia law in newly Muslim countries, women will also lose ground— not only to the cultural values of the non-Western world but also to the far-right movements if they succeed in establishing themselves as the principal defenders of the existing social order.

EXCUSING A BREAKDOWN IN THE RULE OF LAW

This is what rolling back women's rights looks like. It is a brochure produced by the Swedish government's National Board of Health and Welfare (Socialstyrelsen) for newcomers in 2018 with the title "Information for You Who Are Married to a Child."[12]

Socialstyrelsen   Migrationsverket

**Information till dig
som är gift med
ett barn**

It dispassionately states that in Sweden it is illegal to marry a child under 18 years of age and criminal to have sex with someone under the age of 15. However, the only consequence for those who are living with a sexual partner considered a child by law, as the brochure gently spells out, is that social services "may suggest that you do not live together for a shorter or longer period." The brochure does not suggest that the law will be enforced. The government department responsible offered no condemnation of child marriage, a well-established human rights abuse, until it was criticized in the media for taking such a permissive stance. The pamphlet has since been retracted and a new law put into place stating that Sweden does not recognize foreign child marriages. However, the law does not automatically invalidate existing child marriages and the government continues to provide welfare benefits, housing, and child support to married children and their offspring.

Child marriage is not a new phenomenon in Sweden. It is an established practice in some poorly integrated communities. Like other "honor culture" practices, such as honor violence and female genital mutilation, child marriage is imposed on young women, who rarely have the resources, education, or freedom to resist. In my work as a translator in the Netherlands more than twenty years ago and today as the head of a women's rights foundation in the United States, I see cases of young girls and women controlled by their families, married against their will, and effectively raped by older husbands. Very rarely do these cases make it onto the front pages, and even more rarely do they appear in official statistics. One recent example from southeastern Sweden stands out for the timid response of the authorities involved. In 2016, social services in a small town called Mönsterås permitted a couple to continue "living together" even though he was a 20-year-old asylum seeker and she was just 13.[13] Despite numerous visits from social workers putting "risk assessment procedures into place" and attempting to "persuade" the couple to live separately, the girl was left in the household. Months later she became pregnant, and the couple confirmed that they had already been married. According to the municipal authority, the girl's situation did not meet the requirements for coercive measures under the law, and if the girl would not voluntarily move away from her husband, it could not force her to. As a direct consequence of the case, the social services in Mönsterås had to move to a different location after receiving threats.[14]

This is a blatant breakdown in the rule of law. This girl's rights were not protected by those who are paid by Swedish taxpayers to enforce the law against child marriage. And there are many more like her. In the United States, an estimated 248,000 children, some as young as 12, were married between 2000 and 2010.[15] In Germany, too, the problem of child marriage arose as asylum-seeker numbers increased. In 2016, the Federal Ministry of the Interior, Building and Community reported that 1,475 refugee minors were married, three-quarters of them girls and 361 of them under the age of 14.[16] In response to these figures, the following year, the German government passed a law stating that the minimum marriage age is 18 years. In an attempt to pander to Muslim constituents, both the Left and the Greens voted against the law for being "too general."[17]

SHARIA COUNCILS AND LEGAL DOUBLE STANDARDS

Societies that permit the existence of parallel communities resign themselves to the growth of parallel legal systems. This is the case with sharia courts that apply Islamic law to the marital affairs of believers. Dutch researcher Machteld Zee's study of sharia councils in the United Kingdom estimates that between ten and eighty-five sharia councils operate there.[18] Zee documents cases of women seeking divorce being sent back to abusive husbands by sharia courts and being denied the legal protections that non-Muslim wives receive under UK law. In addition to a rant attacking Zee as a member of "the Unholy Trinity" (along with Donald Trump and Baroness Caroline Cox, the founder of Humanitarian Aid Relief Trust), the Islamic Sharia Council published statistics of its caseload in 2010. Of the seven hundred applications received that year, 83 percent had been from women, one-third had been complaints of domestic violence, and another third had been complaints about neglect or a lack of financial support. As the council explains on its website: "To date, the Council has dealt with over 10,000 cases. The majority of these cases concern divorce. In some cases the wife has obtained a civil divorce which is not accepted by the husband, who considers such a divorce to be unacceptable with no bearing upon his right as a husband."

Though frowned upon by the legal establishment, sharia courts continue to operate in the United Kingdom. In its 2019 *Integrated Communities Strategy Green Paper*, the UK government admitted that there was "evidence that some sharia councils may be working in a discriminatory and unacceptable way—for example by seeking to legitimise forced marriage and making arrangements on divorce that are unfair to women."[19] Why, then, allow these courts to continue operating? I find it even more troubling when sharia court decisions are taken into account by secular courts. In March 2018, the district court in the Stockholm suburb of Solna released a man for abusing his wife on the ground that she should have turned first to the man's relatives for help, as sharia law prescribes, rather than to the police. (This same advice is given to Muslims on the English-language web forum Ummah.com.)[20]

For decades Western authorities have turned a blind eye to unequal treatment of women in immigrant communities not only when it comes to marriage and divorce but also in regard to education.

Examples of voluntary gender segregation at university student events may seem like minor encroachments on equal rights, but when university heads defend gender segregation, we should be concerned. In 2013, the University of Leicester's Islamic Society seated women at the back of the room for a training course.[21] Rather than condemning the discrimination, the head of Universities UK, Nicola Dandridge, defended it, suggesting that segregation of the sexes was "not completely alien to our culture." More recently, in 2017, the London School of Economics failed to prevent a gender-segregated event by the university's Islamic Society, which sold separate tickets for men and women and then separated the sexes in the room with a screen. (After students complained, the university eventually conceded that the event had been discriminatory.)[22]

All these seemingly small incidents add up. Institutions that make such concessions to minority groups are unwittingly resetting the norms for whole communities. And this is happening not only in European universities.

EVASION, WITHDRAWAL, RETREAT

The stereotype of northern Europeans spending leisure time in the nude has often been the butt of jokes in other Western countries. How eccentric it seems to most Americans that Germans play tennis in the nude, that Swedes view mixed naked bathing as a part of their national identity, or that the Dutch are enthusiasts for unisex saunas. The Europeans I first encountered in the 1990s believed that such customs were signs of progress toward a more civilized society. Today, however, this progress is in reverse as institutions adapt to the preferences of those who insist on "modesty" and gender segregation.

In the nineteenth century, Sweden became the first European

country to permit mixed-gender swimming. In December 2016, however, the Swedish Equality Ombudsman (Diskrimineringsombudsmannen, or DO) decided that discriminatory gender-segregated hours were permissible in public swimming pools in order to accommodate women whose religious convictions prohibited them from swimming with men.[23] Sweden is not alone in making such concessions. Gender-segregated bathing has been introduced in some municipal pools in the German city of Bonn,[24] whereas in 2015, local authorities in Duisburg, near Essen, resisted demands for segregated swimming pools by Muslim associations.[25] Of course, the people making these decisions are partially resegregating their facilities in an effort to be culturally tolerant. Yet few are thinking through the implications of their decisions for society at large.

Religious conviction is not the only reason native Swedes have begun accommodating women-only swimming, however. Soon after the 2015 migration wave began, a growing number of female swimmers started to report being harassed in the water. Pool lifeguards and patrons reported groups of immigrant men staring at, harassing, encircling, groping, and sexually intimidating female swimmers. One of many examples took place on a Saturday afternoon in 2016 at Vänersborg swimming pool: A mother was grabbed by the hips by a man who pressed himself against her body numerous times. She could not fend him off, as she was holding on to her young daughter to prevent her falling under the water. "I was completely paralyzed and couldn't defend myself," she later said.[26]

Stockholm's largest swimming complex, Eriksdalsbadet, introduced gender-segregated Jacuzzis in January 2016 following an increase in complaints from women about male groping.[27] The head of the pool declined to reveal the number of complaints. In the Swedish town of Kalmar, a pool located near a home for unaccompanied migrant minors had so many cases of harassment in 2016 that local

women formed their own "grope watch" (*tafsvakten*) to police the
pool.[28] The pool's acting manager admitted, "Many customers are
coming to me and saying, 'We don't want to come and swim if someone is going to come and leer at us.'" Yet she still claimed that "We
have no problem here." The "grope watch" founder said she had
acted simply because local women were afraid to use the pool and
not enough was being done to protect them. According to the journalist Paulina Neuding, Swedish police reported that 80 percent of
complaints at swimming pools were about foreigners, most of them
without national ID numbers—in other words, asylum seekers waiting to be processed by authorities.[29]

In 2017, police in Krefeld, Germany, reported an alleged molestation by a group of five Syrian boys on two girls in the Bockum
swimming pool. In Düsseldorf, a 27-year-old Afghan was accused
of exposing himself and propositioning a 14-year-old girl at a swimming pool. A Bornheim pool banned asylum-seeker men over 18
years of age after six reports of "sexually offensive behavior of some
migrant men at the pool." In response to such behavior, the Munich
municipal authorities produced a brochure with an illustration de-

picting a hand reaching toward a bikini-clad blond woman's bottom with a red "forbidden" symbol over it. The leaflets were designed for new migrants and have been published in a number of languages, including Arabic, French, Pashto, and Somali.[30]

This kind of problem is also occurring on the other side of the Atlantic. In 2017, a 39-year-old Syrian refugee named Soleiman Hajj Soleiman was charged with sexually assaulting six girls aged 13 to 15 who had been celebrating a birthday at a swimming pool in Edmonton, Canada.[31] One of the victims, a 14-year-old girl, said the man had touched her breasts and buttocks under the water in the wave pool. Immediately after the arrest, a spokesperson from the local Islamic Family and Social Services Association expressed dismay that the man's nationality and immigration status had been publicly revealed. Eighteen months later, Soleiman was acquitted of the six counts of sexual assault and six counts of sexual contact with a child due to a lack of "reliable evidence."

NOT-SO-FREE BODY CULTURE

As a newcomer to the Netherlands, I was startled when I encountered social nudity. It was explained to me that many Europeans enjoy spas, saunas, beaches, and lakes in the nude. Men, women, and children of all ages frolic together, uninhibited and stark naked. I remember my Dutch girlfriends complaining that they were unable to sunbathe topless on holidays in places such as Thailand; they thought the Thais absurdly prudish for not allowing them to strip off. Coming from a culture obsessed with shrouding women's bodies, I couldn't believe that such displays of naked flesh were treated so nonchalantly. I came to accept that naturism was a good thing that contributed to individual self-confidence by reducing the feelings of shame about human anatomy that other cultures instill. While reading about the spate of groping by asylum seekers in European swimming pools, I wondered if they had also come into contact with this "free body culture." I asked Mikolai, the owner of a German nude bathing company I met in London, if many new immigrant men had visited his resorts. Yes, he said.[32]

"We've had many incidents of young immigrants coming in expecting sex and making people feel uncomfortable. We tried to explain that we are not a sex institution."

I asked, "How did you convey what your resorts are to men from Iraq and Afghanistan? People who have never seen anyone walking around naked like that?"

"Our philosophy is based on the Roman Empire," he replied. "In ancient Rome free people had the opportunity to enjoy their idea of paradise in the sunshine. As everyone knows, this was not everlasting, so we have created a place like Rome with marble decor and tropical plants where people can buy a slot of time to enjoy their idea of paradise. Whether it's a Saturday afternoon reading a book, swimming, enjoying a glass of champagne, they can have their paradise. And we have a zero-tolerance policy for those who disrupt others' slice of paradise. The minute these young guys, or anyone else, breaks one of our rules by leering or making others feel uncomfortable, they are removed from the facility and banned."

Has that policy worked? "Well the German government accused us of discrimination for this. For the first time we have had to put CCTV cameras up." He looked close to tears as he went on, "Now the naturist area is separated for men and women."

Sadly, this is not an isolated experience. In 2016, a group of naturists near Dresden was ordered to cover up at a lake campsite that had welcomed nudity since 1905. The reason for the change in policy? An asylum seekers' center had been built across the lake.[33] During summer 2016, a group of "Mediterranean-looking men" was removed from a naturist beach in Geldern, North Rhine–Westphalia. Swimmers complained that the men shouted "Allahu akbar" at them, calling the men and children "infidels" and the women "sluts."[34]

This may go some way to explaining why naturism is waning in Europe. A spokesperson for the FamilienSportBund Erftland-Ville in the Rhineland said that its membership numbers had dropped by two-thirds in the last decade.[35] Similarly, since the 1990s, membership at naturist clubs in Dortmund and Witten has roughly halved. A 2017 survey of eight thousand women by IFOP, an international market research group, reported a decline beginning in 2009 in the numbers of European women who practice either nudity or toplessness on beaches.[36] In France, topless bathing has halved over a generation, especially for young women, who are one-quarter as likely to go topless as those aged 60 and above. The researcher who led the study commented that body consciousness, sedentary lifestyles, and concerns for skin health might have caused the change in women's behavior. But Kurt Fischer, the president of the German Federation of Naturist Clubs (Deutscher Verband für Freikörperkultur, or DFK), says that another reason for the decline is that "Young people with immigrant backgrounds and from Muslim cultures, where the unclothed body remains taboo, have proven impervious to the lure of nudism."[37]

WHOLE COMMUNITIES ARE FINDING THEIR LIBERTIES RETRACTED

I am writing this book mainly because I see women's rights being eroded as a consequence of mismanaged immigration and failing integration. But I want to make it clear here that it is not only women who are being affected. LGBTQ and Jewish communities are also being targeted by immigrants from cultures hostile to their very existence. Having only liberated themselves from systematic persecution in the West in the second half of the twentieth century, members of both communities are again on the receiving end of verbal and physical abuse in the streets of Europe.

Homosexuality is stigmatized and forbidden in Islam.[38] Many countries in North Africa and the Middle East, the regions from which the majority of immigrants to Europe come, criminalize homosexuality. Likewise, mosques and governments in these parts of the world produce a steady stream of anti-Jewish propaganda. As children in Somalia, we were taught to hate Jews and blame them for all that was wrong in the world. I don't find it surprising that newcomers crossing the border into Europe hold homophobic and anti-Semitic views. What is surprising is the doublethink of European elites who tolerate this hate by a minority out of fear of appearing racist or hateful themselves.

Considering how quickly social values change, Europe's LGBTQ population should be on guard about the impact that changing demographics are likely to have on their hard-won rights. Take the United Kingdom, for example. The majority of Britons, including practicing Christians, are now in favor of gay marriage.[39] But surveys of British Muslims show that more than half believe that gay sex should be illegal.[40] LGBTQ people are reporting being harassed by hostile young immigrants, even in what were once considered gay neighborhoods. Some gay couples say they no longer walk hand in hand in cities such as Brussels.[41]

OPEN ANTI-SEMITISM RETURNS TO EUROPE

In recent years, Jewish children in Berlin schools have begun to encounter a new form of persecution. At Jungfernheide School in 2016, a Jewish boy reported a fellow student as saying "If a Jew were in this class, I would kill him." In Tempelhofer Elementary School, a Jewish child received death threats from classmates, and in Friedenau a Jewish student was beaten up for his faith.[42]

Such anti-Semitic attacks do not stop at the school gate. Attacks on Jews in public places in Berlin are also rising. The Department for Research and Information on Antisemitism Berlin (RIAS Berlin), an NGO monitoring anti-Semitism, reported a 14 percent increase in anti-Semitic incidents in Berlin, from 951 incidents in 2017 to 1,083 in 2018.[43]

In an incident captured on video in an upmarket suburb of Berlin in April 2018, a Syrian man shouted "Yahudi" (Arabic for "Jew") while belting two men wearing kippas (Jewish skullcaps). The head of the Central Council of Jews in Germany (Zentralrat der Juden in Deutschland) responded by recommending that Jewish men refrain from wearing kippas in public.[44] Similar stories could be told about the experience of Jews in Denmark, Great Britain, France, and elsewhere. Twice the number of Belgian Jews relocate to Israel each year as did in the early 2000s.[45] The numbers of French Jews decamping for Israel quadrupled following the *Charlie Hebdo* attacks.

FLIGHT AND WITHDRAWAL

Jewish flight is only part of a wider picture of relocation in response to mass migration. A much maligned way in which native populations adapt to mass migration is the phenomenon of "white flight." Immigrants and their descendants tend to settle in communities close to their kin. As the numbers of immigrants increase, some native-born residents move out. Researchers studying this phenomenon suggest that white flight is a chain reaction in which even those who favor diversity leave once the proportion of newcomers reaches a certain tipping point, particularly in schools.[46] For decades, policy makers and municipal authorities have sought to discourage white flight in the belief that it deepens the isolation of ethnic minorities and diminishes their opportunities to interact with the host society. When I was in politics in the early 2000s, the Dutch government was working with various municipalities to arrest this trend in Amsterdam. Like so many integration programs, however, the interventions we made did not work.

White flight changes the appearance of European neighborhoods, but most communities continue to function peacefully, albeit with significant government support. Some, however, deteriorate and become ghettoes afflicted by grime and crime. In such areas, disaffected young people with few prospects for material success too often gravitate toward drugs and antisocial behavior. Property crime, drug dealing, intimidation, and violence take place openly in such blighted suburbs. In Sweden, so-called vulnerable areas have become notorious for car burnings, shootings, and grenade attacks. The police acknowledge that a high proportion of perpetrators are first- and second-generation migrants.[47]

Such neighborhoods—for example, La Chapelle–Pajol in Paris and Laeken in Brussels—aren't just unsafe areas for women; they are "no-go zones" that have become unsafe for those carrying out public services as well. Postal and delivery services have at times been suspended in Malmö.[48] In suburban Stockholm, parking wardens did not work in Tensta for months and libraries in Hässelby were closed in the afternoons in 2015 due to attacks on librarians.[49] In some Swedish neighborhoods, paramedics and fire services wait for police protection before responding to emergency calls in no-go zones.[50] In a 2015 report, the Swedish Police Authority identified fifty-three such "vulnerable areas." Police report a lack of cooperation by residents, which leads to fewer arrests and successful prosecutions and exacerbates the sense that the rule of law simply does not apply in those neighborhoods.[51]

Cai Berger, a longtime Uniting Church of Sweden pastor in Stockholm's infamous area of Tensta, says it has been this way for thirty years. "This has become a way of life. Cars are torched, kids are mugged or beaten up, but the state does nothing about the problem. Some of my closest friends live in these areas, and they are afraid to talk openly about it."

Berger is a typically tall, tanned, blond Swede who married an Iranian asylum seeker in 2018. "I've been working in these areas for so long, and I know firsthand that the gangs responsible for the crimes are an ethnic and religious mix," he said. "It's not just Muslims or recent arrivals, as some have suggested in the media. Some kids join the gangs because they were school buddies with a member. But when police come to a mainly white suburb, the residents don't come out throwing rocks at them."

He is careful to qualify his point: "Whether or not it's immigrant related, the issues of migration, crime, security, and competing for public resources tend to cluster in people's minds in Sweden."[52]

Less willing to discuss the problem of "no-go zones" are Europe's political leaders. In 2015, the mayor of Paris, Anne Hidalgo, threatened to sue Fox News for alleging that her city had such Muslim-only areas.[53] The following year, in an opinion article cowritten with the mayors of New York and London, she reiterated the need to "continue to pursue an inclusive approach to resettlement [of refugees and migrants] in order to combat the growing tide of xenophobic language around the globe. . . . We know policies that embrace diversity and promote inclusion are successful."[54] In 2016, the mayor of Argenteuil in northwestern Paris was outraged that his arrondissement was being compared to the jihadi hot spot Molenbeek in Brussels. However, two years after Cologne's infamous New Year's

Eve attacks, even Chancellor Angela Merkel finally had to admit that there were parts of Germany "where nobody dares to go."[55]

A RETREAT FROM LIBERALISM

Following the hundreds of Islamist terrorist attacks of the past two decades, Europeans have grown accustomed to seeing armed police and soldiers on their streets. Now, however, enhanced security measures are also being used to deter less political forms of crime by new immigrant arrivals. In Linz in 2016, the police "Lentos" unit, which is usually deployed to subdue football hooligans, was called in to deal with "a group of, largely, North African men" at the train station who had "been up to all sorts of things—from sexual harassment to public drunkenness, drug taking, even causing actual bodily harm."[56] While visiting Vienna in 2018, my researcher observed officers of all shapes, sizes, and genders, some in riot gear or with police dogs, patrolling the city streets, stopping cars to question drivers and passersby. It seemed to her as if there were police on every corner.

The problem is not only that a visibly growing police presence seems to run counter to the spirit of an open and free society. It also costs a great deal. In the ancient German university town of Tübingen, to give just one example, the municipal government built a special apartment complex to house problematic migrants at a cost of €400,000 a year and doubled the number of city police officers.[57] As the Danish MP Henrik Dahl explained, such are the hidden costs of mass migration.

> In the day-to-day bureaucratic business of a politician, you have to find money in the national budget for security. Each year more money needs to be found. All governments going

through this process year after year must ask themselves why they must increase the security budget far more than inflation would suggest. Obviously because there's a problem. How come you have to pass legislation to define how units of the armed forces work under the supervision of the police to protect synagogues? I mean, this was not necessary ten or fifteen years ago. It's necessary now.[58]

LIBERTY OR SECURITY?

In an effort to restore their monopoly on violence, governments have to ramp up security spending, increasing police numbers or (as in the United Kingdom) introducing surveillance systems based on large numbers of cameras. This change requires societies to reassess the delicate balance between liberty and security. A liberal society that wants to survive understands that there is a trade-off and seeks to strike the right balance.

The location of that point of balance between freedom and security is not self-evident, however. It struck me in the course of writing this book how many people I spoke to had paid a personal penalty for speaking freely about their concerns. Openly discussing the bad behavior of immigrant men, like discussing the dangers of political Islam, can get you into all kinds of trouble. In the early 2000s, it seemed novel that I needed bodyguards. The first article I ever published was in response to the 9/11 terrorist attacks in 2001, observing that the attackers had had a religious motivation that it was foolish to deny. At that time, the only people who had security in the Netherlands were the royal family, the American, British, and Israeli ambassadors, and (for some weird reason) the Swedish ambassador. By October 2002, I had police protection and was being moved from safe house to safe house to avoid assassination. Some journalists accused me of being an alarmist. My response to them was "You don't understand the jihadi threat and the honor culture of clans. Pretty soon we will all be needing security."

Certainly, there are many more people in my situation today than there were eighteen years ago. Take the case of Seyran Ateş. She is a feminist Muslim, the author of the book *Islam Needs a Sexual Revolution*, and the founder of a liberal mosque in the middle of Berlin.[59] Fatwas have been placed on her in three countries: Turkey, the country of her birth; Egypt; and Iran. Egypt's Dar al-Ifta al-Misriyyah (a center for Islamic research) has condemned her for allowing women and men to pray side by side; Al-Azhar University in Cairo condemns the very concept of a liberal mosque; while the fatwa of the Turkish Diyanet (Directorate of Religious Affairs) says that there is "nothing more depraving and ruining religion" than mixed-sex prayers.[60] She was called a Gülen supporter, thus a terrorist supporter. Her mosque is referred to by the Diyanet as the Gülen-sect mosque.[61]

Speaking to my colleagues and me in 2018, Seyran seemed like a fairy-tale princess tucked away at the top of a tower. Walking up many flights of dark, musty stairs to meet her, we received nods from numerous German police stationed throughout the building as we passed them. It seemed incongruous that such a gentle and obviously kind woman could be perceived as a threat to anyone. I asked her how she is holding up.

She replied, "Sometimes one has to take the first step and the rest will come until things become normal. Ruby Bridges was six years old when she started school as the only black kid in a white Louisiana school. She had marshals around her and police protection for a year. In the second year, she didn't need police protection anymore. So it took only one year for people to get used to that."

I wanted her to explain what it is about her liberal mosque that drives Islamists to wish to destroy her. "It's that our mosque is not gender segregated," she told me. "Men and women pray shoulder to shoulder. However, this is only pictorial, as in all other mosques. People stand close together, but everyone on their own carpet, so there is no physical touch during prayer. Some Muslims go absolutely crazy about it. They say a man cannot concentrate on God when a woman is near him; he will just think about having sex with her. It doesn't matter which woman it is, what she looks like, her age, or anything. Their idea is that every man wants to fuck every woman nearby him. I'm sorry to say it so directly. It is really about sexuality. The head scarf is also about sexuality, and here we have women without head scarves. It's so hard for them to accept that they are willing to kill me for it."[62]

Seyran's ally and fellow Turkish immigrant Efgani Dönmez, an Austrian MP, also requires security, especially for public events.[63] Like me, he has been called a "racist," a "right-wing populist," and an "Islamophobe." "When I think about where the insults are coming from," he told me, "I wear them as a badge of honor." Eskild Dahl Pedersen, the Danish security chief of a housing cooperative, was given police protection on one occasion, after he spoke publicly about the problems of failed integration and exposed an immigrant community leader who had used the cooperative's surveillance cameras to monitor local girls.[64] Düzen Tekkal is another courageous individual who has received threats, in her case for speaking out in Germany about the plight of Iraq's Yazidi women. "I am told, 'Be quiet, it will be better for you,' and sometimes I feel guilty for my family, because it affects them. Many of my friends are now taking security. [But] I remind myself that fear is not an option and we have to go on."[65]

For Hamed Abdel-Samad, a German author and commentator, it started in 2013. While he was giving a lecture tour in Cairo, an Islamic professor called for his death on live television. His photo and home address were circulated online with a call to action: "Wanted Dead."

"German members of ISIS fighting in Syria wrote home to their German friends instructing them to kill me," he told me. "Now I have five or more bodyguards with me to fly on a plane or walk to the store to buy bread. In every European country I have security. No one thinks about people like us and the way immigration is constantly increasing our risk."

He is frustrated. "We are the real liberals," he said. "It is immigrants like us [who are] risking our lives to defend the liberal values that drew us to Europe in the first place. But we are called 'self-hating Muslims' or 'Islamophobes' by those who instead defend the Muslim Brotherhood."[66]

I, too, have struggled with this hypocrisy in the West. It appears that those immigrants with illiberal and misogynistic ideas are protected but we liberal feminists are not.

Threats drive some of us from our homes. The Iranian-born ex-Muslim Jaleh Tavakoli, a fierce critic of honor culture, was forced to move out of her Copenhagen home.[67]

Others speaking about these issues find their careers stalling. Outspoken academics such as the Swedish sociologist Göran Adamson found himself denied promotion. The British member of Parliament Sarah Champion was unceremoniously dumped from Labour's shadow cabinet for exposing the sexual exploitation of minors in her constituency.

Yet it is just this sort of appeasement of the forces of illiberalism that leads to the rise of the populist Right. As the legitimate authorities shut down the free speech of those who seek to defend the open society, they inadvertently create an opportunity for forces that are not much more committed to liberal values than those they seek to expel or exclude from Europe.

Chapter 17

THE POPULIST PROBLEM

It is commonplace to observe that the wave of migration has had a major impact on European politics since 2015, boosting right-wing populist parties. But how big and how enduring has that political impact been?

THE POPULIST WAVE

European voters are regularly asked by Eurobarometer, "What do you think are the two most important issues facing your country at the moment?" During the period of the financial crisis and its aftermath (2009–2012), immigration was named by around one in ten voters (9 to 11 percent), far below unemployment (named by over half of voters in early 2013), the economic situation, and inflation. The composite issue of "health and social security" was also mentioned by more voters than immigration. That began to change in the course of 2013, and by the end of 2015, immigration was named by 36 percent of voters as one of the two most important issues, on an equal footing with unemployment. However, immigration subsequently fell back to 21 percent in 2018, below both unemployment and social security.[1]

There is considerable variety among countries. In Portugal and Spain, as well as in most new member states in central and eastern Europe—with the notable exception of Hungary—immigration is not seen as a major issue for the national government. The countries in which a quarter of voters or more name it as one of the top-two issues for government are, in ascending order, Sweden (25 percent), Belgium, Germany, Austria, Denmark, Italy, and Malta (39 percent). However, immigration rises to the top if voters are asked, "What do you think are the most important issues facing the EU at the moment?" The issue overtook the other issues in late 2015, when 58 percent named it. Significantly, terrorism came in second. Those two issues have remained the top-two issues seen as facing the European Union, with immigration declining to 38 percent and terrorism spiking to 44 percent in early 2017 before falling back to 29 percent in early 2018. By comparison, climate change was named as a top EU issue by just 11 percent of voters. In a majority of EU member states, more than two-fifths of voters regard immigration as one of the top-two issues the European Union has to deal with.

Interestingly, and perhaps surprisingly, men care slightly more than women about the issue for both national governments and the European Union, but the difference is not significant. Younger generations also worry less about immigration than older generations, but again the difference is not huge. (A third of voters aged 15 to 24 named immigration as a top-two issue for the European Union, compared with two-fifths of those aged over 55.) In 2018 polls, there was an approach to unanimity in support of additional measures to fight illegal immigration: 88 percent said they favored additional measures, as opposed to one-tenth of that number—8.8 percent—who were against additional measures. In no country was the proportion favoring additional measures less than 87.8 percent; the maximum recorded was for Sweden: 88.7 percent. On this issue, men and women also concur, as do the generations.

Mainstream European politicians and commentators are often critical of US president Donald Trump and especially his views on immigration. The irony is that European voters are now well to the right of Americans on this issue. In a 2017 survey, researchers found that a "larger than expected" proportion of Dutch citizens (40 percent) wanted a ban on additional Muslim immigrants.[2] But that was low compared to a Chatham House survey of ten European countries, which revealed that on average 55 percent favored a ban on Muslim immigration (65 percent in Austria, 53 percent in Germany, 51 percent in Italy, and 47 percent in the United Kingdom). In Sweden, twice the number of voters (60 percent) wanted fewer refugees in 2018 as before the migrant crisis in 2015, and the proportion wanting an increase halved, to 12 percent.[3]

Not surprisingly under these circumstances, parties favoring restrictions on immigration have done well in Europe in recent years. It would of course be a mistake to lump together all the right-wing populist parties as anti-immigration, as policies vary significantly from country to country. In some countries, for example, populists are more overtly hostile to the European Union than in others. Some populists—for example, Alternative für Deutschland—are more overt than others in attacking "Islamization." Nevertheless, there is a common strain of opposition to immigration that unites a broad populist movement across Europe.

In France, the National Rally (until June 2018 the National Front) remains the principal opposition to President Emmanuel Macron's En Marche!, its leader, Marine Le Pen, having won a third of the votes in the second round of the 2017 presidential election. Previously a one-man independent in the Dutch Parliament, Geert Wilders remains the leading Dutch populist, though his Party for Freedom performed poorly in the 2019 Dutch provincial elections, losing ground to the new Forum for Democracy. Alternative für Deutschland skyrocketed from nowhere in Germany's staid and steady political culture to win 13 percent of the national vote in 2017. Without the threat posed by the UK Independence Party, it is hard to believe that Prime Minister

David Cameron would ever have committed his Conservative government to a referendum on EU membership, and its successor, the Brexit
Party, remains a significant political force on the right. Although
Brexit is a multifaceted issue, there is no question that immigration
was a central theme of the successful "Leave" campaign in 2016. Italy's populist Lega, led by Matteo Salvini, entered government with the
left-wing populists known as the Five Star Movement after the 2018
election and promptly made the restriction of immigration the principal focus of government policy. The Sweden Democrats went from
being deliberately sidelined by mainstream parties in the Riksdag to
a legitimate force, tripling their presence in Parliament with 17.5 percent of the vote in 2018. The dramatic rise from obscurity of these and
other populist parties shows how seriously the issue of immigration is
taken by European voters.

Based on votes in the most recent national elections, right-wing
populist parties won more than 10 percent of the votes in fourteen
European countries.

Table 15: Right-Wing Populist Parties in Europe, May 2019

Country	Party	Share of Vote in Most Recent National Election (%)
Hungary	Fidesz	49.0
Hungary	Jobbik	19.0
Austria	Freedom Party	26.0
Switzerland	Swiss People's Party	25.8
Denmark	Danish People's Party	21.0
Belgium	New Flemish Alliance	20.4
Estonia	Conservative People's Party	17.8
Finland	The Finns	17.7
Sweden	Sweden Democrats	17.6
Italy	The League	17.4
Spain	Vox	15.0

France	National Rally	13.0
Netherlands	Freedom Party	13.0
Germany	Alternative for Germany	12.6
Czech Republic	Freedom and Direct Democracy	11.0

Source: Extracted from "Europe and Right-Wing Nationalism: A Country-by-Country Guide," BBC News, November 13, 2019, https://www.bbc.com/news/world-europe-36130006.

However, these most recent election results may understate the extent of popular support for policies intended to limit immigration. The populists generally did better in the 2019 elections to the European Parliament. To be sure, few anti-immigration populists are actually in power. Matteo Salvini lost power in 2019 after a misjudged bid to trigger new elections in Italy. In May 2019, Austria's Freedom Party was forced out of its coalition with the conservatives when its leader was filmed offering contracts to a purported Russian businesswoman in exchange for illicit funding. Yet pressure from populists has forced established parties to adopt tighter policies on immigration. As the former Australian prime minister John Howard once observed, "Whenever a government is seen to have immigration flows under control, public support for immigration increases; when the reverse occurs hostility to immigration rises." This has applied in most European countries since 2015, if not before. In Denmark, the populist Danish People's Party's share of the vote dropped from 20 percent in 2015 to 9 percent in 2019 because the Social Democratic Party campaigned for tougher border controls and laws enabling the repatriation of migrants. The Social Democratic prime minister, Mette Frederiksen, put it simply: "Voters who have deserted us over recent years, who thought our immigration policy was wrong, have come back this time."[4]

Opinion polls enable us to track the ebb and flow of immigration as a political issue. In the case of Germany, Alternative für Deutschland (AfD) came into existence as recently as 2013. Between then and the end of 2015, it never attracted more than 8 percent of support and even dwindled to 3 percent in August 2015. Just over a year later, however, as the full implications of the immigration crisis sank in, its popularity surged to 14 percent. After losing ground in 2017, the party performed strongly in 2018 and 2019, catching up with the Social Democrats in September 2018 and tying with them for third place at 14 percent in polls at the time of writing (November 2019). In regional elections in the formerly East German state of Thuringia in October 2019, AfD came in second, behind the far-left Die Linke but ahead of Chancellor Merkel's Christian Democrats. It is worth noting, nevertheless, that the Green Party has significantly outperformed AfD in the past year, suggesting the growing importance of environmental issues to German voters.[5]

WHAT THE POPULISTS WANT

The lesson of the past decade seems clear: if pro-immigration progressives refuse to listen to citizens' concerns or dismiss them as racism, right-wing populists will gain an audience. As Daniel Schwammenthal of the American Jewish Committee's Transatlantic Institute told me in Belgium in 2018, "The iron rule of politics is that if there are real problems in society and responsible parties don't deal with it, the irresponsible parties will jump on them."[6]

Populist parties do a good job of articulating voters' grievances when no one else is willing to do so. However, the populists are seldom well versed in the arts of parliamentary politics, which in Europe essentially means coalition building. Even in opposition, the populists struggle to establish their credibility. AfD's parliamentary manager in the Bundestag, for example, accidentally voted against a bill limiting family reunification for migrants.[7]

In any case, promises to "kick out" illegal migrants or to "stop the boats" are easier to make than to fulfill. The "drawbridge up" mentality will not stop the flow of migrants from abroad, unless there is a huge increase in the security of Europe's southern borders and a massive improvement in economic conditions in the Muslim world; it is even less likely to solve the problems of integration within Europe. Experience strongly suggests that most of the immigrants who have recently arrived in Europe will be staying for good, just like the guest workers two generations before them, even if their asylum applications are mostly rejected and even if they are formally liable to deportation. This is why Europe must face facts and create the right incentives for immigrants and native populations to succeed together.

THE MULTICULTURAL DRAMA

As Paul Scheffer wrote in his essay "The Multicultural Drama," it is the working classes who feel the impact of immigration as new migrants settle in their neighborhoods. They are the ones who worry about the competition for scarce jobs and resources. Counting on postwar welfare systems to provide them with cradle-to-grave security, they are the ones who fear receiving a thinner slice of the pie as migrants who have not paid into the welfare system claim their share of the benefits. In 2018, a German food bank, Essener Tafel, restricted its food distribution to migrants, as their use of the service had increased threefold. The head of the charity, Jörg Sartor, explained that the restriction was in place because so many of the elderly women and single mothers who had previously used the charity had ceased to do so. It was not long before the word "Nazis" was spray-painted on the organization's delivery vans.[8]

Terms such as "racist," "bigot," and "xenophobe" are overused today in order to shut down debate. When I first campaigned for the right-of-center People's Party for Freedom and Democracy (Volkspartij voor Vrijheid en Democratie, or VVD) in the Netherlands, I was warned that the constituents I would meet were racist. But the people I met were anything but bigots. They had a sense of community, volunteered at local schools, and kept their neighborhoods immaculately clean. When they told me of their concerns about immigration and integration, they never brought up the skin color of immigrants or their religion. Rather, it was specific social behaviors they complained about. The British writer David Goodhart estimates that about 3 to 5 percent of the British population are truly xenophobic, perhaps rising to 7 to 10 percent on some issues. "But the vast majority of people, when they are asked, are opposed to large-scale immigration," he told me. "They don't think it benefits them economically or culturally, and they're probably right about both those things."[9]

True white supremacists want to enslave, subjugate, or annihilate nonwhites—much as true jihadis think that those who refuse to submit to Islam ought to die. Ordinary Europeans who express concern that waiting lists for hospital services and housing will worsen as more migrants enter the country are not white supremacists. However, simply ignoring their concerns or labeling them racist will only create political opportunities for true racists.

I have been a beneficiary of the asylum system and of a successful integration program. I have emigrated twice in my life. I would be a monstrous hypocrite if I lent support to the proponents of deportation and immigration restriction. What I want to see is many others like me enjoying the same opportunities that I enjoyed and contributing, as I believe I have, to the health of the West's open societies. But without drastic reforms of Europe's immigration and integration systems, that is not going to happen.

Chapter 18

A NEW APPROACH TO INTEGRATION

If European leaders continue to stick their heads in the sand, then I believe that within a decade or two there will be a meaningful rolling back of women's rights. Public spaces will look noticeably different. We will no longer see women walking confidently, unaccompanied, in the streets or taking public transit alone. The constraints will not merely be on the women within certain minority communities; they will be felt—to varying degrees, depending on where they live—by a significant proportion of all women.

The driving force for this change will be large-scale immigration from Muslim-majority countries where people grow up with a radically different view of the place of women in society. But just as important in causing this change will be Europe's misguided immigration and integration policies. By treating this as a minor problem and hoping it will go away quietly, European leaders have succeeded in making immigration one of the dominant political issues of our time. And it is set to get even bigger. My purpose in writing this book is to urge Europeans to act differently before it is too late. European leaders claim that they want to help refugees. But they refuse to create the conditions on the ground that will allow refugees to flourish in European society.

Fundamental changes can and should be made to the existing policy order. European leaders in the late twentieth century visualized a united Europe. They succeeded in transforming the continent's political institutions. My criticism of today's leaders is that they look at the problem of immigration and offer incremental measures that only increase the existing complexity. We could fill a library with the rules and regulations on immigration across the various states. The system is so elaborate, contradictory, and confusing that it is in dire need of an overhaul. We need the old kind of visionary thinking about Europe to be applied to this new and pressing problem that barely crossed the minds of the original signatories of the Treaty of Rome. My suggestions for the changes that should be made are as follows.

1. REPEAL THE EXISTING ASYLUM FRAMEWORK

The global asylum and refugee system is no longer fit for its stated purpose. As a beneficiary of that system, I do not make such a statement lightly. But the reality is that this outdated asylum system can no longer cope with the challenges posed by mass violence and global migration today.

The world's population has trebled since 1951, when the Convention Relating to the Status of Refugees was ratified in Geneva. It was created in a completely different global context from the one that exists today. It was devised following the mass displacement and attempted genocide of European Jews during World War II and aimed to offer a safe haven to relatively small numbers of individuals from countries fleeing explicit, documented political persecution by governments. It was intended as a temporary solution to a postwar problem, not as a long-term system.

In 1967, the convention was extended universally so that anyone living in a dangerous place, not just those personally persecuted by the state, had grounds for asylum. Millions—potentially hundreds of millions—of people now qualify. The Office of the United Nations High Commissioner for Refugees (UNHCR) reported almost 25 million refugees worldwide in 2018 and another 3.5 million asylum seekers waiting for decisions.[1] Consequently, the distinction between migrant and asylum seeker has become blurred to such an extent that it is no longer useful. If we step back and take a dispassionate view, it is clear that we need a better definition of what refugees are and how they can be best helped. The first step, therefore, is to repeal the existing asylum laws and replace them with a much simpler framework.

As someone who has been through the asylum system and translated for dozens of other asylum seekers, I understand the appeal of using asylum as a legal basis for migration. But what is wrong with being an economic migrant in search of a better life? It is clear that we need to change the artificial classification that differentiates between asylum seekers, refugees, and economic migrants.

Rather than focusing on where people come from and their motivations for leaving, I believe the main criterion for granting residence should be how far they are likely to abide by the laws and adopt the values of their host society. People like me would have been better off being given an option to prove our ability to adapt instead of having to shoehorn our life stories into the Geneva Convention's framework. Rather than leaving it to a bureaucratic lottery, migrants should therefore be selected on the basis of their likelihood of adapting and flourishing in the West. These would be individuals with the highest probability of entering the labor market, rather than the welfare state, and those who genuinely wish to become Dutch, French, or British and live among, as opposed to just near, their fellow citizens.

Today, armies of officials review asylum applications and ask applicants ridiculous questions. They spend hours scrutinizing asylum seekers' stories to determine whether they are telling the truth about their identity, their age, their country of origin, and how they arrived in the West. They ask what seat they sat in on the plane, what the conductor on the train was wearing, and it goes on and on. Rather than wasting time on such formalistic detective work, officials should spend the time asking what migrants know about the culture, laws, and norms of the society they wish to join. They should find out what skills they have and have a frank conversation about what life will be like for them in Germany or France. They should give them a sense of the reality they will face and how emotionally, economically, and psychologically hard it will be. When asylum seekers are given health checkups, they should be screened by a psychologist, too, to assess their ability to adapt.

Those migrants who are unwilling to embrace the laws and values of the host society should be given a reasonable time frame to demonstrate their adaptation to the West, say a year or two, and if this is unsuccessful, they should be ordered to leave or be deported. Rather than languishing in reception centers dependent on handouts for years while their asylum applications and appeals are assessed, new arrivals could prove their capacity for life in the West.

2. ADDRESS THE PUSH FACTORS . . .

It is impossible to reform the asylum system or solve failed integration policies without first addressing the causes of mass migration. Western countries will have to invest resources to address the security and economic issues in the countries from which migrants are coming, or millions more will risk their lives crossing the Mediterranean and the English Channel. The European Union and individual countries already have relationships with numerous refugee-producing countries. Trade agreements, development aid, and diplomatic pressure should be tied to progress on the migration issue, such as forcing countries to accept the return of their repatriated migrants. In societies that have been overrun by militias and people smugglers, Europeans should send military and civilian forces to help build institutions and the rule of law.

Second, Europe must stop pretending that the stabilization of the Muslim world is somebody else's problem. More than "soft power" is required to restore order to the countries from which so many immigrants are coming. The half-baked transatlantic intervention in Libya and the belated and inadequate US intervention in Syria have had disastrous results, as has the effective abandonment of Iraq, which once again teeters on the brink of anarchy. EU member states must be willing to engage in leadership and, if necessary, to intervene militarily to restore order in international conflict areas rather than continuing to depend on the United States to deal with each crisis. As it stands, European defense budgets are unjustifiably low considering the rapidly escalating violence of the regions to the south and east of the Mediterranean. Despite repeated US complaints, only seven European NATO members (among them the United Kingdom) spend more than 2 percent of their gross domestic product on defense, while the United States spends just over 3.4 percent.

Border enforcement in Europe is also underfunded. Without secure borders and an effective deportation system, Europe's immigration policies and interventions to alleviate the push factors will fail. In 1985, Prime Minister Margaret Thatcher refused to sign the United Kingdom up to the Schengen Agreement, saying "It is a matter of plain common sense that we cannot totally abolish frontier controls if we are also to protect our citizens from crime and stop the movement of illegal immigrants." Her judgment was correct. As it stands, the Schengen states are unable to enforce their borders. In 2018, while they held the presidency of the European Union, the Austrians arranged for ten thousand EU soldiers to be deployed to support Frontex in securing Europe's borders against irregular migration.[2] Unlike with the German chancellor in 2015, the political will was present, and the troops are expected to be in place by 2020.[3] But that is just a beginning.

3. . . . AS WELL AS THE PULL FACTORS

A crucial part of the overhaul is reconsidering the attractiveness of western Europe's generous welfare states. The social contract between citizen and state is breaking down in places where welfare schemes are accommodating large numbers of beneficiaries whose families have never contributed to the system. The original welfare state was predicated on a notion of reciprocity, but to newcomers it looks more like universal basic income. The Nobel laureate Milton Friedman said that you can have free immigration or you can have a welfare state, but you cannot have both.[4] Welfare states are national, not universal. There must therefore be meaningful limits on what outsiders can claim based on the feat of having crossed a nation's border.

The Austrian government has been demonized for trying to inject reciprocity back into its welfare systems. Since 2018, migrants have had to sign an Integration Declaration, committing them to meeting obligations in order to continue to receive government assistance and maintain their residential status in Austria. Those who do not comply with integration requirements, such as German-language proficiency, values training, and workforce participation, face sanctions. After two years, those who still do not comply can be sent back to their home countries. This threat of penalties—in the form of cuts to welfare—works. When my research team visited the Austrian Integration Fund (Österreichischer Integrations Fonds, or ÖIF) in Vienna a few months after the Integration Declaration was instituted, large numbers of people were lined up throughout the building and out the doors, all registering for courses and language training. In one class for newcomers, thirty or so men and women of different ages and nationalities sat on chairs in a circle, engaged in a conversation with a facilitator about gender relations in Austria. Some participants, particularly the younger males, smirked and giggled at the idea that girls in Austria are allowed to go out at night just like boys. Others nodded in agreement. By the end of the discussion, one woman quietly lowered her head scarf. To me, her subtle action symbolized exactly what an integration course should do: provide exposure to the values of one's new society and give them the confidence to adopt them for themselves.

The all-encompassing nature of western Europe's welfare states makes "carrot and stick" integration reform relatively easy. For example, in Denmark, the state provides housing, education, and health care as well as social assistance payments. By connecting the provision of those services to the behavior of recipients, the government is trying to break the social and cultural habits that have effectively locked so many Muslim immigrants out of the open society. Children in migrant neighborhoods must now be separated from their families for twenty-five hours per week and learn Danish values, or their parents will have their welfare payments cut.[5] In addition, curfews for under-18s are intended to minimize their involvement in street gangs.[6] This policy was later withdrawn for being too severe.

4. REINSTATE THE RULE OF LAW

Europe's national governments must also review their criminal justice systems. They are simply too lenient toward violent offenders and permit unconscionable exceptions to the rule of law for migrants.

I have thought deeply about the seeming paradox of using illiberal means to achieve liberal ends, but the rule of law without enforcement is mere misrule. As well as a sufficient level of physical police presence, there are now smarter ways of enforcing the rule of law. It is not only authoritarian governments such as China's that can use CCTV, facial recognition technology, and artificial intelligence to monitor their populations. To a remarkable extent, security in the United Kingdom, as well as in Israel, already depends on such camera-based surveillance. Such solutions may seem unpalatable to privacy-obsessed Germans, but a case for their limited use in troubled neighborhoods can surely be made. When citizens in Tübingen were asked by the metropolitan government whether they were willing to accept video surveillance and increased policing in exchange for greater safety, they overwhelmingly agreed.[7]

Technology has a role to play. But there is no substitute for humans with expertise. National and regional police forces need special units dedicated to the protection of women and girls, not to mention Jewish communities, LGBTQ communities, and the dissidents of Islam.

5. LISTEN TO THE SUCCESSFUL IMMIGRANTS

It has struck me time and again as I researched this book that successfully integrated immigrants are the people doing the most to crack this debate open. I think we should therefore hear much more from those people who have migrated from the Muslim world and come out of the process as well-adjusted liberal Europeans. Surely, their advice is what policy makers should be taking into consideration.

In Germany, these include Hamed Abdel-Samad, the son of an Egyptian imam; Düzen Tekkal and Seyran Ateş, both Turks brought up in Germany; and Efgani Dönmez, a Turkish-Austrian politician. Swedes such as the Afghani Mustafa Panshiri, the Iranian Tino Sanandaji, and the Kurd Gulan Avci, a deputy member of Parliament, all argue for not just offering but insisting on liberal values for migrants. Outspoken women such as the Iranian-born Dane Jaleh Tavakoli, the Belgian politician Assita Kanko from Burkina Faso, and the Yemini-Swiss academic Elham Manea all agree that the religion and culture of their homeland are not easily compatible with the ideals of individual freedom in the West. The British Pakistanis Nazir Afzal, Rumy Hasan, and Maajid Nawaz, the founder of Quilliam, argue that carving out exceptions for Muslim immigrants will only hold them back from integrating.

I am in agreement with each of these people on the necessary conditions for integrating Muslims into European societies. The core of their views, and mine, is that we must defend liberal values more robustly, that the rule of law must be enforced, that individual responsibility is crucial, and that the taboo on open discussion of these issues has only made them worse, especially for women.

Rather than propping up ineffective integration programs and pandering to unrepresentative Islamist "spokesmen," Western governments should reallocate their resources to support the ideas of these successful adapters and the integration infrastructure should be geared toward speeding up the adaptation process. It is not enough for immigrants simply to learn the rudiments of the local language and get menial jobs. They must also be willing to adopt the values of the country that has given them sanctuary. The obligation of government is to see to it that immigrants are familiarized with those values and that they are taught by instructors who appreciate what is at stake.

6. PROVIDE SEX EDUCATION TO ALL CHILDREN

Nazir Afzal is the brave and outspoken former Crown prosecutor who tried the first "grooming gang" cases in the United Kingdom. He has long been a fierce advocate for women's rights, and he speaks frankly about the problems of honor culture. In prosecuting some of the grooming gang perpetrators, Nazir noticed that even after being convicted they did not believe they had done anything wrong. As he explained to me:

> They have strict families. They may have a forced or arranged marriage and feel constricted in their home life. They're looking for freedom. And they have never been educated; there is no sex education or relationship education for young men in many of these communities. They don't know what a good relationship is or how to make one. So going up and touching somebody, unlawfully and without consent, is something natural for them.

Nazir argued that the first step in reversing these attitudes must be mandatory sex education and relationship education for all children. I asked whether there was any appetite to lift the taboo around sex in the Muslim community. He admitted that it was an uphill struggle.

An imam got in touch with me here in the UK. He was struck
by the grooming gangs issue and wanted to do something in
response. So he offered sex education classes in his Rochdale
mosque. But he found it impossible to get young children to
come along; their parents wouldn't let them attend. And yet
he was an imam, he had respect and authority. The only way
to solve this is mandating sex and relationship education.[8]

The type of sex education Nazir advocates is more than the nuts
and bolts of sexual intercourse and reproduction. It is education
about healthy relationships, about consent as well as violence, and
about the harms that children and young people can be exposed to.
Children should be taught that they will explore their bodies when
they are young, that they will fall in love and want to have sex, and
that sex comes with responsibilities—not only the possibility of creating babies but also the risk of contracting a disease and the need
for consent. Young men and women need to be taught to respect
each other's physical boundaries and, when they are in doubt, to
stop pursuing sexual contact. Boys must be brought up with the idea
that girls are fellow human beings with an equal right to sexual self-
determination.

Jess Phillips, a firebrand feminist and member of Parliament in
the United Kingdom, advocates mandatory sex and relationship education for all children. Speaking from her office in the House of
Commons, she told me in her strong Birmingham accent:

I've spoken at hundreds of schools and with countless parents
about this. In my electorate I've door-knocked streets of entirely British Pakistani families, and they've never once said
they don't want their kids to have sex education. They just want
to be told that they have to do it—whether they can wear the

niqab or not or whether they have to attend sex ed. They want certainty, and to do that sex ed must be made mandatory.

I asked Jess why policy makers like herself have not made this happen. Her response was that "It's the 'twelve men' who don't want mandatory relationship education."[9] The "twelve men" Jess refers to are the self-appointed community spokesmen. The "twelve men" generally reflect not the views of the community but rather those of a minority of religious conservatives. They intervene on behalf of the immigrant community, claiming that they are not ready to change or that adapting their culture to local norms will be harmful. I, too, saw the "twelve men" at work during my time in politics in the Netherlands. Since interviewing Jess in 2018, the policy makers did succeed in making sex and relationship education mandatory.

Policy change is only half of the solution; the other is parents. It is up to mothers and fathers in the Muslim community to end the taboos on discussing sex and relationships. Some Muslims are putting their communities' well-being before religious dogma and are beginning to address the issue. One woman doing just this is a Canadian blogger who goes by the unlikely name of "The Salafi Feminist."[10] In her niqab and motorbike leathers, Zainab bint Younus is an incongruous figure, her views not matching her appearance. She favors polygamy and claims that the niqab is a feminist statement. But she also wants women to speak in the mosque and sit at the front with men.

As a first step, Younus advocates "Islamic sex education" to help children understand the changes in their bodies and to protect themselves from sexual exploitation. She got to the heart of the matter in a speech to women in her community, calling on parents to teach their sons respect for girls as individuals and "when she says 'no,' you leave her alone. . . . It doesn't even matter how they're dressed." She went on:

There's also a very important aspect in teaching the difference between caring for someone and controlling them. . . . [We must] talk to them about what it means to deal with conflict, to deal with communication, again, emotional maturity is another subject in and of itself, and boys especially need to be taught this. . . . Young men, young boys, they get away with so much. We tell them, "boys will be boys," we make so many excuses for them, not realizing that we are harming ourselves, we're harming them, and we're harming the Ummah at large by maintaining these attitudes.[11]

To me, "Salafi Feminist" is an oxymoron. She still advocates sticking to the letter of the Quran when it comes to lowering the female gaze in interactions with the other sex and preventing girls from having male friends. Still, she has created an opening, and I believe she is on the right track. Compared with the "twelve men" approach, she is a breath of fresh air.

With the funds, networks, and lobbying power at their disposal, Western feminists could play a constructive role in ensuring that women's individual autonomy remains cherished in the West and is not eroded by the import of the "modesty doctrine." But this will require a greater willingness on their part to confront and challenge non-Western cultures, societies, and religious tenets that are oppressive to women, to discuss them openly, and to propose constructive changes. Seyran Ateş suggests sending students of gender studies and women's studies on field trips to Afghanistan, Iran, or Pakistan. There they will see for themselves what it is like to lack basic human rights solely because of one's sex. That may not be a realistic proposition, for obvious reasons. But there may be other ways to open the eyes of feminists to the pitfalls of cultural regression.

CONCLUSION: THE ROAD TO GILEAD

As much as we would wish it to be so, progress is not a given. Revolutions inspire counterrevolutions, and rights are more easily rescinded than established. I have seen women's liberties rolled back shockingly fast in the Middle East and Africa in my lifetime. The force that has done most to reverse women's rights is patriarchal institutions underpinned by Islamist ideology.

Margaret Atwood published *The Handmaid's Tale* in 1985 to warn that American evangelical Christians might one day succeed in establishing a patriarchal regime in the United States—or at least part of it, as "Gilead" is supposed to be New England.[1] Most of her readers appear to have missed the fact that something very like this had already happened in the Muslim world as religious ideologues seized power in the 1970s and '80s in Afghanistan, Iran, Saudi Arabia, and Somalia. Islamic dystopias completely changed the circumstances of women in these countries—particularly better-off women in the larger cities, who, in the 1950s and '60s, had enjoyed at least some of the freedoms of women in the West. Islamists turned back the clock for women by claiming the public space for men with a religious fiat. Women were reduced to the role of mere breeders of sons.

It has been said before, but it is worth looking again at the photographs of women in Kabul in the 1960s.[2] These images are now relics of a time before women's liberties were erased by the Taliban's religious oppression. They show young women in tight-fitting sweaters; women in shift dresses with bare arms, their legs visible from the knee down; women walking in the streets unchaperoned, with elaborate 1960s coiffures and Jackie O–style bobs; girls seated alongside boys in school and college classrooms. With the imposition of Islamic autocracy in the 1990s, women and girls were forced out of the schools, harassed off the streets, shrouded in burkas, and confined to their homes to breed the next generation of jihadis. The Taliban turned back time for Afghan women.

Something similar had already happened in Iran, where the 1979 Islamic revolution had wiped away the rights of Iranian women. Under the shah's regime—which was of course autocratic and repressive in other ways—rich Persian women had danced to psychedelic pop music in bell-bottoms and hot pants. They had freely moved unveiled through the streets of Tehran. Today their daughters and granddaughters are hounded by the Basij (religious police) and jailed for removing their hijabs or dancing in public.

Older Saudi women still remember being able to walk alone in public, their hair uncovered, and to socialize with men in restaurants. However, wary of the rise of Iran's Shiite theocracy and a failed millenarian revolt at Mecca in 1979, Saudi Arabia's King Khalid extended the powers of the Wahhabi clerics. Women's liberties were a prime target for the fanatical bearded men of the religious police, the Mutaween.

Similarly, women's rights in Egypt have taken one step forward and two steps back. In 1953, President Gamal Abdel Nasser elicited uproarious laughter when he told an Egyptian audience that the Muslim Brotherhood wanted to force all women to wear the hijab in public.[3] Only decades later, what had seemed a joke became reality. Farther south, in Somalia, it was the same story. In the 1970s, I remember men comfortably mixing with women dressed in Italian fashion or transparent dresses with their midriffs bare. By the 1990s, after taking over the madrassa system and Quran schools, the Muslim Brotherhood moved from the fringes to the mainstream. Devout Somali men then opted for Arab dress, their spindly ankles and wispy beards setting them up for humorous comparison with their Arab brothers. Less amusing was their practice of whipping women with electrical cables in the streets if any part of their body was visible. Two decades later, Somali women have been driven from the streets or move around fearfully, covered from head to toe.

To be sure, all these societies still lagged far behind the West in the 1970s. The images of past liberation I have described above are nearly all of women who belonged to the social elite in systems that were anything but politically liberal. But at least some women were going to school and to work, wearing whatever they liked, and mingling freely with men.

Of course, I am not predicting that European women will meet exactly the same fate. History is unlikely to move as far back in time in Sweden or Germany as it has done in Iran and Somalia. It would be hyperbolic to suggest that Europe is sliding toward sharia law. Yet the recent wave of sexual violence and harassment in Europe is subtly but undeniably changing the nature of female life in Europe for the worse. The failure to resist an encroaching chauvinistic culture is driving women from the streets of parts of Stockholm, Berlin, and Paris. Do we want a Europe in which photographs of female life taken before 2015 become objects of fascination, like the pictures in the books that the central character censors in Atwood's sequel to *The Handmaid's Tale, The Testaments*? If we wish to avoid it, we must imagine Old Europe as Gilead. It is already a closer fit than New England.

LEAVING SOME WOMEN IN THE PAST

As I said, the photos I referred to above depicted the lives of an urban elite in Kabul, Tehran, and Cairo. In the countryside and among strictly observant families, women did not enjoy much equality with men. Nevertheless, in those days feminists still aspired to extend women's liberation to all women. They did not accept that some women, simply because they were born into a patriarchal religion, were unworthy of the freedoms they themselves were fighting for. Today, by contrast, feminists steeped in multicultural ideology excuse the inequality imposed upon women across the Muslim world, including in the parallel societies of Europe. They pointedly "respect" this misogynistic culture rather than agitating for it to evolve. Western feminists have effectively relegated their Muslim sisters to the past. They are sleepwalking as their own rights begin to be eroded.

We must not forget that the very concept that women are equal to men is a relatively new one. It emerged only in the West and despite its advancements—from the right to vote to protection from discrimination in the workplace—has yet to achieve the complete equality to which feminists aspire. This fragile near equality, which exists in law if not in every home and workplace, has existed for only a fraction of time, and history has shown us that such achievements can be quickly reversed. The Communist regimes in the Soviet Union and China also promised women equality as part of their revolutions but delivered a reality that fell far short.

The mythical "arc of history" that progressives assume bends toward human progress is better described as a pendulum, at least when it comes to women's rights. It has swung backward and forward, extending and rescinding liberties to women, depending on the prevailing ideology of the time. In the Victorian era, religion was not the sole reason European women had a more circumscribed existence. In England, for example, there was a reaction against the perceived moral decline, "easy virtue," and permissiveness of the eighteenth century. As in many Muslim societies in more recent times, the threat of public violence—of assault and rape—was used to confine women to the private sphere.[4] Women donned more re-strictive clothing, reduced their contact with men, were policed out of certain areas, and lived more spatially constrained lives than in the decades before. It was a backlash that dismayed John Stuart Mill and his collaborator and wife, Harriet Taylor Mill. Their argument in *The Subjection of Women* (completed in 1861) was

> That the principle which regulates the existing social relations between the two sexes—the legal subordination of one sex to the other—is wrong in itself, and [is] now one of the chief hindrances to human improvement; and that it ought to be re-placed by a principle of perfect equality, admitting no power or privilege on the one side, nor disability on the other.[5]

Mill published that essay in 1869, after his wife's death. All over the Western world, many of the changes he and his wife so persua-sively advocated have slowly but surely been implemented, even though there is as yet no perfect equality. Yet I fear that what has been achieved to improve and protect the rights of girls and women over the past century and a half, since the publication of that great essay, is now at risk because of a badly mismanaged wave of immi-gration.

The pendulum is swinging back toward misogyny as liberal Europe changes to accommodate migrant cultures. Adaptation is happen-ing, but it's happening the other way around. Progress is not only not inevitable; in this case, it is reversing.

In writing this book, I have come to the conclusion that we need a new women's movement, one that views the world not in terms of multiculturalism and intersectionality but in universal terms and that, in the spirit of John Stuart and Harriet Taylor Mill, is prepared to stand up for the rights of all women.

Women's safety from predatory men is the issue around which all true feminists must rally and coalesce.

We women can and must refuse to be relegated, as we have been in the past—as I have been in my own lifetime—to the status of prey. I hope you will join me in this endeavor.

ACKNOWLEDGMENTS

This book would have no meaning without Western civilization. It allows for liberties and freedoms unlike any other civilization. The passionate desire to preserve it is what drove me to write this book.

Over the last decade, I've seen the problems discussed in these pages challenge Western norms. I've seen a crumbling of confidence and pride in our values. I've seen Western nations too insecure to stand up and fight against cultural practices that are incompatible with liberalism—too insecure to defend the women and girls who cannot fight for themselves. This book was written in honor of all the defenders of Western civilization and the giants whose shoulders we stand on.

This book would also not have existed without the brave women who spoke to me, including the victims of unconscionable assaults, some of whom survived multiple attacks, some of whom remain unflinching in their acceptance of immigrants, refugees, and those unlike themselves.

The immigrant men who spoke to me have defied criticism and shaming from some of their peers for working within and for the European system. They have displayed chivalry and courtesy to the women and girls who've been affected by these violent attacks. These men are personifications of courage. I thank, in particular, Hamed Abdel Samad, Mustafa Panshiri, and Nazir Afzal.

Many European institutions have failed in numerous ways, but there is a whole group of people that I would like to acknowledge who often remain unacknowledged: the police, the social workers, the forensic science technicians, the judges, and the teachers.

I would also like to thank my team, who shifted through masses of data, read through horrific cases, and worked tirelessly to support me. I want to thank Leonie Phillips for her extraordinary work ethic and patience as she traveled around Europe, researching the "ground truth" and writing drafts. I want to thank Jurgen Reinhoudt, for tirelessly researching and fact-checking, even when the data were updated or the definitions changed. And I want to thank Alex Still for the thousands of hours she devoted to the different versions of this book. She kept us all sane with endless grace.

I am also grateful to Susanna Lea, my agent but also, more importantly, my dear friend; and to my team at HarperCollins, Eric Nelson, Hannah Long, and everyone behind the scenes. You have had the patience and endurance to see this book through.

I would like to express my wholehearted gratitude for everyone who reviewed and commented on this book, each of whom strengthened it in their own way. I particularly would like to acknowledge Elizabeth Cobbs, Chris DeMuth, Kyle Kinnie, Paulina Neuding, Amanda Parker, Andrew Roberts, Dan Seligson, and Robert Wickers.

I'd also like to thank Christopher Caldwell, Dame Louise Casey, Senator Tom Cotton, Megyn Kelly, Dr. Henry Kissinger, Mark Levin, Andrew McCarthy, Douglas Murray, Andrew Norfolk, Trevor Phillips, Peter Robinson, Senator Ben Sasse, and Christina Hoff Sommers, for reading and supporting the book.

Finally, this book would not have been possible without my husband, Niall Ferguson, who read and edited the manuscript, and our children, who lent me the time to be away from them.

NOTES

CHAPTER 1: THE CLOCK TURNS BACK

1. Rainer Bauböck and Milena Tripkovic, eds., *The Integration of Migrants and Refugees: An EUI Forum on Migration, Citizenship and Demography*, European University Institute, 2017, https://cadmus.eui.eu/bitstream/handle/1814/45187/Ebook_IntegrationMigrants Refugees2017.pdf?sequence=3&isAllowed=y, 93.
2. "Violence Against Women," World Health Organization, November 29, 2017, https:// www.who.int/news-room/fact-sheets/detail/violence-against-women.
3. "So reagiert die Politik auf den Mordfall Maria," *Bild*, December 4, 2016, https://www .bild.de/politik/inland/todesfall/studentin-vergewaltigt-ermordet-49066016.bild.html.

CHAPTER 2: THE FIFTH WAVE

1. Peter Gatrell, *The Unsettling of Europe: How Migration Reshaped a Continent* (New York: Basic Books, 2019).
2. "Migratory Map," Frontex, 2019, https://frontex.europa.eu/along-eu-borders/migratory -map/.
3. "Data Explorer," European Union, https://appsso.eurostat.ec.europa.eu/nui/.
4. Bojan Pancevski, "Steady Flow of Refugees Fuels Nationalist Gains in Europe," *Wall Street Journal*, April 30, 2019, https://www.wsj.com/articles/steady-flow-of-refugees-fuels- nationalist-gains-in-europe-11556628273.
5. "Abschiebungen in andere EU-Staaten auf Höchststand," Spiegel Online, January 21, 2019, https://www.spiegel.de/politik/deutschland/fluechtlinge-abschiebungen-in- andere-eu-staaten-auf-hoechststand-a-1249008.html.
6. "The Dublin System in the First Half of 2018: Key Figures from Selected European Countries," European Council on Refugees and Exiles, October 2018, http://www .asylumineurope.org/sites/default/files/aida_2018halfupdate_dublin.pdf, 6.
7. Pancevski, "Steady Flow of Refugees Fuels Nationalist Gains in Europe." Peter Cluskey, "Most Fleeing to Europe Are 'Not Refugees,' EU Official Says," *Irish Times*, January 26, 2016, https://www.irishtimes.com/news/world/europe/most-fleeing-to-europe-are-not -refugees-eu-official-says-1.2511133.
8. Valerie Boyer, "Assemblee Nationale, Constitution du 4 October 1958," http://www .assemblee-nationale.fr/dyn/15/rapports/cion_afetr/l15b2303-tvii_rapport-avis.pdf.
9. Michèle Tribalat, micheletribalat.fr, and personal correspondence, June 2018.
10. Yue Huang and Michael Kvasnicka, "Immigration and Crimes Against Natives: The 2015 Refugee Crisis in Germany," IZA Institute of Labor Economics Discussion Paper Series, no. 12469, July 2019, http://ftp.iza.org/dp12469.pdf.
11. "Interactive Data Table: World Muslim Population by Country," Pew Research Center, No- vember 17, 2017, https://www.pewforum.org/chart/interactive-data-table-world-muslim -population-by-country/.
12. "Asylum and First Time Asylum Applicants by Citizenship, Age and Sex Annual Aggre- gated Data (Rounded)," Eurostat, March 12, 2019, http://appsso.eurostat.ec.europa.eu /nui/show.do?dataset=migr_asyappctza&lang=en.

13. "Asylum and Migration in the EU: Facts and Figures," European Parliament, July 22, 2019, http://www.europarl.europa.eu/news/en/headlines/society/20170629STO78630 /asylum-and-migration-in-the-eu-facts-and-figures.
14. Ibid.
15. Phillip Connor and Jeffrey S. Passel, "Europe's Unauthorized Immigrant Population Peaks in 2016, Then Levels Off," Pew Research Center, November 13, 2019, https:// www.pewresearch.org/global/2019/11/13/europes-unauthorized-immigrant-population -peaks-in-2016-then-levels-off.
16. Ibid.
17. Ibid.
18. "Europe's Growing Muslim Population," Pew Research Center, November 29, 2017, https://www.pewforum.org/2017/11/29/europes-growing-muslim-population/.

CHAPTER 3: SEXUAL VIOLENCE BY NUMBERS
1. World Health Organization, *Global and Regional Estimates of Violence against Women: Prevalence and Health Effects of Intimate Partner Violence and Non-Partner Sexual Violence* (Geneva: World Health Organization, 2013), https://apps.who.int/iris/bitstream/handle /10665/85239/9789241564625_eng.pdf?sequence=1&isAllowed=y.
2. Ibid., 4.
3. Ibid., 31.
4. Ibid., 8.
5. "Gender Equality Index 2017: Measuring Gender Equality in the European Union 2005–2015—Report," European Institute for Gender Equality, October 10, 2017, https:// eige.europa.eu/publications/gender-equality-index-2017-measuring-gender-equality -european-union-2005-2015-report.
6. "Recorded Offences by Offence Category—Police Data," Eurostat, 5, accessed January 24, 2020, https://ec.europa.eu/eurostat/documents/64346/10008371/Recorded_offences _by_offence_category_2017.pdf.
7. "Recorded Offences by Offence Category—Police Data," Eurostat, October 29, 2019, http://appsso.eurostat.ec.europa.eu/nui/show.do?query=BOOKMARK_DS-559176 _QID_1727C2DE_UID_-3F171EB0&layout=ICCS,L,X,0;UNIT,L,X,1;GEO,L,Y,0 ;TIME,C,Z,0;INDICATORS,C,Z,1;&zSelection=DS-559176TIME,2015;DS-559176 INDICATORS,OBS_FLAG;&rankName1=INDICATORS_1_2_-1_2&rankName2 =TIME_1_0_0_0&rankName3=ICCS_1_2_0_0&rankName4=UNIT_1_2_1_0 &rankName5=GEO_1_2_0_1&rStp=&cStp=&rDCh=&cDCh=&rDM=true&cDM =true&footnes=false&empty=false&wai=false&time_mode=ROLLING&time_most _recent=true&lang=EN&cfo=%23%23%23%2C%23%23%23.%23%23%23.
8. "LIGEBP1: Victims of Offenses Against the Person by Type of Offence, Age and Sex," Statistics Denmark, https://www.statbank.dk/statbank5a/SelectVarVal/Define.asp ?MainTable=LIGEPB1&PLanguage=1&PXSId=0&wsid=cftree.
9. "Sexual offences in England and Wales: Year Ending March 2017," Office for National Statistics, February 8, 2018, https://www.ons.gov.uk/peoplepopulationandcommunity /crimeandjustice/articles/sexualoffencesinenglandandwales/yearendingmarch2017.
10. Matt Watts and Ross Lydall, "Half of Women Feel at Risk of Harassment on London Public Transport," *Evening Standard*, May 19, 2016, https://www.standard.co.uk/news/transport /half-of-women-feel-at-risk-of-harassment-on-london-public-transport-a3252051.html.
11. "Insécurité et délinquance en 2018: premier bilan statistique," Ministère de l'Intérieur, January 31, 2019, https://www.interieur.gouv.fr/Interstats/Actualites/Insecurite-et -delinquance-en-2018-premier-bilan-statistique.

12. Amandine Lebugle, "Young Women in Large Cities are the Main Victims of Violence in Public Space," *Population & Societies* 550 (December 2017), https://www.ined.fr/fichier /s_rubrique/27216/550_ang_population.societies.decembre.violence.en.pdf.

13. *Violence Against Women: An EU-Wide Survey: Main Results* (Vienna: European Union Agency for Fundamental Rights, 2014), https://fra.europa.eu/sites/default/files/fra_uploads /fra-2014-vaw-survey-main-results-apr14_en.pdf.

14. Zoe Tabary, "220,000 Women Sexually Harassed on Public Transport in France: Study," Reuters, December 21, 2017, https://www.reuters.com/article/us-women-france-sexcrimes /220000-women-sexually-harassed-on-public-transport-in-france-study-idUSKBN1EF2J2.

15. All data from "Police Crime Statistics," Bundeskriminalamt, https://www.bka.de/EN /CurrentInformation/PoliceCrimeStatistics/policecrimestatistics_node.html.

16. Brottsförebyggande Rådet, "Våldtäkt och sexualbrott," Brä, October 14, 2019, https:// www.bra.se/statistik/statistik-utifran-brottstyper/valdtakt-och-sexualbrott.html.

17. *Swedish Crime Survey 2016* (Stockholm: The Swedish National Council for Crime Prevention, 2017), https://www.bra.se/bra-in-english/home/publications/archive /publications/2017-02-15-swedish-crime-survey-2016.html.

18. Ibid.

19. Ibid.

20. Betsy Stanko and Emma Williams, "Reviewing Rape and Rape Allegations in London: What Are the Vulnerabilities of the Victims Who Report to the Police?," in *Rape: Challenging Contemporary Thinking*, ed. Miranda Horvath and Jennifer Brown (Cullompton, UK: Willan, 2009), 207–255.

21. "Sexual Offences in England and Wales: Year Ending March 2017," Office for National Statistics, February 8, 2018, https://www.ons.gov.uk/peoplepopulationandcommunity /crimeandjustice/articles/sexualoffencesinenglandandwales/yearendingmarch2017. Laura Backes, Anna Clauss, Maria-Mercedes Hering, et al., "Fact-Check: Is There Truth to Refugee Rape Reports?," Spiegel Online, January 17, 2018, https://www.spiegel.de /international/germany/is-there-truth-to-refugee-sex-offense-reports-a-1186734.html. Michael Planty, Lynn Langton, Christopher Krebs, et al., "Female Victims of Sexual Violence, 1994–2010," U.S. Department of Justice, Office of Justice Programs, May 31, 2016, https://www.bjs.gov/content/pub/pdf/fvsv9410.pdf, 4. Det Kriminalpræventive Råd, 2016.

22. Brottsförebyggande Rådet, "Rape and Sexual Offences," Brå, https://www.bra.se /bra-in-english/home/crime-and-statistics/rape-and-sex-offences.html. Brottsföre byggande Rådet, *Våldtäkt mot personer 15 år och äldre: Utveecklingen under åren 1995–2006* (Stockholm: Brå, 2008), https://www.bra.se/download/18.cba82f7130f475 a2f180008010/1371914724593/2008_13_valdtakt_mot_personer_over_15_ar.pdf.

23. Federal Ministry for Family Affairs, Senior Citizens, Women and Youth, *Health, Well-Being and Personal Safety of Women in Germany: A Representative Study of Violence Against Women in Germany*, Summer 2004, https://www.bmfsfj.de/blob/93906/9c0076f c66b1be6d0eb28258fe0aa569/frauenstudie-englisch-gewalt-gegen-frauen-data .pdf, 8–9.

24. Ibid., 13–14.

25. Ibid., 9.

26. Ibid., 14.

27. Ibid., 23.

28. Ibid., 28.

29. Deborah F. Hellmann, Max W. Kinninger, and Sören Kliem, "Sexual Violence Against Women in Germany: Prevalence and Risk Markers," *International Journal of Environmental Research and Public Health* 15, no. 1613 (July 2018): 1–19.

30. Ibid., 8–9.

31. I am grateful to Renée DiResta of the Stanford Internet Observatory for this information.

32. Backes et al., "Is There Truth to Refugee Rape Reports?"

33. Ibid.

34. *Kriminalitätsbericht: Statistik und Analyse, 2017*, Bundesministerium Inneres, 2017, https:// www.bmi.gv.at/508/files/SIB_2017/03_SIB_2017-Kriminalitasetsbericht_web.pdf.

35. Ibid.

36. "LIGEBP1: Victims of Offenses Against the Person by Type of Offence, Age, and Sex."

37. Paulina Neuding, "Sweden's Sexual Assault Crisis Presents a Feminist Paradox," Quillette, October 10, 2017, https://quillette.com/2017/10/10/swedens-sexual-assault-crisis -presents-feminist-paradox/.

38. Ibid.

39. Ibid.

40. Joachim Kerpner, Kerstin Weigl, and Alice Staaf, "Unik granskning: 112 pojkar och män dömda för gruppvåldtäkt," *Aftonbladet*, May 6, 2018, https://www.aftonbladet.se /nyheter/a/rLKwKR/unik-granskning-112-pojkar-och-man-domda-for-gruppvaldtakt.

41. Ibid.

42. "UG-referens: Dömda för våldtäkt," *SVT Nyheter*, October 11, 2018, https://www.svt.se /nyheter/granskning/ug/domda-for-valdtakt-1.

43. David Crouch, "Swedish Police Accused of Covering Up Sex Attacks by Refugees at Music Festival," *The Guardian*, January 11, 2016, https://www.theguardian.com/world/2016 /jan/11/swedish-police-accused-cover-up-sex-attacks-refugees-festival.

44. Mattis Wikström and Kim Malmgren, "De är män som våldtar kvinnor tillsammans," *Expressen*, March 20, 2018, https://www.expressen.se/nyheter/brottscentralen/qs/de-ar -mannen-som-valdtar-tillsammans/.

45. "Fiche #3 Violences Sexuelles: Insecurite et delinquance en 2018: premier bilan statis-tique," Interstats, 2018.

46. "Reality Check: Are Migrants Driving Crime in Germany?," BBC News, September 13, 2018, https://www.bbc.com/news/world-europe-45419466.

47. Marcel Leubecher, "Gewalt von Zuwanderern gegen Deutsche nimmt zu," *Welt*, April 9, 2019, https://www.welt.de/politik/deutschland/article191584235/BKA-Lagebild-Gewalt -von-Zuwanderern-gegen-Deutsche-nimmt-zu.html.

48. *Bundeslagebild Kriminalität im Kontext von Zuwanderung 2017*, Bundeskriminalamt, May 8, 2018, https://www.bka.de/SharedDocs/Downloads/DE/Publikationen /JahresberichteUndLagebilder/KriminalitaetImKontextVonZuwanderung /KriminalitaetImKontextVonZuwanderung_2017.pdf.

49. Ibid.

50. Christian Pfeiffer, Dirk Baier, and Sören Kliem, *Zur Entwicklung der Gewalt in Deutsch-land Schwerpunkte: Jugendliche und Flüchtlinge als Täter und Opfer*, Institut für Delin-quenz und Kriminalprävention, Zürcher Hochschule für Angewandte Wissenschaften, January 2018, https://pdfs.semanticscholar.org/8cf4/655e7090ac6b11a7a0f02f8530d d1ae5676e.pdf, 71–91.

51. Yue Huang and Michael Kvasnicka, "Immigration and Crimes Against Natives: The 2015 Refugee Crisis in Germany," IZA Institute of Labor Economics Discussion Paper Series, no. 12469, July 2019, http://ftp.iza.org/dp12469.pdf, abstract.

52. Ibid., 3.

53. Ibid., 25.

54. Ibid., 34.

55. Ibid., 21–22.

56. Ibid., 25.

57. Ibid.

CHAPTER 4: *TAHARRUSH GAMEA* (THE RAPE GAME) COMES TO EUROPE
1. Susi Wimmer, "Joggerinnen attackiert und vergewaltigt: 28-Jähriger vor Gericht," *Süddeutsche Zeitung*, March 25, 2018, https://www.sueddeutsche.de/muenchen/proz essauftakt-joggerinnen-attackiert-und-vergewaltigt-28-jaehriger-vor-gericht-1.3918813.
2. "Nach sexuellen Ubergriff aux Spaziergängerin: Täter festgenommen," *Merkur*, September 3, 2017, https://www.merkur.de/lokales/garmisch-partenkirchen/garmisch-partenkirchen -ort28711/sexueller-uebergriff-auf-garmsich-partenkirchnerin-taeter-gefasst-8643128 .html.
3. "Strullendorf: Somalier (17) vergewaltigt 43-jährige in Fussgängertunnel," TVO, March 14, 2017, https://www.tvo.de/strullendorf-teenager-vergewaltigt-43-jaehrige-im -fussgaengertunnel-234536.
4. Ibid.
5. "Drei Männer vergewaltigen 16-jähriges Mädchen auf offener Strasse," *Die Welt*, September 16, 2017, https://www.welt.de/vermischtes/article168708906/Drei -Maenner-vergewaltigen-16-jaehriges-Maedchen-auf-offener-Strasse.html.
6. "POL-HH: 190128-4. Zeugenaufruf nach Sexualdelikt in Hamburg-Bramfeld," Polizei Hamburg, January 27, 2019, https://www.presseportal.de/blaulicht/pm/6337/4178172.
7. Silvia Zöller, "'Weil er Sex wollte' 19-Jähriger gesteht versuchte Vergewaltigung von 74-Jähriger," *Mitteldeutsche Zeitung*, January 8, 2019, https://www.mz-web.de/halle-saale /-weil-er-sex-wollte-19-jaehriger-gesteht-versuchte-vergewaltigung-von-74-jaehriger -31842548.
8. "Verraten die Angeklagten heute den 12. Verdächtigen?," *Bild*, June 26, 2019, https://www.bild.de/regional/stuttgart/stuttgart-aktuell/freiburg-prozessauftakt -nach-gruppenvergewaltigung-vor-disco-62879682.bild.html.
9. "Gruppenvergewaltigung einer 18-Jährigen in Freiburg: Elf junge Männer auf Anklagebank," Focus Online, June 26, 2019, https://www.focus.de/politik/gerichte -in-deutschland/verbrechen-erschuetterte-deutschland-gruppenvergewaltigung -in-freiburg-prozess-gegen-elf-junge-maenner-beginnt_id_10860345.html.
10. Christine Kensche, "'Das ist doch nur eine Frau,' sagte Hussein K.," *Welt*, January 25, 2018, https://www.welt.de/vermischtes/article172868730/Mordprozess-in-Freiburg -Das-ist-doch-nur-eine-Frau-sagte-Hussein-K.html.
11. "Hussein K. Given Life Sentence for Rape and Murder of Freiburg Student," The Local de, March 22, 2018, https://www.thelocal.de/20180322/hussein-k-given-life-sentence -for-rape-and-murder-of-freiburg-student.
12. "In Deutschland habe er dann die Möglichkeit zum Zugang zu Frauen, auch zu sexuellen Kontakten gehabt und gezielt nach sehr jungen, noch unsicheren Mädchen gesucht." "Weder Reue noch Mitgefühl," *Frankfurter Allgemeine*, July 10, 2019, https://www.faz .net/aktuell/rhein-main/im-mordfall-susanna-bekommt-ali-bashar-lebenslange-haft -16277361.html. (Author's translation.)
13. Von Wiebke Ramm, "In seinen Augen war sie seins," Spiegel Online, February 5, 2019, https://www.spiegel.de/panorama/justiz/flensburg-mord-an-mireille-warum-das-gericht -ahmad-s-schuldig-sprach-a-1251740.html. (Author's translation.)
14. Alessandra Ziniti, "Pensionata violentata in spiaggia ad Ortona da un rifugiato. 'Credevo che volesse uccidermi,'" *La Repubblica*, November 15, 2018, https:// www.repubblica.it/cronaca/2018/11/15/news/donna_violentata_in_spiaggia _ad_ortona_da_un_somalo_aveva_appena_ottenuto_la_protezione_sussidiaria -211710833.
15. "Ragazza di 16 anni attirata in una trappola e stuprata dal branco degli stranieri," *Leggo*, September 6, 2018, https://www.leggo.it/italia/cronache/ragazza_stuprata_branco _stranieri_avezzano-3956226.html.

16. "Desirée Mariottini Killing: Migrants Held in Italy over Girl's Death," BBC News, October 25, 2018, https://www.bbc.com/news/world-europe-45976450.
17. Roland Gauron, "Une interprète violée et un journaliste agressé aux abords de la «jungle» de Calais," *Le Figaro*, October 18, 2016, http://www.lefigaro.fr/actualite-france/2016/10/18/01016-20161018ARTFIG00122-une-interprete-violee-et-un-journaliste-agresse-aux-abords-de-la-jungle-de-calais.php.
18. Edouard de Mareschal, "Calais: un migrant érythréen mis en examen pour viol aggravé," *Le Figaro*, November 3, 2017, http://www.lefigaro.fr/actualite-france/2017/11/03/01016-20171103ARTFIG00260-calais-un-migrant-erythreen-mis-en-examen-pour-viol-aggrave.php.
19. Samuel Cogez, "Croisilles: Six mois de prison pour le migrant qui s'était frotté à une fille de 11 ans," *La Voix du Nord*, July 13, 2018, https://www.lavoixdunord.fr/416074/article/2018-07-13/six-mois-de-prison-pour-le-migrant-qui-s-etait-frotte-une-fille-de-11-ans.
20. "Un migrant soupçonné d'agressions sexuelles sur deux adolescents de 14 ans," *Valeurs Actuelles*, October 12, 2017, https://www.valeursactuelles.com/faits-divers/un-migrant-soupconne-dagressions-sexuelles-sur-deux-adolescentes-de-14-ans-89687.
21. "Våldtog och hotade 'skära halsen' av flicka—nu döms Mohomed till ett par veckors ungdomstjänst," FriaTider, July 16, 2018, https://www.friatider.se/v-ldtog-och-hotade-sk-ra-halsen-av-flicka-nu-d-ms-mohomed-till-ett-par-veckors-ungdomstj-nst.
22. "Man häktad för fyra år gammal dubbelvåldtäkt," *Aftonbladet*, November 21, 2019, https://www.aftonbladet.se/nyheter/a/K3KvxG/man-haktad-for-fyra-ar-gammal-dubbelvaldtakt.
23. Alison Smale, "Migrant Crimes Add Volatile Element to Austria's Election," *New York Times*, May 21, 2016, https://www.nytimes.com/2016/05/22/world/europe/migrant-crimes-add-volatile-element-to-austrias-election.html.
24. "Vergewaltigung: Täter ist kein Unbekannter," *Heute*, June 20, 2018, https://www.heute.at/s/vergewaltigung-tater-ist-kein-unbekannter-57896221.
25. "Wien: Frau im Beisein von zwei Kleinkindern sexuell missbraucht," Kurier, February 14, 2017, https://kurier.at/chronik/wien/mutter-im-beisein-von-zwei-kleinkindern-auf-der-wiener-donauinsel-sexuell-missbraucht/246.520.687. Rebecca Perring, "Afghan Migrant 'Sexually Assaults Mother-of-Two as She Pushes Young Children in Pram,'" *Express*, February 14, 2017, https://www.express.co.uk/news/world/767301/Afghan-migrant-sex-attack-mother-pram-children-Austria. Cheryl Benard, "I've Worked with Refugees for Decades. Europe's Afghan Crime Wave Is Mind-Boggling," *The National Interest*, July 11, 2017, https://nationalinterest.org/feature/ive-worked-refugees-decades-europes-afghan-crime-wave-mind-21506.
26. Smale, "Migrant Crimes Add Volatile Element to Austria's Election."
27. Gábor Sarnyai, "Budapest Police Hunt for Man Accused of Sexual Assault," Hungary Today, September 10, 2018, https://hungarytoday.hu/budapest-police-hunt-for-man-accused-of-sexual-assault/. Szemán László János, "Tíz évet kaphat az erőszakoló afgán," *Magyar Nemzet*, April 30, 2019, https://magyarnemzet.hu/belfold/tiz-evet-kaphat-az-eroszakolo-afgan-6876137/.
28. Ulrik Bachmann, "Afghansk dreng vil frifindes for voldtægt af 14-årig: 'Satan fristede mig,'" *Ekstra Bladet*, October 30, 2018, https://ekstrabladet.dk/112/afghansk-dreng-vil-frifindes-for-voldtaegt-af-14-aarig-satan-fristede-mig/7374771.

CHAPTER 5: HOW WOMEN'S RIGHTS ARE BEING ERODED

1. "Written submission from a member of the public (SPP0005)," referenced in *Sexual harassment of women and girls in public places: Sixth Report of Session 2017–19*, http://data.parliament.uk/writtenevidence/committeeevidence.svc/evidencedocument/women

-and-equalities-committee/sexual-harassment-of-women-and-girls-in-public-places
/written/76790.html.

2. Evie Burrows-Taylor, "Women in Paris Tell Their Stories of Being Groped, Pestered and Sexually Harassed," The Local fr, July 30, 2018, https://www.thelocal.fr/20180730 /women-in-paris-tell-their-stories-of-sexual-harassment.

3. Aude Bariéty, "L'agresseur de Marie Laguerre condamné à six mois de prison ferme," *Le Figaro*, October 4, 2018, http://www.lefigaro.fr/actualite-france/2018/10/04/01016 -20181004ARTFIG00344-l-agresseur-de-marie-laguerre-condamne-a-six-mois-de -prison-ferme.php. Louis Chahuneau, "Affaire Marie Laguerre: son agresseur condamné à 6 mois de prison ferme," *Le Point*, October 4, 2018, https://www.lepoint.fr/societe /affaire-marie-laguerre-le-harcelement-de-rue-en-proces-04-10-2018-2260206_23.php.

4. Tatjana Hörnle, "The New German Law on Sexual Assault and Sexual Harassment," *German Law Journal* 18, no. 6 (November 2017): 1309–30, https://www.cambridge.org /core/journals/german-law-journal/article/new-german-law-on-sexual-assault-and -sexual-harassment/C8FAD908DD7B6ECC28C6CF36BD9603BE.

5. "Dramatisk ökning av trakasserier mot Migrationsverkets personal," SVT Nyheter, November 12, 2016, https://www.svt.se/nyheter/inrikes/hot-vanligaste-incidenten -hos-migrationsverket.

6. Isabelle Nordström, "Ringde 166 gånger till kvinnlig anställd och skrek könsord," *Aftonbladet*, October 5, 2017, https://www.aftonbladet.se/nyheter/samhalle/a/rooOR /ringde-166-ganger-till-kvinnlig-anstalld-och-skrek-konsord.

7. Paulina Neuding, "Social oro ger stök pä bibblan," *Svenska Dagbladet*, May 16, 2015, https://www.svd.se/social-oro-ger-stok-pa-bibblan.

8. "Refugee Women and Children Face Heightened Risk of Sexual Violence amid Tensions and Overcrowding at Reception Facilities on Greek Islands," UNHCR, February 9, 2018, https://data2.unhcr.org/en/news/20607.

9. Maria von Welser, *No Refuge for Women: The Tragic Fate of Syrian Refugees* (Vancouver: Greystone Books, 2017). Laura Backes, Anna Clauss, Maria-Mercedes Hering, et al., "Fact-Check: Is There Truth to Refugee Rape Reports?," Spiegel Online, January 17, 2018, https://www.spiegel.de /international/germany/is-there-truth-to-refugee-sex-offense-reports-a-1186734.html.

10. Jorg Diehl, "Hunderte Opfer, fast keine Tater," *Spiegel Panorama*, March 11, 2019, https:// www.spiegel.de/panorama/justiz/koelner-silvesternacht-ernuechternde-bilanz-der-justiz -a-1257182.html.

11. "Schwerpunkt: Silvester & die Folgen," *Emma*, February 25, 2016, https://www.emma .de/artikel/koeln-die-folgen-dieser-nacht-331595.

12. Von Georg Mascolo and Britta von der Heide, "1200 Frauen wurden Opfer von Silvester -Gewalt," *Süddeutsche Zeitung*, July 10, 2016, https://www.sueddeutsche.de/politik /uebergriffe-in-koeln-1200-frauen-wurden-opfer-von-silvester-gewalt-1.3072064.

13. Marina Koren, "Angela Merkel's Response to the New Year's Eve Assaults," *The Atlantic*, January 12, 2016, https://www.theatlantic.com/international/archive/2016/01/cologne -refugees-migrants-merkel/423708/.

14. "Young Women Sexually Harassed, Robbed at Berlin Street Festival," DW, May 15, 2016, https://www.dw.com/en/young-women-sexually-harassed-robbed-at-berlin-street -festival/a-19259780-0.

15. Alison Smale, "Women Report Assaults at German Music Festival," *New York Times*, May 31, 2016, https://www.nytimes.com/2016/06/01/world/europe/darmstadt-germany -migrants-assaults.html.

16. "Frauen bei Open-Air-Festival in Bremen sexuell belästigt," *Welt*, July 18, 2016, https:// www.welt.de/vermischtes/article157139678/Frauen-bei-Open-Air-Festival-in-Bremen -sexuell-belaestigt.html.

17. "Utredning av polisens agerande I samband med ungdomsfestivalen We Are Sthlm, sommaren 2015," Polisregion Stockholm, February 23, 2016, https://tino.us/wp-content /uploads/2016/08/avskrivning-WAS-2015-final.pdf.

18. Johan Furusjö, "Massövergreppen i Kungsträdgården: Vad vi vet," *Aftonbladet*, January 13, 2016, https://www.aftonbladet.se/nyheter/a/jProgn/massovergreppen-i-kungstrad garden-vad-vi-vet. (Author's translation.)

19. Nicola Frank, personal interview, November 28, 2018.

20. Christian Pfeiffer, Dirk Baier, and Sören Kliem, *Zur Entwicklung der Gewalt in Deutschland Schwerpunkte: Jugendliche und Flüchtlinge als Täter und Opfer*, Institut für Delinquenz und Kriminalprävention, Zürcher Hochschule für Angewandte Wissenschaften, January 2018, https://pdfs.semanticscholar.org/8cf4/655e7090ac6b11a7a0f02f8530d d1ae5676e.pdf, 71–91.

21. Paulina Neuding, personal interview, April 6, 2018.

22. Belgian woman, interviewed in *La Femme de la Rue*, 2012.

23. Cécile Beaulieu, "Paris: des femmes victimes de harcèlement dans les rues du quartier Chapelle-Pajol," *Le Parisien*, May 18, 2017, http://www.leparisien.fr/paris-75018/harcele ment-les-femmes-chassees-des-rues-dans-le-quartier-chapelle-pajol-18-05-2017-6961779 .php. (Author's translation.)

24. Ibid.

25. Michael van der Galien, "Shocking Video: Muslim Immigrants Ban Women from Entire Neighborhoods in France," PJ Media, December 15, 2016, https://pjmedia.com/news -and-politics/michael-van-der-galien/2016/12/15/shocking-video-muslim-immigrants -ban-women-from-entire-neighborhoods-in-france-n49337.

26. Sofie Peeters, *Femme de la Rue*, 2012.

27. Sofie Peeters, personal interview, March 31, 2018.

28. "Documentary-Maker Dresses like a Whore," VRT News, August 3, 2012, http://deredactie .be/cm/vrtnieuws.english/News/1.1389654#.

29. "Meine Tochter hat am Linzer Bahnhof Angst," *Kronen Zeitung*, February 12, 2016, https://www.krone.at/495747. (Author's translation.)

30. Ulrich Mendelin, "Flüchtlingskriminalität am Bahnhof Sigmaringen: Die Stimmung ist angespannt," Schwäbische, March 29, 2018, https://www.schwaebische.de/landkreis /landkreis-sigmaringen/sigmaringen_artikel,-flüchtlingskriminalität-am-bahnhof -sigmaringen-die-stimmung-ist-angespannt-_arid,10843541.html.

31. Seyran Ateş, personal interview, April 5, 2018.

32. Barney Henderson, "German Rail Operator Launches Women-Only Train Carriages Following Sex Attacks," *The Telegraph*, March 28, 2016, https://www.telegraph.co.uk /news/2016/03/28/german-rail-operator-launches-women-only-train-carriages -followi/.

33. "POL-ST: Lienen, Dorfkirmes, sexuelle Belästigung und Körperverletzungsdelikte durch Zuwanderer," Polizei Steinfurt, March 4, 2018, https://www.presseportal.de /blaulicht/pm/43526/3882290.

34. "Activity Inequality Project," Stanford University, 2017, http://activityinequality .stanford.edu.

35. *Violence Against Women: An EU-Wide Survey: Main Results* (Vienna: European Union Agency for Fundamental Rights, 2014), https://fra.europa.eu/sites/default/files/fra_uploads /fra-2014-vaw-survey-main-results-apr14_en.pdf.

36. "Better Life Index—Edition 2017," Organisation for Economic Co-operation and Development, 2017, https://stats.oecd.org/index.aspx?DataSetCode=BLI.

37. "100 Women: The 'Right Amount' of Panic for Women in Public," BBC News, October 16, 2017, https://www.bbc.com/news/world-41614720.

38. "Boom in Demand for Self-Defence Weapons," The Local at, January 13, 2016, https://www.thelocal.at/20160113/boom-in-demand-for-weapons-in-vienna-and-styria.
39. Leonie Phillips, personal interview, April 17, 2018.
40. Lavanya Ramanathan, "Locking Panties and Man-Repelling Bracelets: Is This What the Women of 2018 Need?," *Washington Post*, January 19, 2018, https://www.washingtonpost.com/lifestyle/style/locking-panties-and-man-repelling-bracelets-is-this-what-the-women-of-2018-need/2018/01/18/c74a2abe-f6fc-11e7-b34a-b85626af34ef_story.html?noredirect=on&utm_term=.57ca43246239.
41. Lin Taylor, "In wake of #MeToo, anti-rape shorts aim to ease assault fears," Reuters, February 23, 2018, https://www.reuters.com/article/us-women-rape/in-wake-of-metoo-anti-rape-shorts-aim-to-ease-assault-fears-idUSKCN1G7218.

CHAPTER 6: IS THE LAW AN ASS?

1. Brottsförebyggande Rådet, *Våldtäkt mot personer 15 år och äldre: Utvecklingen under åren 1995–2006* (Stockholm: Brå, 2008), https://www.bra.se/download/18.cba82f7130f475a2f180008010/1371914724593/2008_13_valdtakt_mot_personer_over_15_ar.pdf . Brottsförebyggande Rådet, "Våldtäkt och sexualbrott," Brå, October 14, 2019, https://www.bra.se/statistik/statistik-utifran-brottstyper/valdtakt-och-sexualbrott.html.
2. Maximiliane Koschyk, "Why Are Sexual Assaults in Bavaria on the Rise?," DW, September 20, 2017, https://www.dw.com/en/why-are-sexual-assaults-in-bavaria-on-the-rise/a-40613027. "Kriminalstatistik 2014 vorgestellt: Mehr Täter, mehr Taten!," Bund Deutscher Kriminalbeamter, May 6, 2015, https://www.kripo-akademie.de/der-bdk/aktuelles/pressemitteilungen/kriminalstatistik-2014-vorgestellt-mehr-taeter-mehr-taten.
3. Andy Myhill and Jonathan Allen, *Rape and Sexual Assault of Women: The Extent and Nature of the Problem: Findings from the British Crime Survey* (London: Home Office Research, Development and Statistics Directorate, 2002), https://www.sericc.org.uk/pdfs/1211_homeoffice2372002.pdf..
4. Brottsförebyggande Rådet, *Våldtäkt mot personer 15 år och äldre.* Janet Phillips and Malcolm Park, "Measuring Domestic Violence and Sexual Assault Against Women: A Review of the Literature and Statistics," Parliament of Australia, 2006, https://www.aph.gov.au/about_parliament/parliamentary_departments/parliamentary_library/publications_archive/archive/violenceagainstwomen.
5. Miranda Horvath and Jennifer Brown, eds., *Rape: Challeging Contemporary Thinking* (Cullompton, UK: Willan, 2009), 77.
6. Brottsförebyggande Rådet, "Rape and Sexual Offences," Brå, 2017, https://www.bra.se/bra-in-english/home/crime-and-statistics/rape-and-sex-offences.html. *Sexual Harassment of Women and Girls in Public Places* (London: House of Commons Women and Equalities Committee, 2018), https://publications.parliament.uk/pa/cm201719/cmselect/cmwomeq/701/701.pdf.
7. Paulina Neuding, "Sweden's Sexual Assault Crisis Presents a Feminist Paradox," Quillette, October 10, 2017, https://quillette.com/2017/10/10/swedens-sexual-assault-crisis-presents-feminist-paradox/.
8. "France Urges Women to Report World Cup Sexual Assaults—but Victims Have No Faith in the System," Agence France-Presse, July 19, 2018, https://www.scmp.com/news/world/europe/article/2155908/france-urges-women-report-world-cup-sexual-assaults-victims-have. "'Me Too Football': Women in France Denounce Sex Assaults During World Cup Celebrations," The Local fr, July 17, 2018, https://www.thelocal.fr/20180717/me-too-football-women-in-france-denounce-sex-assaults-during-world-cup-celebrations.

9. Lizzie Dearden, "Grooming Gangs Abused More than 700 Women and Girls Around Newcastle After Police Appeared to Punish Victims," *Independent*, February 23, 2018, https://www.independent.co.uk/news/uk/crime/grooming-gangs-uk-britain-newcastle -serious-case-review-operation-sanctuary-shelter-muslim-asian-a8225106.html.

10. Jody Raphael, *Rape Is Rape: How Denial, Distortion, and Victim Blaming Are Fueling a Hidden Acquaintance Rape Crisis* (Chicago: Chicago Review Press, 2013).

11. Ruud Koopmans, personal interview, April 10, 2018.

12. Country Coordinator Portugal, "Portugal: How to Collect Data on Ethnicity and Race?," European Web Site on Integration, European Commission, February 5, 2018, https://ec .europa.eu/migrant-integration/news/portugal-how-to-collect-data-on-ethnicity-and-race.

13. Valerie Hudson, personal interview, May 14, 2018.

14. "German Legal Research Guide," Georgetown Law Library, http://guides.ll.georgetown .edu/c.php?g=363443&p=2455532.

15. "Trial Starts of Asylum Seeker over Brutal Rape in Munich's English Garden," The Local de, March 26, 2018, https://www.thelocal.de/20180326/trial-starts-of-asylum-seeker -over-brutal-rape-in-munichs-english-garden.

16. "Polizeiliche Kriminalstatistik 2018," Polizei Hamburg, 2018, https://www.polizei.hamburg /daten-und-fakten/12140070/pks-2018/, 42.

17. AD vs. AM, 2017, Landgericht Hamburg. (Author's translation.)

CHAPTER 7: ACTIONS HAVE CONSEQUENCES

1. "WATCH: Merkel's Awkward Interaction with Tearful Palestinian Girl," NPR, July 16, 2015, https://www.npr.org/sections/thetwo-way/2015/07/16/423554204/watch -merkels-awkward-interaction-with-tearful-palestinian-girl.

2. "Merkel says German multicultural society has failed," BBC, October 17, 2010, https:// www.bbc.com/news/world-europe-11559451.

3. Robin Alexander, personal interview, April 30, 2018. (Author's translation.)

4. "Entwicklung der Asylantragszahlen seit 1953," *Aktuelle Zahlen zu Asyl*, August 2018, BAMF, 3, https://www.bamf.de/SharedDocs/Anlagen/DE/Statistik/AsylinZahlen /aktuelle-zahlen-zu-asyl-august-2018.pdf?___blob=publicationFile&v=6.

5. Ayla Albayrak, "Drop in Asylum Applications Relieves European Burden," *Wall Street Journal*, February 1, 2018, https://www.wsj.com/articles/drop-in-asylum-applications -relieves-european-burden-1517504475.

6. Rainer Bauböck and Milena Tripkovic, eds., *The Integration of Migrants and Refugees: An EUI Forum on Migration, Citizenship and Demography*, European University Institute, 2017, https://cadmus.eui.eu/bitstream/handle/1814/45187/Ebook_IntegrationMigrants Refugees2017.pdf?sequence=3&isAllowed=y, 8.

7. Mahmoud Darwesh and Nawas Darraji, "Interview: Libyan Official Says 1.5 Mln Illegal Immigrants Outside Immigrant Shelters," Xinhaunews, May 12, 2018, http://www .xinhuanet.com/english/2018-05/12/c_137173055.htm.

8. "World Population Prospects 2019," United Nations Department of Economic and Social Affairs, https://population.un.org/wpp/DataQuery/.

9. David Pilling, "Migration Is as Old as Humanity and Should Be Welcomed," *Financial Times*, April 10, 2019, https://www.ft.com/content/fb9600c8-5b68-11e9-939a-341f5a da9d40.

10. Stephen Smith, *La ruée vers l'Europe: La jeune Afrique en route pour le Vieux Continent* (Paris: Grasset, 2018).

11. Neli Esipova, Anita Pugliese, and Julie Ray, "More Than 750 Million Worldwide Would Migrate if They Could," Gallup, December 10, 2018, accessed January 23, 2020, https:// news.gallup.com/poll/245255/750-million-worldwide-migrate.aspx.

12. "Europe Is Sending African Migrants Home. Will They Stay?," *The Economist*, March 28, 2018, https://www.economist.com/middle-east-and-africa/2018/03/28/europe-is -sending-african-migrants-home-will-they-stay. "About Half or More in Several sub -Saharan African Countries Would Move to Another Country," Global Attitudes Survey, Spring 2017, Q140, https://www.pewresearch.org/global/2018/03/22/at-least-a-million -sub-saharan-africans-moved-to-europe-since-2010/.

13. Guy Delauney, "Migrant Crisis: Explaining the Exodus from the Balkans," BBC News, September 8, 2015, https://www.bbc.com/news/world-europe-34173252. Shirin Hakimzadeh, "Iran: A Vast Diaspora Abroad and Millions of Refugees at Home," Migration Policy Institute, September 1, 2006, https://www.migrationpolicy.org/article/iran -vast-diaspora-abroad-and-millions-refugees-home. "Pakistan," Amnesty International, https://www.amnesty.org/en/countries/asia-and-the-pacific/pakistan/.

14. Michael Jansen, "Syria, Iraq and Eritrea: Why People Are Fleeing," *Irish Times*, September 11, 2015, https://www.irishtimes.com/news/world/europe/syria-iraq-and-eritrea -why-people-are-fleeing-1.2347795.

15. Ibid. Patricia Gossman, "Dispatches: Why Afghans are Leaving," Human Rights Watch, September 16, 2015, https://www.hrw.org/news/2015/09/16/dispatches-why-afghans -are-leaving. Melissa Fleming, "Six Reasons Why Syrians Are Fleeing to Europe in Increasing Numbers," *The Guardian*, October 25, 2015, https://www.theguardian.com /global-development-professionals-network/2015/oct/25/six-reasons-why-syrians-are -fleeing-to-europe-in-increasing-numbers.

16. "Asylum and Migration in the EU: Facts and Figures," European Parliament, July 22, 2019, http://www.europarl.europa.eu/news/en/headlines/society/20170629STO78630 /asylum-and-migration-in-the-eu-facts-and-figures.

17. Elian Peltier and Eloise Stark, "Rescuing Migrants Fleeing Through the Frozen Alps," *New York Times*, February 22, 2018, https://www.nytimes.com/interactive/2018/02/22 /world/europe/alpine-rescue.html.

18. "Latest: France Says Some Aid Groups Help Smugglers," Associated Press, April 5, 2019, https://www.apnews.com/255e2e1baf5f45309fd9ed9e70834a62. "Iraqi Migration to Europe: IOM Report," International Organization for Migration, August 16, 2016, https://www.iom.int/news/iraqi-migration-europe-iom-report. Fleming, "Six Reasons Why Syrians Are Fleeing to Europe in Increasing Numbers."

19. Tino Sanandaji, personal interview, April 7, 2018.

20. Jonathan Eyal, "Migrants' Integration Woes Spook Europe," *Straits Times*, January 14, 2018, https://www.straitstimes.com/world/europe/migrants-integration-woes-spook -europe.

21. Dominik Schreiber, "So kriminell sind Ausländer wirklich," Kurier, March 7, 2017, https:// kurier.at/chronik/oesterreich/so-kriminell-sind-auslaender-wirklich/250.253.044.

22. Boris Palmer, personal interview, June 18, 2018.

23. "Gesetz zur erleichterten Ausweisung von straffälligen Ausländern und zum erweiterten Ausschluss der Flüchtlingsanerkennung bei straffälligen Asylbewerbern," *Bundesgesetzblatt* 1, no. 12 (March 2016): 394–95, http://www.bgbl.de/xaver/bgbl/start.xav?startb- k=Bundesanzeiger_BGBl&jumpTo=bgbl116012.pdf.

24. Carla Bleiker, "Deportation Laws in Germany—What You Need to Know," DW, January 3, 2019, https://www.dw.com/en/deportation-laws-in-germany-what-you-need-to-know /a-46950234.

25. Simon Gosvig, "Rigsadvokaten kritiserer fejl i voldtægtssager," Anklagemyndigheden, November 20, 2017, https://anklagemyndigheden.dk/da/rigsadvokaten-kritiserer- fejl-i-voldtaegtssager.

26. Swedish Supreme Court Ruling B5931-18, Paragraph 26, 9, https://www.domstol.se

/globalassets/filer/domstol/hogstadomstolen/avgoranden/2019/b-5931-18.pdf.
(Author's translation.) "Sweden's Supreme Court Overturns Deportation Decision for
Convicted Rapist," The Local se, April 25, 2019, https://www.thelocal.se/20190425
/swedens-supreme-court-overturns-deportation-decision-for-convicted-rapist.

27. "A Year in Review: First 12 Months of the European Border and Coast Guard Agency,"
Frontex, 2017, https://frontex.europa.eu/assets/Publications/General/A_Year_in
_Review.pdf.

28. Bojan Pancevski, "Steady Flow of Refugees Fuels Nationalist Gains in Europe," *Wall
Street Journal*, April 30, 2019, https://www.wsj.com/articles/steady-flow-of-refugees
-fuels-nationalist-gains-in-europe-11556628273. Matthew Karnitschnig, "German Far
Right Fuels Muslim 'Takeover' Fears," Politico, April 19, 2019, https://www.politico
.eu/article/germany-islam-chemnitz-far-right-demonstration/. "Migration Enforcement
in the EU—Latest Figures," Eurostat, July 9, 2018, https://ec.europa.eu/eurostat/web
/products-eurostat-news/-/DDN-20180709-1?inheritRedirect=true&redirect=%2
Feurostat%2Fweb%2Fmain.

29. Udo Bauer, "Are Deportations from Germany on the Rise?," InfoMigrants, August 2,
2019, https://www.infomigrants.net/en/post/18555/are-deportations-from-germany
-on-the-rise.

30. Maria Repitsch, "Tusentals avviker från utvisningar," Sveriges Radio, May 2, 2018,
https://sverigesradio.se/sida/artikel.aspx?programid=83&artikel=6944493.

31. David Wood, personal interview, June 26, 2019.

32. "Enforcement of immigration legislation statistics," *Eurostat Statistics Explained*, July
2020, https://ec.europa.eu/eurostat/statistics-explained/index.php/Enforcement_of
_immigration_legislation_statistics#Latest_developments_in_enforcement_statistics.

33. Erik Magnusson, "Malmös bidrag till papperslösa blir fråga för finansministern,"
Svdsvenskan, May 29, 2018, https://www.sydsvenskan.se/2018-05-29/malmos-bidrag
-till-papperslosa-blir-fraga-for.

34. Pancevski, "Steady Flow of Refugees Fuels Nationalist Gains in Europe."

35. Karnitschnig, "German Far Right Fuels Muslim 'Takeover' Fears."

36. "English Channel Migrant Crossings," Home Affairs Committee, Parliament, United
Kingdom, February 26, 2019, https://www.parliamentlive.tv/Event/Index/30d138ae
-13f4-478e-9786-54fb8b132fe0.

37. *Refugees in Europe: Review of Integration Practices & Policies*, European Foundation for
Democracy, 2018, https://emnbelgium.be/publication/refugees-europe-review-integra-
tion-practices-policies-european-foundation-democracy.

38. Fazlur Rahman Raju, "Germany Deported 31 Undocumented Bangladeshis Under
Repatriation Agreement," *Dhaka Tribune*, April 17, 2018, https://www.dhakatribune
.com/bangladesh/2018/04/17/germany-deported-31-undocumented-bangladeshis
-repatriation-agreement/.

39. "EUTF for Africa," European Union, May 15, 2019, https://ec.europa.eu/trustfundforafrica
/sites/euetfa/files/facsheet_eutf_generic_long_online_publication_15.5.19.pdf.

40. "Europe Is Sending African Migrants Home. Will They Stay?"

41. "EUTF for Africa."

42. David Brown, "Deportee 'Saved' by Airline Passengers Raped Teenager," *The Times*,
October 15, 2018, https://www.thetimes.co.uk/article/deportee-saved-by-airline
-passengers-raped-teenage-girl-zf2l6xkg6.

43. "Hundra demonstrerar mot tvångsutvisningarna i Kållered," *Dagens Nyheter*, April 9, 2018,
https://www.dn.se/nyheter/sverige/hundra-demonstrerar-mot-tvangsutvisningarna
-i-kallered/.

44. "Stockholm—fjärde veckan av de afghanska barnfamiljernas sittstrejk," happytogobattle,

July 30, 2019, https://happytogobattle.wordpress.com/2019/07/30/stockholm-fjarde
-veckan-av-de-afghanska-barnfamiljernas-sittstrejk/.

45. Polizeipräsidium Aalen, "POL-AA: Ellwangen: Abschiebung aus der LEA mit Gewalt
verhindert," Presse Portal, May 2, 2018, https://www.presseportal.de/blaulicht/pm
/110969/3932909.

46. "200 Migrants in South German Town Prevent Deportation of Man," The Local de, May
2, 2018, https://www.thelocal.de/20180502/200-migrants-in-south-german-town
-prevent-deportation-of-man-to-congo.

47. "Talking Migration Data: Data on African Migration to Europe," Migration Data Portal,
February 20, 2019, https://migrationdataportal.org/blog/talking-migration-data-data
-african-migration-europe.

48. Karnitschnig, "German Far Right Fuels Muslim 'Takeover' Fears."

49. "Rapport D'Information," Asemblée Nationale, October 4, 1958, http://www.assemblee
-nationale.fr/15/rap-info/i1014.asp#P87_9097. "Collomb: 'Autour de 300.000 étrangers
en situation irrégulière,'" France 24, August 11, 2017, https://www.france24.com/fr
/20171108-collomb-autour-300000-etrangers-situation-irreguliere.

50. Von Aljoscha-Marcello Dohme, "Trotz Prämien: 2017 verließen Deutschland wieder
weniger Asylbewerber," *Kölner Stadt-Anzeiger*, March 27, 2018, https://www.ksta.de/politik
/trotz-praemien-2017-verliessen-deutschland-wieder-weniger-asylbewerber-29933874.

51. David Wood, *Controlling Britain's Borders: The Challenge of Enforcing the UK's Immigration Rules* (London: Civitas, 2019), http://www.civitas.org.uk/content/files
/controllingbritainsborders.pdf.

52. See, e.g., "I Sold All I Had to Go to Europe—Now I'm Home, and Broke," BBC News,
May 7, 2018, https://www.bbc.com/news/stories-44007932.

53. Patrick Kingsley, "Libya's People Smugglers: Inside the Trade That Sells Refugees Hopes of a
Better Life," *The Guardian*, April 24, 2015, https://www.theguardian.com/world/2015
/apr/24/libyas-people-smugglers-how-will-they-catch-us-theyll-soon-move-on. Will
Huddleston, Aysem Biriz Karacay, and Marina Nikolova, *Study on Smuggling of Migrants:
Characteristics, Responses and Cooperation with Third Countries: Case Study 4: Nigeria—
Turkey—Bulgaria*, European Commission, DG Migration & Home Affairs, https://ec.europa
.eu/home-affairs/sites/homeaffairs/files/case_study_4_nigeria_-_turkey_-_bulgaria.pdf.

54. Celia Mebroukine, "French Police Clear out Paris Migrants Camp," Reuters, May 30,
2018, https://www.reuters.com/article/us-europe-migrants-paris-evacuation/french
-police-clear-out-paris-migrants-camp-idUSKCN1IV0FE.

55. "Exposed Areas: Social Order, Criminal Structure and Challenges for the Police,"
National Operational Department of Intelligence Unit, Police Sweden, June 2017,
https://polisen.se/siteassets/dokument/ovriga_rapporter/utsatta-omraden-social
-ordning-kriminell-struktur-och-utmaningar-for-polisen-2017.pdf, 32.

56. Bojan Pancevski, "An Ice-Cream Truck Slaying, Party Drugs and Real-Estate Kings:
Ethnic Clans Clash in Berlin's Underworld," *Wall Street Journal*, October 17, 2018, https://
www.wsj.com/articles/ethnic-crime-families-provoke-german-crackdown-1539604801.

57. Ibid.

CHAPTER 8: THE BROKEN WINDOWS OF LIBERAL JUSTICE

1. Hannes Heine, "Wir müssen unsere Regeln durchsetzen," *Der Tagesspiegel*, March 7,
2018, https://www.tagesspiegel.de/berlin/andreas-geisel-zu-angstraeumen-in-belin
-wir-muessen-unsere-regeln-durchsetzen/21041726.html.

2. Jody Raphael, *Rape Is Rape: How Denial, Distortion, and Victim Blaming Are Fueling a
Hidden Acquaintance Rape Crisis* (Chicago: Chicago Review Press, 2013).

3. Mustafa Panshiri, personal interview, May 25, 2018.
4. Soeren Kern, "Germany: Surge in Migrant Attacks on Police," Gatestone Institute, November 29, 2017, https://www.gatestoneinstitute.org/11459/germany-migrants -attack-police.
5. Mustafa Panshiri, personal interview, May 25, 2018. See also Jens Ganman and Mustafa Panshiri, *Det lilla landet som kunde* (Stockholm: Vulkan, 2018), 88.
6. Ulrich Rosenhagen, "From Stranger to Citizen? Germany's Refugee Dilemma," *Dissent*, Summer 2017, https://www.dissentmagazine.org/article/from-stranger-to-citizen -germanys-refugee-dilemma-integration.
7. Polizei Essen, "POL-E: Essen: Polizeibeamtin bei Einsatz schwer verletzt-Bürger greifen beherzt ein-Kontrolle einer Shisha-Bar eskaliert," Presse Portal, September 9, 2018, https://www.presseportal.de/blaulicht/pm/11562/4056309.
8. *Bundeslagebild Kriminalität im Kontext von Zuwanderung 2016*, Bundeskriminalamt, April 24, 2017, https://www.bka.de/SharedDocs/Downloads/DE/Publikationen/ JahresberichteUndLagebilder/KriminalitaetImKontextVonZuwanderung/Kriminali taetImKontextVonZuwanderung_2016.html.
9. Jörg Diehl and Ansgar Siemens, "So schätzen Polizisten die Sicherheitsanlage an," Spiegel Online, November 18, 2018, https://www.spiegel.de/panorama/justiz/kriminelle -migranten-was-sagen-polizisten-und-wie-ist-das-einzuschaetzen-a-1237348.html. (Author's translation.)
10. Hildegard Michel-Hamm, "SOS from a German Policewoman" (video), DW, August 7, 2019, https://www.dw.com/en/sos-from-a-german-policewoman/av-19227664.
11. Ibid.
12. Ellen Barry and Christina Anderson, "Hand Grenades and Gang Violence Rattle Sweden's Middle Class," *New York Times*, March 3, 2018, https://www.nytimes .com/2018/03/03/world/europe/sweden-crime-immigration-hand-grenades.html.
13. Damien McElroy, "Swedish Policeman Pins Violent Crime on Migrants," *The Sunday Times*, February 26, 2017, https://www.thetimes.co.uk/article/swedish-policeman -pins-violent-crime-on-migrants-8xm609l9n.
14. "Exposed Areas: Social Order, Criminal Structure and Challenges for the Police," National Operational Department of Intelligence Unit, Police Sweden, June 2017, https://polisen.se/siteassets/dokument/ovriga_rapporter/utsatta-omraden-social -ordning-kriminell-struktur-och-utmaningar-for-polisen-2017.pdf, 29.
15. "'It's a Massacre': One French Police Officer Commits Suicide Every Four Days," The Local fr, April 9, 2019, https://www.thelocal.fr/20190409/its-a-massacre-one-french -police-officer-commits-suicide-every-four-days.
16. "Exposed Areas," 36.
17. Bojan Pancevski, "Teens Roam Streets with Rifles as Crime Swamps Sweden," *The Sunday Times*, January 21, 2018, https://www.thetimes.co.uk/article/teens-roam-streets -with-rifles-as-crime-swamps-sweden-q83g055k9.
18. Jürgen Lauterbach, "Sex mit Gewalt, aber keine Vergewaltigung," *Märkische Allgemeine*, April 20, 2017, https://www.maz-online.de/Lokales/Brandenburg-Havel/Sex-mit -Gewalt-aber-keine-Vergewaltigung.
19. Aude Bariéty, "L'agresseur de Marie Laguerre condamné à six mois de prison ferme," *Le Figaro*, October 4, 2018, http://www.lefigaro.fr/actualite-france/2018/10/04/01016 -20181004ARTFIG00344-l-agresseur-de-marie-laguerre-condamne-a-six-mois-de -prison-ferme.php.
20. Samuel Cogez, "Croisilles: Six mois de prison pour le migrant qui s'était frotté à une fille de 11 ans," *La Voix du Nord*, July 13, 2018, https://www.lavoixdunord.fr/416074/article /2018-07-13/six-mois-de-prison-pour-le-migrant-qui-s-etait-frotte-une-fille-de-11-ans.

21. "Bub vergewaltigt—Iraker kommt in Kürze frei!," *Kronen Zeitung*, May 23, 2017, https://www.krone.at/570811.

22. Katrin Bennhold, "A Girl's Killing Puts Germany's Migration Policy on Trial," *New York Times*, January 17, 2018, https://www.nytimes.com/2018/01/17/world/europe/germany-teen-murder-migrant.html.

23. "Germany: Asylum-seeker who killed Kandel teen found dead in prison cell," *DW*, October 11, 2019, https://www.dw.com/en/germany-asylum-seeker-who-killed-kandel-teen-found-dead-in-prison-cell/a-50769693.

24. Michael Zgoll, "Messerattacke: Fünf Jahre Haft für 17-jährigen Syrer," *Hannoversche Allgemeine*, September 14, 2018, https://www.haz.de/Hannover/Aus-der-Stadt/Landgericht-Hannover-urteilt-nach-Tat-in-Grossburgwedel-Fuenf-Jahre-Haft-fuer-syrischen-Messerstecher.

25. Ibid.

26. "Messerattacke in Burgwedel: Jugendhaft für 17-Jährigen, der Vivien K. ein Messer in den Bauch rammte," RTL.de, September 11, 2018, https://www.rtl.de/cms/messerattacke-in-burgwedel-jugendhaft-fuer-17-jaehrigen-der-vivien-k-ein-messer-in-den-bauch-rammte-4220010.html.

27. Diamant Salihu, Åse Asplid, and Michael Syrén, "Här är anmälningarna från 'We are Sthlm,'" *Expressen*, January 13, 2016, https://www.expressen.se/nyheter/har-ar-anmalningarna-fran-we-are-sthlm/.

28. Ibid.

29. Kate Connolly and Mark Tran, "Cologne Police 'Struggled to Gain Control During Mass Sexual Assaults,'" *The Guardian*, January 7, 2016, https://www.theguardian.com/world/2016/jan/07/cologne-police-struggled-to-gain-control-of-mass-sexual-assaults-new-years-eve.

30. Mara Bierbach, "Parliamentary Report: Police Could Have Prevented Cologne New Year's Eve Attacks," DW, March 31, 2017, https://www.dw.com/en/parliamentary-report-police-could-have-prevented-cologne-new-years-eve-attacks/a-38226193.

31. Alice Schwarzer, "Der Shchock—the New Year's Eve of Cologne," *Emma*, February 2017. (Author's translation.)

32. Ben Knight, "Cologne Sexual Assault Case Collapses," *The Guardian*, May 6, 2016, https://www.theguardian.com/world/2016/may/06/cologne-sex-assault-attacks-case-collapses.

33. Rick Noack, "Leaked Document Says 2,000 Men Allegedly Assaulted 1,200 German Women on New Year's Eve," *Washington Post*, July 11, 2016, https://www.washingtonpost.com/news/worldviews/wp/2016/07/10/leaked-document-says-2000-men-allegedly-assaulted-1200-german-women-on-new-years-eve/?noredirect=on. Rainer Wendt, "'The perpetrators laugh at us!,'" *Emma*, November–December 2016.

34. "Being Christian in Western Europe," Pew Research Center, May 29, 2018, https://www.pewforum.org/2018/05/29/being-christian-in-western-europe/.

35. *Brottsförebyggande rådet* (Stockholm: Swedish National Council for Crime Prevention, 2018), 16.

CHAPTER 9: THE PLAYBOOK OF DENIAL

1. "Three Refugees Charged for Groping at Danish Festival," The Local dk, August 1, 2016, https://www.thelocal.dk/20160801/three-asylum-seekers-charges-for-groping-girl-at-festival.

2. Paulina Neuding, "Sweden's Violent Reality Is Undoing a Peaceful Self-image," Politico, April 16, 2018, https://www.politico.eu/article/sweden-bombings-grenade-attacks-violent-reality-undoing-peaceful-self-image-law-and-order/.

3. Maria von Welser, *No Refuge for Women: The Tragic Fate of Syrian Refugees* (Greystone Books, 2017).
4. Mattis Wikström and Kim Malmgren, "De är män som våldtar kvinnor tillsammans," *Expressen*, March 20, 2018, https://www.expressen.se/nyheter/brottscentralen/qs /de-ar-mannen-som-valdtar-tillsammans/. (Author's translation.)
5. Joachim Kerpner, Kerstin Weigl, and Alice Staaf, "Unik granskning: 112 pojkar och män dömda för gruppvåldtäkt," *Aftonbladet*, October 21, 2019, https://www.aftonbladet.se /nyheter/a/rLKwKR/unik-granskning-112-pojkar-och-man-domda-for-gruppvaldtakt. (Author's translation.)
6. Christian Pfeiffer, Dirk Baier, and Sören Kliem, *Zur Entwicklung der Gewalt in Deutschland Schwerpunkte: Jugendliche und Flüchtlinge als Täter und Opfer*, Institut für Delinquenz und Kriminalprävention, Zürcher Hochschule für Angewandte Wissenschaften, January 2018, https://pdfs.semanticscholar.org/8cf4/655e7090ac6b11a7a0f02f8530dd1ae5676e .pdf. Maximiliane Koschyk, "Why Are Sexual Assaults in Bavaria on the Rise?," DW, September 20, 2017, https://www.dw.com/en/why-are-sexual-assaults-in-bavaria-on-the-rise/a-40613027.
7. Brottsförebyggande Rådet, *Våldtäkt mot personer 15 år och äldre: Utvecklingen under åren 1995–2006* (Stockholm: Brå, 2008), https://www.bra.se/download/18.cba82f7130f47 5a2f180008010/1371914724593/2008_13_valdtakt_mot_personer_over_15_ar.pdf. Ronet Bachman and Linda E. Saltzman, "Violence Against Women: Estimates from the Redesigned Survey," Washington, DC: Office of Justice Programs, U.S. Department of Justice, 1995, https://www.bjs.gov/content/pub/pdf/FEMVIED.PDF.
8. "Stimmen die Meldungen über vergewaltigende Flüchtlinge?," *Der Spiegel*, January 6, 2018, https://www.spiegel.de/spiegel/stimmen-die-meldungen-ueber-vergewaltigende -fluechtlinge-a-1186254.html.
9. Vilija Blinkevičiūtė, "Mano parlamentinė veikla," Darbas Europos Parlamente, http:// www.blinkeviciute.eu/darbas-europos-parlamente/mano-parlamentine-veikla.
10. Interview with Austrian government employee, Vienna, June 21, 2018.
11. Eliza Gray, "Swedish Feminists Thread Needle Between Sexism and Racism in Migrant Controversy," *Time*, January 19, 2016, https://time.com/4182186/sweden-feminists -sexual-assault-refugees/.
12. "'Anti-deportation Industry' Named Germany's Non-Word of the Year 2018," DW, January 15, 2019, https://www.dw.com/en/anti-deportation-industry-named-germanys -non-word-of-the-year-2018/a-47086095.
13. Kate Connolly, "Populist Talkshows Fuel Rise of Far Right, German TV Bosses Told," *The Guardian*, June 13, 2018, https://www.theguardian.com/world/2018/jun/13/populist -talkshows-fuel-rise-of-far-right-german-tv-bosses-told.
14. Soeren Kern, "Germany's Migrant Rape Crisis: Where Is the Public Outrage?," October 26, 2016, http://soerenkern.com/2016/10/26/germanys-migrant-rape-crisis-public -outrage/.
15. "Anmerkung der Redaktion" and "Neunter Tarverdächtiger festgenommen," *Süddeutsche Zeitung*, November 30, 2018. (Author's translation.)
16. "Zum Geleit," *Süddeutsche Zeitung*, October 6, 1945, 1.
17. James Dennison and Teresa Talò, "Explaining Attitudes to Immigration in France," Working Paper RSCAS 2017/25, Migration Policy Centre, Robert Schuman Centre for Advanced Policy Studies, May 2017, https://cadmus.eui.eu/bitstream/handle /1814/46245/RSCAS_2017_25.pdf?sequence=1&isAllowed=y, executive summary.
18. Anthony Heath and Lindsay Richards, "How Do Europeans Differ in Their Attitudes to Immigration? Findings from the European Social Survey, 2002/03–2016/17," OECD Social, Employment and Migration Working Papers No. 222, OECD Publishing, 2019, https:// pdfs.semanticscholar.org/02e8/28a5fad3cbd36b695d8c4b160c154b2ef442.pdf?

_ga=2.60475301.968125941.1577491817-1227194247.1574373344. Richard Wike, Bruce Stokes, and Katie Simmons, "Europeans Fear Wave of Refugees Will Mean More Terrorism, Fewer Jobs," Pew Research Center, July 11, 2016, https://www.pewresearch.org /global/2016/07/11/europeans-fear-wave-of-refugees-will-mean-more-terrorism-fewer-jobs/.

19. Miriam Ticktin, "Sexual Violence as the Language of Border Control: Where French Feminist and Anti-immigrant Rhetoric Meet," *Signs: Journal of Women in Culture and Society* 33, no. 4 (2008), 863–89.

20. Ruud Koopmans, personal interview, April 10, 2019.

21. Hugh Schofield, "Algerian Novelist Kamel Daoud Sparks Islamophobia Row," BBC News, March 7, 2016, https://www.bbc.com/news/world-europe-35653496.

22. "Sarrazin vs the Saracens," *The Economist*, September 1, 2010, https://www.economist .com/newsbook/2010/09/01/sarrazin-vs-the-saracens.

23. "Suhrkamp-Verlag distanziert sich vom 'Turm'-Autor," *Frankfurter Allgemeine*, March 10, 2018, https://www.faz.net/aktuell/feuilleton/suhrkamp-distanziert-sich-von-seinem -autor-uwe-tellkamp-15487159.html.

24. Hamed Abdel-Samad, personal interview, June 27, 2018.

25. Bill de Blasio, Anne Hidalgo, and Sadiq Khan, "Our Immigrants, Our Strength," *New York Times*, September 20, 2016, https://www.nytimes.com/2016/09/20/opinion/our -immigrants-our-strength.html.

26. Marina Koren, "Angela Merkel's Response to the New Year's Eve Assaults," *The Atlantic*, January 12, 2016, https://www.theatlantic.com/international/archive/2016/01/cologne -refugees-migrants-merkel/423708/.

27. "Norway Educates Migrants on Treatment of Women" (video), VOA Europe, January 15, 2016, https://www.voanews.com/episode/norway-educates-migrants-treatment-women-3709921.

28. "Three Refugees Charged for Groping at Danish Festival."

29. Johan Furusjö, "Massövergreppen i Kungsträdgården: Vad vi vet," *Aftonbladet*, January 13, 2016, https://www.aftonbladet.se/nyheter/a/jProgn/massovergreppen-i-kungstradgarden -vad-vi-vet. (Author's translation.)

30. Hartwig Pautz, "Constructing the 'Immigrant': Germany's Radical Left in the Refugee Crisis," *German Politics* 27, no. 3 (2017): 424–41, https://www.tandfonline.com/doi/abs /10.1080/09644008.2017.1312351?af=R&journalCode=fgrp20.

CHAPTER 10: THE FEMINIST PREDICAMENT

1. Eliza Gray, "Swedish Feminists Thread Needle Between Sexism and Racism in Migrant Controversy," *Time*, January 19, 2016, https://time.com/4182186/sweden-feminists -sexual-assault-refugees/.

2. Sofie Peeters, personal interview, March 31, 2018.

3. Ibid.

4. "'Reality Check': Police Union Head Criticizes Uni After String of Sexual Assaults," The Local de, February 5, 2018, https://www.thelocal.de/20180205/reality-check -police-union-head-criticizes-uni-after-string-of-sexual-assaults.

CHAPTER 11: THE MODESTY DOCTRINE

1. Brottsförebyggande Rådet, *Våldtäkt mot personer 15 år och äldre: Utvecklingen under åren 1995–2006* (Stockholm: Brå, 2008), https://www.bra.se/download/18.cba8 2f7130f475a2f180008010/1371914724593/2008_13_valdtakt_mot_personer _over_15_ar.pdf.

2. *Bundeslagebild Kriminalität im Kontext von Zuwanderung 2017*, Bundeskriminalamt, May 8, 2018, https://www.bka.de/SharedDocs/Downloads/DE/Publikationen/Jahres

berichteUndLagebilder/KriminalitaetImKontextVonZuwanderung/Kriminalitaet
ImKontextVonZuwanderung_2017.pdf.

3. "Asylum and First Time Asylum Applicants by Citizenship, Age and Sex Annual Aggregated Data (Rounded)," Eurostat, March 12, 2019, http://appsso.eurostat.ec.europa.eu/nui /show.do?dataset=migr_asyappctza&lang=en.

4. Valerie Hudson, "Europe's Man Problem," Politico, January 6, 2016, https://www.politico .eu/article/europes-man-problem/.

5. Andrea Den Boer and Valerie Hudson, "Bare Branches: The Security Implications of Asia's Surplus Male Population," Cambridge: MIT Press, 2005.

6. Hudson, "Europe's Man Problem."

7. Louisa Leontiades, Dalia Gazah, and Jörg Luyken, "Life in Suspense: The Refugees in Germany Who Can't Reunite with Their Families," The Local de, November 16, 2017, https://www.thelocal.de/20171116/life-in-suspense-the-refugees-in-germany-who -cant-reunite-with-their-families.

8. "Reality Check: Are Migrants Driving Crime in Germany?," BBC News, September 13, 2018, https://www.bbc.com/news/world-europe-45419466.

9. Laura Backes, Anna Clauss, Maria-Mercedes Hering, et al., "Fact-Check: Is There Truth to Refugee Rape Reports?," Spiegel Online, January 17, 2018, https://www.spiegel.de /international/germany/is-there-truth-to-refugee-sex-offense-reports-a-1186734.html.

10. Christian Pfeiffer, Dirk Baier, and Sren Kliem, "Zur Entwicklung der Gewalt in Deutschland Schwerpunkte: Jugendliche und Flüchtlinge als Täter und Opfer," Institut für Delinquenz und Kriminalpr.vention, Zürcher Hochschule für Angewandte Wissenschaften, January 2018, https://pdfs.semanticscholar.org/8cf4/655e7090ac6b11a7a0f02f8530dd1ae5676e .pdf, 71–91.

11. Camille Paglia, Sexual Personae: Art and Decadence from Nefertiti to Emily Dickinson, vol. 1 (New Haven, CT: Yale University Press, 1990), 23. Page number per Google Books.

12. Barney Zwartz and Sarah Smiles, "Melbourne Sheik Backs Calls to Legalise Polygamy," Sydney Morning Herald, June 26, 2008, https://www.smh.com.au/national/melbourne -sheik-backs-calls-to-legalise-polygamy-20080625-2wv9.html.

13. Anne McCants and Dan Seligson, "Polygamy, the Commodification of Women, and the Erosion of Trust," unpublished manuscript, August 2019, http://pseweb.eu/ydepot /seance/513535_McCants_Seligson_Polygamy_Sversion.pdf.

14. Walter Scheidel, "Monogamy and Polygyny, Version 1.0," Princeton/Stanford Working Papers in Classics, January 2009, http://www.princeton.edu/~pswpc/pdfs /scheidel/010903.pdf.

15. Dan Seligson, personal interview, June 11, 2018.

16. Knut S. Vikør, Between God and the Sultan: A History of Islamic Law (Oxford, UK: Oxford University Press, 2005), 324.

17. Abdullahi Ahmed An-Na'im, Toward an Islamic Reformation: Civil Liberties, Human Rights, and International Law (Syracuse, NY: Syracuse University Press, 1990), 161–81, esp. 171.

18. Imad Ad-Din (228–30), quoted in Francesco Gabrieli, ed., Arab Historians of the Crusades (Dorset Press, 1989 [1957]), 204.

19. Rudolph Peters, Crime and Punishment in Islamic Law: Theory and Practice from the Sixteenth to the Twenty-first Century (Cambridge, UK: Cambridge University Press, 2005), 14–15, 177. Arafat Mazhar, "Raped Women Should Keep Quiet," The Express Tribune (Pakistan), July 9, 2011, https://tribune.com.pk/story/206049/raped-women-should -keep-quiet/.

20. Vikør, Between God and the Sultan, 283.

21. "Women and *Hajj*, Rapists, and Minors," Islamic Research Foundation International, Inc., May 8, 1999, https://www.irfi.org/questions_answers/women_and_hajj.htm.

22. Mona Eltahawy, *Headscarves and Hymens: Why the Middle East Needs a Sexual Revolution* (New York: HarperCollins, 2015), 52.

23. Riazat Butt, "Our Dirty Little Secret," *The Guardian*, April 21, 2008, https://www .theguardian.com/commentisfree/2008/apr/21/ourdirtylittlesecret. See also Dilshad Ali, "The Trifecta of Rape Culture, Sexual Abuse and Muslim Communities— Debunking False Statements," Patheos, October 11, 2018, https://www.patheos .com/blogs/altmuslim/2018/10/the-trifecta-of-rape-culture-sexual-abuse-and -muslim-communities/.

24. Judy Bachrach, "Twice Branded: Western Women, Muslim Lands," *World Affairs* 172, no. 1 (Summer 2009): 84–92.

25. Amena Bakr, "Dubai Jails Norwegian Woman for Illicit Sex After She Reports Rape," *The Star* (Toronto), July 21, 2013, https://www.thestar.com/news/world/2013/07/21 /dubai_jails_norwegian_woman_for_illicit_sex_after_she_reports_rape.html.

26. "Oh, Boy: Are Lopsided Migrant Sex Ratios Giving Europe a Man Problem?," *The Econo-mist*, January 16, 2016, https://www.economist.com/europe/2016/01/16/oh-boy.

27. Bachrach, "Twice Branded: Western Women, Muslim Lands."

28. Eltahawy, *Headscarves and Hymens*.

29. Ibid., 76–77.

30. Lorraine Brown and Hanaa Osman, "The Female Tourist Experience in Egypt as an Islamic Destination," *Annals of Tourism Research* 63 (March 2017): 12–22.

31. *Understanding Masculinities: Results from the International Men and Gender Equality Sur-vey (IMAGES)—Middle East and North Africa* (UN Women and Promundo-US, 2017), https://promundoglobal.org/wp-content/uploads/2017/05/IMAGES-MENA-Multi -Country-Report-EN-16May2017-web.pdf.

32. Marnia Lazreg, *Questioning the Veil: Open Letters to Muslim Women* (Princeton, NJ: Princeton University Press, 2009).

33. "Egyptian Lawyer Jailed for Saying Women in Ripped Jeans Should Be Raped," BBC News, December 2, 2017, https://www.bbc.com/news/world-middle-east-42209755.

34. Vivian Yee and Hwaida Saad, "For Lebanese Women, a Beach of Their Own," *New York Times*, September 10, 2018, https://www.nytimes.com/2018/09/10/world/middleeast /lebanon-women-beach.html.

35. Janice Dickson, "Refugee Women Live in Fear, Avoiding Washrooms Because of Sexual Ha-rassment," *National Post*, October 15, 2018, https://nationalpost.com/pmn/news-pmn/canada -news-pmn/refugee-women-live-in-fear-avoiding-washrooms-because-of-sexual-harassment.

36. Maria von Welser, *No Refuge for Women: The Tragic Fate of Syrian Refugees* (Vancouver: Greystone Books, 2017).

37. *Desperate and Dangerous: Report on the Human Rights Situation of Migrants and Refugees in Libya*, United Nations Support Mission in Libya and Office of the High Commis-sioner for Human Rights, December 20, 2018, https://www.ohchr.org/Documents /Countries/LY/LibyaMigrationReport.pdf, 31.

38. Rumy Hasan, *Multiculturalism: Some Inconvenient Truths* (London: Politico's Publishing, 2010), 1217. Jaclyn Friedman and Jessica Valenti, eds., *Yes Means Yes! Visions of Female Sexual Power and a World Without Rape* (Berkeley: Seal Press, 2008).

39. Brad Perry, "Hooking Up with Healthy Sexuality: The Lessons Boys Learn (and Don't Learn) About Sexuality, and Why a Sex-Positive Rape Prevention Paradigm Can Benefit Everyone Involved," in Friedman and Valenti, *Yes Means Yes!*, ed. Jaclyn Friedman and Jessica Valenti (Berkeley: Seal Press, 2008), 193–207.

40. Alia Amer, "Sex in Islam: What Every Muslim Teenager and Adult Needs to Know about Sexuality," Zawaj.com, https://www.zawaj.com/articles/teenager_know.html.
41. Isabel Teotonio, "Parents Experiencing Back-to-School Jitters About Sex-Ed Rollback," *The Star* (Toronto), September 4, 2018, https://www.thestar.com/news/gta/2018/09/04/parents-experiencing-back-to-school-jitters-amid-sex-ed-rollback.html.
42. Nazia Parveen, "Birmingham Primary School to Resume Modified LGBT Lessons," *The Guardian*, July 3, 2019, https://www.theguardian.com/world/2019/jul/03/birmingham-primary-school-to-resume-modified-lgbt-lessons.
43. Oliver Harvey, "Worlds Collide as Gay Assistant Head Teaches Kids about Homosexuality in 98 Per Cent Muslim Community," *The Sun*, February 1, 2019, https://www.thesun.co.uk/news/8334977/homosexuality-birmingham-saltley-islam.
44. Forum conversation on ummah.com, September 29, 2018, https://www.ummah.com/forum/forum/islam/jinns-ruqya-unseen/12580704-chronic-wet-dreams-issue. Forum conversation on ummah.com, August 12, 2010, https://www.ummah.com/forum/forum/lounge-v2/286898-who-is-to-blame-for-a-man-s-lust-for-women. Forum conversations on ummah.com, July 28, 2016, https://www.ummah.com/forum/forum/misc/anonymous-posting-counselling-forum/488482-my-hormones-can-t-handle-all-the-women-in-public.
45. Kamel Daoud, "The Sexual Misery of the Arab World," *New York Times*, February 12, 2016, https://www.nytimes.com/2016/02/14/opinion/sunday/the-sexual-misery-of-the-arab-world.html.
46. Lara Logan, personal interview, November 5, 2018.
47. Alice Schwartzer, "Was war da los?," *Emma*, March–April 2016.
48. Magdi Abdelhadi, "Cairo Street Crowds Target Women," BBC News, November 1, 2006, http://news.bbc.co.uk/2/hi/middle_east/6106500.stm.
49. Angie Abdelmonem, "Reconceptualizing Sexual Harassment in Egypt: Longitudinal Assessment of *el-Taharrush el-Ginsy* in Arabic Online Forums and Anti-sexual Harassment Activism," *Kohl: A Journal for Body and Gender Research* 1 (2015): 23–41, https://s3-eu-west-1.amazonaws.com/harassmap/media/uploaded-files/reconceptualizing-sexual-harassment-in-egypt-1.pdf.
50. Eltahawy, *Headscarves and Hymens*.
51. Marina Koren, "Angela Merkel's Response to the New Year's Eve Assaults," *The Atlantic*, January 12, 2016, https://www.theatlantic.com/international/archive/2016/01/cologne-refugees-migrants-merkel/423708/.
52. Alison Smale, "As Germany Welcomes Migrants, Sexual Attacks in Cologne Point to a New Reality," *New York Times*, January 14, 2016, https://www.nytimes.com/2016/01/15/world/europe/as-germany-welcomes-migrantssexual-attacks-in-cologne-point-to-a-new-reality.html.
53. Alice Schwarzer, "Der Schock—the New Year's Eve of Cologne," *Emma*, February 2017.
54. Ibid. Jürgen Mathies and Alice Schwarzer in conversation with the author, December 30, 2016.

CHAPTER 12: CULTURE CLASH

1. Samuel Huntington, "The Clash of Civilizations?," *Foreign Affairs*, Summer 1993, https://www.foreignaffairs.com/articles/united-states/1993-06-01/clash-civilizations.
2. Bastien Chabé-Ferret, Joël Machado, and Jackline Wahba, "Remigration Intentions and Migrants' Behavior," *Regional Science and Urban Economics* 68 (January 2018): 56–74.
3. Ibid.
4. Antje Röder, "Immigrants' Attitudes Toward Homosexuality: Socialization, Religion,

and Acculturation in European Host Societies," *International Migration Review* 49, no. 4 (2015): 1042–70.

5. World Values Survey, http://www.worldvaluessurvey.org/wvs.jsp.

6. "Live Cultural Map over Time 1981 to 2015," World Values Survey, http://www.world valuessurvey.org/WVSContents.jsp?CMSID=Findings.

7. "Asylum and First Time Asylum Applicatants by Citizenship, Age and Sex Annual Ag-gregated Data (Rounded)," Eurostat, March 12, 2019, http://appsso.eurostat.ec.europa .eu/nui/show.do?dataset=migr_asyappctza&lang=en.

8. "How Important Is Religion in Respondent's Life," World Values Survey V9, http:// www.worldvaluessurvey.org/wvs.jsp. "Justifiable: For a Man to Beat His Wife," World Values Survey V208, http://www.worldvaluessurvey.org/wvs.jsp. ["Online analysis," select 2010–2014, select countries, then questions.]

9. Sofie Peeters, personal interview, March 31, 2018.

10. Cai Berger, personal interview, April 6, 2018.

11. Efgani Dönmez, personal interview, June 22, 2018.

12. Joachim Kerpner, Kerstin Weigl, and Alice Staaf, "Unik granskning: 112 pojkar och män dömda för gruppvåldtäkt," *Aftonbladet*, May 6, 2018, https://www.aftonbladet.se /nyheter/a/rLKwKR/unik-granskning-112-pojkar-och-man-domda-for-gruppvaldtakt.

13. Mustafa Panshiri, personal interview, May 25, 2018.

14. "Youmo in Practice," Myndigheten för ungdoms- och civilsamhällesfrågor, October 11, 2018, https://www.mucf.se/publikationer/youmo-practice.

15. "Tonårselev mördade sin lärarinna efter sexrelation," GT, October 11, 2019, https:// www.expressen.se/gt/ung-man-atalas-for-lararmordet-i-kil-/.

16. Hamed Abdel-Samad, personal interview, June 27, 2018.

17. Agnès Leclair, "Dans la Manche, l'affaire du réfugié acquitté d'un viol fait polémique," *Le Figaro*, November 23, 2018, http://www.lefigaro.fr/actualite-france/2018/11/23/01016 20181123ARTFIG00310-acquitte-d-un-viol-car-il-n-avait-pas-les-codes-culturels.php. (Author's translation.)

18. "Selon lui, l'accusé 'considère les femmes françaises comme des p****, il a un comportement de prédateur.'" Ibid.

19. Jess Phillips, personal interview, May 15, 2018.

20. Jody Raphael, *Rape Is Rape: How Denial, Distortion, and Victim Blaming Are Fueling a Hidden Acquaintance Rape Crisis* (Chicago: Chicago Review Press, 2013), 55.

21. Rhiana Wegner, Antonia Abbey, Jennifer Pierce, et al., "Sexual Assault Perpetrators' Justifications for Their Actions: Relationships to Rape Supportive Attitudes, Incident Characteristics and Future Perpetration," *Violence Against Women* 21, no. 8 (August 2015): 1018–37, https://www.ncbi.nlm.nih.gov/pmc/articles/PMC4491036/.

22. Nazir Afzal, personal interview, March 28, 2018.

23. "Immigrant Sex Fiend Claims He 'Did Not Know It Was Illegal to Grope Women,'" *Express*, July 26, 2018, https://www.express.co.uk/news/world/994736/Immigrant -grope-illegal-Germany. Hans H. Nibbrig, "Mann soll 13 Frauen in U-Bahnen sexuell belästigt haben," *Berliner Morgenpost*, July 24, 2018, https://www.morgenpost.de /berlin/article214924057/Mann-soll-13-Frauen-in-U-Bahnen-sexuell-belaestigt -haben.html.

24. Jalal Baig, "The Perils of #MeToo as a Muslim," *The Atlantic*, December 21, 2017, https:// www.theatlantic.com/international/archive/2017/12/tariq-ramadan-metoo/548642/.

25. Ella Hill, "As a Rotherham Grooming Gang Survivor, I Want People to Know About the Religious Extremism Which Inspired My Abusers," *Independent*, March 18, 2018, https://www.independent.co.uk/voices/rotherham-grooming-gang-sexual-abuse -muslim-islamist-racism-white-girls-religious-extremism-a8261831.html.

26. Richard Kerbaj, "Muslim Leader Blames Women for Sex Attacks," *The Australian*, October 26, 2006, https://www.theaustralian.com.au/news/nation/muslim-leader-blames -women-for-sex-attacks/news-story/d8b6a183c6a976752cb07be532543afd.

27. Mark Hughes and Jerome Taylor, "Rape 'impossible' in marriage, says Muslim cleric," *Independent*, October 14, 2010, https://www.independent.co.uk/news/uk/home-news /rape-impossible-in-marriage-says-muslim-cleric-2106161.html. Mikael Jalving, "Dansk imam taget med bukserne nede, men var det en hunhund?," *Jyllands Posten*, March 5, 2013, https://web.archive.org/web/20130311122604/http://blogs.jp.dk/frontalt/2013 /03/05/dansk-imam-taget-med-bukserne-nede-men-var-det-en-hunhund/.

28. Iris Andriessen, Henk Fernee, and Karin Wittebrood, *Perceived Discrimination in the Netherlands* (The Hague: Netherlands Institute for Social Research, 2014).

29. Ahu Alanya, Marc Swyngedouw, Veronique Vandezande, and Karen Phalet, "Close Encounters: Minority and Majority Perceptions of Discrimination and Intergroup Relations in Antwerp, Belgium," International Migration Review 51, no. 1 (Spring 2017), 191–217, https://onlinelibrary.wiley.com/doi/full/10.1111/imre.12203.

30. *Refugees in Europe: Review of Integration Practices & Policies*, European Foundation for Democracy, 2018, https://www.europeandemocracy.eu/wp-content/uploads/2019 /03/2018-Refugees-In-Europe-Full-Version.pdf.

31. Olga Khazan, "Inherited Trauma Shapes Your Health," *The Atlantic*, October 16, 2018, https:// www.theatlantic.com/health/archive/2018/10/trauma-inherited-generations/573055/.

32. "How France's Regions Reflect the Country's Diversity," *The Economist*, October 7, 2017, https://www.economist.com/special-report/2017/10/02/how-frances-regions-reflect -the-countrys-diversity.

33. Mohammed Qasim, *Young, Muslim and Criminal: Experiences, Identities and Pathways into Crime* (Bristol: Policy Press, 2018), 49.

34. Nazir Afzal, "Fear of Racism That Let Jihadis Flourish in the UK," *Daily Mail*, June 6, 2017, https://www.dailymail.co.uk/news/article-4575452/Prosecutor-NAZIR-AFZAL-UK -deals-extremism.html.

35. Akbar Ahmed, *Journey into Europe: Islam, Immigration, and Identity* (Washington, DC: Brookings Institution Press, 2018), 477.

36. Camille Paglia, *Free Women, Free Men: Sex, Gender, Feminism* (New York: Pantheon, 2017), xxv.

37. Hamed Abdel-Samad, personal interview, June 27, 2018.

38. "Europe Is Sending African Migrants Home. Will They Stay?," *The Economist*, March 28, 2018, https://www.economist.com/middle-east-and-africa/2018/03/28/europe -is-sending-african-migrants-home-will-they-stay.

39. Paulina Neuding, "Social oro ger stök på bibblan," *Svenska Dagbladet*, May 16, 2015, https://www.svd.se/social-oro-ger-stok-pa-bibblan. Cheryl Benard, "I've Worked with Refugees for Decades. Europe's Afghan Crime Wave Is Mind-Boggling," *The National Interest*, July 11, 2017, https://nationalinterest.org/feature/ive-worked-refugees-decades -europes-afghan-crime-wave-mind-21506. Bassam Tibi, "Syrien und Deutschland," in *Der Schock—Die Silvesternacht von Köln,* mit Beiträgen von Kamel Daoud, Necla Kelek, Bassam Tibi u.a. (Cologne: Kiepenheuer & Witsch, 2016).

40. Bernard Lewis, "Europe and Islam," The Tanner Lectures on Human Values, Brasenose College, Oxford University, February 26, March 5 and 12, 1990, https://tannerlectures .utah.edu/_documents/a-to-z/l/Lewis98.pdf, 134.

CHAPTER 13: WHY INTEGRATION HAS NOT HAPPENED

1. Bernard Lewis, "Europe and Islam," The Tanner Lectures on Human Values, Brasenose College, Oxford University, February 26, March 5 and 12, 1990, https://tannerlectures .utah.edu/_documents/a-to-z/l/Lewis98.pdf, 139.

2. Bill de Blasio, Anne Hidalgo, and Sadiq Khan, "Our Immigrants, Our Strength," *New York Times*, September 20, 2016, https://www.nytimes.com/2016/09/20/opinion/our-immigrants-our-strength.html.

3. Laura Backes, Anna Clauss, Maria-Mercedes Herin, et al., "Fact-Check: Is There Truth to Refugee Rape Reports?," Spiegel Online, January 17, 2018, https://www.spiegel.de/international/germany/is-there-truth-to-refugee-sex-offense-reports-a-1186734.html.

4. Doug Saunders, *Myth of the Muslim Tide: Do Immigrants Threaten the West?* (Toronto: Knopf Canada, 2012).

5. Thomas Liebig and Kristian Rose Tronstad, "Triple Disadvantage?: A First Overview of the Integration of Refugee Women," OECD Social, Employment and Migration Working Papers No. 216, 2018, https://www.oecd-ilibrary.org/employment/triple-disadvantage_3f3a9612-en.

6. Bojan Pancevski, "An Ice-Cream Truck Slaying, Party Drugs and Real-Estate Kings: Ethnic Clans Clash in Berlin's Underworld," *Wall Street Journal*, October 17, 2018, https://www.wsj.com/articles/ethnic-crime-families-provoke-german-crackdown-1539604801.

7. Thomas Sowell, *Migrations and Cultures: A World View* (New York: Basic Books, 1996).

8. Ibid., 47.

9. Ibid., 142, 180.

10. Ibid., 179.

11. Ibid.

12. Ibid., 181.

13. Ibid.

14. Hamed Abdel-Samad, personal interview, June 27, 2018.

15. Ruud Koopmans, *Das verfallene Haus des Islam. Religiöse Ursachen von Unfreiheit, Stagnation und Gewalt* (Munich: CH Beck, 2020).

16. Dan Seligson, personal interview, June 11, 2018.

17. Ayaan Hirsi Ali, *The Challenge of Dawa: Political Islam as Ideology and Movement and How to Counter It* (Stanford, CA: Hoover Institution Press, 2017), https://www.hoover.org/sites/default/files/research/docs/ali_challengeofdawa_final_web.pdf.

18. Christian Pfeiffer, Dirk Baier, and Sören Kliem, *Zur Entwicklung der Gewalt in Deutschland Schwerpunkte: Jugendliche und Flüchtlinge als Täter und Opfer*, Institut für Delinquenz und Kriminalprävention, Zürcher Hochschule für Angewandte Wissenschaften, January 2018, https://www.bmfsfj.de/bmfsfj/service/publikationen/zur-entwicklung-der-gewalt-in-deutschland-/121148.

19. "Muslim Girls in TIGHT Clothes!!! [MUST WATCH]," *Naseeha Sessions*, YouTube, October 24, 2016, https://www.youtube.com/watch?v=2GGYU4QZLSQ. "For Sisters Who Don't Pray [PLEASE WATCH]," *Naseeha Sessions*, YouTube, April 30, 2016, https://www.youtube.com/watch?v=L0VVD6YBry4.

20. Antje Röder, "Explaining Religious Differences in Immigrants' Gender Role Attitudes: The Changing Impact of Origin Country and Individual Religiosity," *Ethnic and Racial Studies* 37, no. 14 (2014): 2615–35.

21. *A Review of Survey Research on Muslims in Britain*, Ipsos MORI Social Research Institute, February 2018, https://www.ipsos.com/sites/default/files/ct/publication/documents/2018-03/a-review-of-survey-research-on-muslims-in-great-britain-ipsos-mori_0.pdf.

22. Mieke Maliepaard and Richard Alba, "Cultural Integration in the Muslim Second Generation in the Netherlands: The Case of Gender Ideology," *International Migration Review* 50, no. 1 (Spring 2016): 70–94.

23. Efgani Dönmez, personal interview, June 22, 2018.

24. *Refugees in Europe: Review of Integration Practices & Policies*, European Foundation for

Democracy, 2018, https://www.europeandemocracy.eu/wp-content/up-loads/2019/03/2018-Refugees-In-Europe-Full-Version.pdf.

25. Seyran Ateş, personal interview, April 5, 2018.
26. Efgani Dönmez, personal interview, June 22, 2018.
27. Jacqueline Stevenson, Sean Demack, Bernie Stiell, et al., *The Social Mobility Challenges Faced by Young Muslims*, Social Mobility Commission, 2017, https://assets.publishing.service.gov.uk/government/uploads/system/uploads/attachment_data/file/642220/Young_Muslims_SMC.pdf, 6.
28. "Gender Equality Index 2017: Measuring Gender Equality in the European Union 2005–2015—Report," European Institute for Gender Equality, October 10, 2017, https://eige.europa.eu/publications/gender-equality-index-2017-measuring-gender-equality-european-union-2005-2015-report. *The Gallup Coexist Index 2009: A Global Study of Interfaith Relations*, Gallup, 2009, http://www.euro-islam.info/wp-content/uploads/pdfs/gallup_coexist_2009_interfaith_relations_uk_france_germany.pdf. *Settling in 2018: Indicators of Immigrant Integration*, OECD Publishing and European Union, 2018, https://doi.org/10.1787/9789264307216-en. Rainer Bauböck and Milena Tripkovic, eds., *The Integration of Migrants and Refugees: An EUI Forum on Migration, Citizenship and Demography*, European University Institute, 2017, https://cadmus.eui.eu/bitstream/handle/1814/45187/Ebook_IntegrationMigrantsRefugees2017.pdf.
29. Saunders, *Myth of the Muslim Tide*.
30. Yassine Khoudja and Fenella Fleischmann, "Labor Force Participation of Immigrant Women in the Netherlands: Do Traditional Partners Hold Them Back?," *International Migration Review* 51, no. 2 (June 2017): 506–41.
31. Bauböck and Tripkovic, *The Integration of Migrants and Refugees*.
32. "Gender Equality Index 2017."
33. *Settling in 2018*.
34. Ibid.
35. "'Rivers of Blood': The Lasting Legacy of a Poisonous Speech," *The Economist*, April 19, 2018, https://www.economist.com/britain/2018/04/19/rivers-of-blood-the-lasting-legacy-of-a-poisonous-speech.
36. Liebig and Tronstad, "Triple Disadvantage?"
37. "'Rivers of Blood.'"
38. *Settling in 2018*.
39. Khoudja and Fleischmann, "Labor Force Participation of Immigrant Women in the Netherlands." Maliepaard and Alba, Cultural Integration in the Muslim Second Generation in the Netherlands."
40. *Settling in 2018*. Liebig and Tronstad, "Triple Disadvantage?"
41. *Integrated Communities Strategy Green Paper: Building Stronger, More United Communities*, HM Government, London, 2018, https://assets.publishing.service.gov.uk/government/uploads/system/uploads/attachment_data/file/696993/Integrated_Communities_Strategy.pdf.
42. Erik Bergström and Kalle Wannerskog, "Parallellt samhälle i utsatta områden," Sveriges Radio, June 21, 2017, https://sverigesradio.se/sida/artikel.aspx?programid=83&artikel=6722015.
43. Bojan Pancevski, "Teens Roam Streets with Rifles as Crime Swamps Sweden," *The Sunday Times*, January 21, 2018, https://www.thetimes.co.uk/article/teens-roam-streets-with-rifles-as-crime-swamps-sweden-q83g055k9. Mikkel Andersson, personal interview, April 8, 2018.
44. Mohammed Qasim, *Young, Muslim and Criminal: Experiences, Identities and Pathways into Crime* (Bristol: Policy Press, 2018), 34.

45. Cai Berger, personal interview, April 6, 2018.
46. Omar Makram, personal interview, January 28, 2019.
47. Rumy Hasan, personal interview, March 20, 2018.
48. Assita Kanko, personal interview, March 30, 2018.
49. Ibid.
50. *Integrated Communities Strategy Green Paper.*
51. "Netherlands: Teachers See Evidence of Increasing Segregation," European Commission, February 1, 2017, https://ec.europa.eu/migrant-integration/news/netherlands -teachers-see-evidence-of-increasing-segregation.
52. Bergström and Wannerskog, "Parallellt samhälle i utsatta områden."
53. "Exposed Areas: Social Order, Criminal Structure and Challenges for the Police," National Operational Department of Intelligence Unit, Police Sweden, June 2017, https://polisen.se/siteassets/dokument/ovriga_rapporter/utsatta-omraden-social -ordning-kriminell-struktur-och-utmaningar-for-polisen-2017.pdf, 32.
54. Qasim, *Young, Muslim and Criminal.*
55. Paul Collier, *Exodus: How Migration Is Changing Our World* (Oxford, UK: Oxford University Press, 2013).
56. Andrea Thomas, "German Towns Filled with Refugees Ask, 'Who is Integrating Whom?,'" *Wall Street Journal*, October 15, 2017, https://www.wsj.com/articles/german -towns-filled-with-refugees-ask-who-is-integrating-whom-1508074522.
57. Ibid.
58. "Results and Country Profiles: Muslims in Europe: integrated, but not accepted?," Bertelsmann Foundation, 6, https://www.bertelsmann-stiftung.de/en/publications /publication/did/results-and-country-profiles-muslims-in-europe.
59. Unni Wikan, *In Honor of Fadime: Murder and Shame* (Chicago: University of Chicago Press, 2008).
60. Johanna Edström, "Larm: Ökatförtryck mot tjejer," Mitt i Stockholm, July 4, 2016, https://mitti.se/nyheter/larm-okatfortryck-mot-tjejer/.
61. Mikkel Andersson, personal interview, April 8, 2018.
62. Edström, "Larm: Ökatförtryck mot tjejer."
63. Jamie Grierson, "Child Sexual Exploitation Offences Increase Fivefold in Manchester," *The Guardian*, March 30, 2017, https://www.theguardian.com/uk-news/2017/mar/30 /child-sexual-exploitation-offences-quadruple-report-greater-manchester.
64. Ric Curtis, Sheyla Delgado, Evan Misshula, et al., "A Comparative Approach to Estimating the Annual Number of Honor Killings in the United States Among People from Middle Eastern, North African, and Southeast Asian (MENASA) Countries," unpublished manuscript, John Jay College of the City of New York, 2014.
65. Nazir Afzal, personal interview, March 28, 2018.
66. Hollie McKay, "Honor Killing in America: DOJ Report Says Growing Problem is Hidden in Stats," *Fox News*, May 3, 2016, https://www.foxnews.com/us/honor-killing-in-america -doj-report-says-growing-problem-is-hidden-in-stats.
67. "Streitende Familie greift Polizisten an," *Frankfurter Allgemeine*, September 10, 2018, https:// www.faz.net/aktuell/rhein-main/streitende-familie-greift-polizisten-an-15780679.html.
68. Statistikbanken, Danmarks Statistik, https://www.statistikbanken.dk/krise2; https:// www.dst.dk/da/Statistik/nyt/NytHtml?cid=30255.
69. "Forced Marriage in Immigrant Communities in the United States: 2011 National Survey Results," Tahirih Justice Center, September 2011, https://www.tahirih.org /wp-content/uploads/2015/03/REPORT-Tahirih-Survey-on-Forced-Marriage-in -Immigrant-Communities-in-the-United-States.pdf.

70. Jennifer Ludden, "Thousands of Young Women in U.S. Forced into Marriage," NPR, 2015, https://www.npr.org/sections/goatsandsoda/2015/04/14/399337562/thousands -of-young-women-in-u-s-forced-into-marriage.
71. Eskild Dahl Pedersen, personal interview, April 9, 2018.

CHAPTER 14: THE INTEGRATION INDUSTRY AND ITS FAILURE

1. Rainer Bauböck and Milena Tripkovic, eds., *The Integration of Migrants and Refugees: An EUI Forum on Migration, Citizenship and Demography,* European University Institute, 2017, https://cadmus.eui.eu/bitstream/handle/1814/45187/Ebook_IntegrationMigrants Refugees2017.pdf?sequence=3&isAllowed=y.
2. "European Countries Should Make It Easier for Refugees to Work," *The Economist,* April 21, 2018, https://www.economist.com/international/2018/04/21/european-countries -should-make-it-easier-for-refugees-to-work?frsc=dg%7Ce.
3. "Netherlands: Refugees Have More Difficulties to Integrate Than Other Migrant Groups," European Commission, June 23, 2017, https://ec.europa.eu/migrant-integration /news/netherlands-refugees-have-more-difficulties-to-integrate-than-other-migrant -groups. "Meeste Syrische asielzoekers hebben eigen woonruimte," Central Bureau voor de Statistiek, June 22, 2017, https://www.cbs.nl/nl-nl/nieuws/2017/25/meeste -syrische-asielzoekers-hebben-eigen-woonruimte.
4. Tom Kornstad, "6 av 10 menn selvforsørget etter 8 år," Statistisk Sentralbyrå, 2016, December 14, 2016, https://www.ssb.no/inntekt-og-forbruk/artikler-og-publikasjoner /6-av-10-menn-selvforsorget-etter-8-ar.
5. Ibid.
6. Bauböck and Tripkovic, *The Integration of Migrants and Refugees.*
7. Chris Cottrell, "Many Refugees in Germany Lack Training or Education: Report," DW, July 20, 2016, https://www.dw.com/en/many-refugees-in-germany-lack-training-or -education-report/a-19414051.
8. Bauböck and Tripkovic, *The Integration of Migrants and Refugees.*
9. Ibid.
10. *Immigrants in Denmark 2017* (Copenhagen: Danmarks Statistik, 2018), 97.
11. Frank Bovenkerk and Tineke Fokkema, "Crime Among Young Moroccan Men in the Netherlands: Does Their Regional Origin Matter?," *European Journal of Criminology* 13, no. 3 (May 2016): 352–71.
12. Mohammed Qasim, *Young, Muslim and Criminal: Experiences, Identities and Pathways into Crime* (Bristol: Policy Press, 2018).
13. "Exposed Areas: Social Order, Criminal Structure and Challenges for the Police," National Operational Department of Intelligence Unit, Police Sweden, June 2017, https:// polisen.se/siteassets/dokument/ovriga_rapporter/utsatta-omraden-social-ordning -kriminell-struktur-och-utmaningar-for-polisen-2017.pdf, 18.
14. Christian Pfeiffer, Dirk Baier, and Sören Kliem, *Zur Entwicklung der Gewalt in Deutschland Schwerpunkte: Jugendliche und Flüchtlinge als Täter und Opfer,* Institut für Delinquenz und Kriminalprävention, Zürcher Hochschule für Angewandte Wissenschaften, January 2018, https://www.bmfsfj.de/bmfsfj/service/publikationen/zur-entwicklung-der-gewalt-in- deutschland-/121148.
15. Sarah Carpentier, Karel Neels, and Karel Van den Bosch, "Do First- and Second- Generation Migrants Stay Longer in Social Assistance than Natives in Belgium?," *Journal of International Migration and Integration* 18, no. 4 (November 2017): 1167–90.
16. Bauböck and Tripkovic, *The Integration of Migrants and Refugees.*
17. Assaf Razin and Jackline Wahba, "Welfare Magnet Hypothesis, Fiscal Burden, and

Immigration Skill Selectivity," Norface Migration Discussion Paper No. 212–36, 2012, http://norface-migration.org/publ_uploads/NDP_36_12.pdf.

18. "The Progressive Case for Immigration," *The Economist*, March 18, 2017, https://www.economist.com/finance-and-economics/2017/03/18/the-progressive-case-for-immigration.

19. "Onderzoek Integratiebeleid," Tweede Kamer der Staten-Generaal, January 119, 2004, https://zoek.officielebekendmakingen.nl/kst-28689-9.html.

20. "Action Plan on the Integration of Third Country Nationals," European Commission, June 7, 2016, https://ec.europa.eu/home-affairs/sites/homeaffairs/files/what-we-do/policies/european-agenda-migration/proposal-implementation-package/docs/20160607/communication_action_plan_integration_third-country_nationals_en.pdf, 4.

21. "Netherlands: New Integration Policies Fail Migrants & Society, Research Shows," European Commission, January 24, 2017, https://ec.europa.eu/migrant-integration/news/netherlands-new-integration-policies-fail-migrants-society-research-shows.

22. Ulrich Rosenhagen, "From Stranger to Citizen? Germany's Refugee Dilemma," *Dissent*, 2017, https://www.dissentmagazine.org/article/from-stranger-to-citizen-germanys-refugee-dilemma-integration.

23. "Auswertung der Befragung zur Sicherheit in Tübingen," Tübingen Universitätsstadt, 2018, https://www.tuebingen.de/gemeinderat/vo0050.php?__kvonr=12512.

24. Österreichischer Integrations Fonds, personal interview, June 21, 2018.

25. Mathias Énard, *2017 Jahresbericht*, Deutscher Akademischer Austauschdienst, 2017, https://www.daad.de/medien/daad_jahresbericht_2017.pdf.

26. "'One-Euro Job' Program for Refugees Off to a Slow Start in Germany," DW, December 2, 2016, https://www.dw.com/en/one-euro-job-program-for-refugees-off-to-a-slow-start-in-germany/a-36618371.

27. "Germany to Cut Funding for Its One-Euro Job Refugees Scheme," Europost, April 21, 2017, http://www.europost.eu/en/a/view/Germany-to-cut-funding-for-its-one-euro-job-refugees-scheme.

28. *VI Justitie en Veiligheid Rijksbegroting 2019*, Ministerie van Justitie en Veiligheid, 2019, https://www.rijksoverheid.nl/ministeries/ministerie-van-justitie-en-veiligheid/documenten/begrotingen/2018/09/18/vi-justitie-en-veiligheid-rijksbegroting-2019, 76.

29. Ibid., 41.

30. "Overview of Federal Budgetary and Financial Data Up to and Including December 2018," Federal Ministry of Finance, Germany, January 31, 2019, https://www.bundesfinanzministerium.de/Content/EN/Standardartikel/Press_Room/Publications/Monthly_Report/Key_Figures/2019-01-federal-budget.html.

31. Andrea Thomas, "Germany Puts Migration-Related Costs at over $86 Billion over Next Four Years," *Wall Street Journal*, July 1, 2016, https://www.wsj.com/articles/germany-puts-migration-related-costs-at-over-86-billion-over-next-four-years-1467392402.

32. Albéric de Montgolfier, *Rapport général, fait au nom de la commission des finances sur le project de loi de finances sur le projet de loi de finances, adopte par l'assemblee nationale, pour 2019*, Tome III, Sénat, France, 2018, http://www.senat.fr/rap/l18-147-316/l18-147-3161.pdf.

33. Roderick Ackermann, Nicolò Franceschelli, and Lucie Debornes, *Democratic Accountability and Budgetary Control of Non-governmental Organisations Financed from the EU Budget—Update*, European Parliament, June 21, 2019, http://www.europarl.europa.eu/meetdocs/2014_2019/plmrep/COMMITTEES/CONT/DV/2019/01-28/Follow-up NGOstudy_EN.pdf, 26.

34. Robin Alexander, personal interview, April 30, 2018.

35. Miriam Mechel and Gregor Peter Schmitz, "Angela Merkel will 'Wir schaffen das' nicht wiederholen," WirtschaftsWoche, September 17, 2016, https://www.wiwo.de/politik

/deutschland/fluechtlingskrise-angela-merkel-will-wir-schaffen-das-nicht-wiederholen
-/14556964.html. (Author's translation.)

CHAPTER 15: GROOMING GANGS
1. Anoosh Chakelian, "'Grooming Rings Are the Biggest Recruiter for the Far Right':
    Rochdale and Telford Prosecutor," *New Statesman*, March 19, 2018, https://www.new
    statesman.com/politics/uk/2018/03/child-sexual-abuse-grooming-rings-are-biggest
    -recruiter-far-right-rochdale-and-telford-prosecutor.
2. Alexis Jay, OBE, *Independent Inquiry into Child Sexual Exploitation in Rotherham,
    1997–2003*, Rotherham Metropolitan Borough Council, August 21, 2014, https://www
    .rotherham.gov.uk/downloads/file/279/independent-inquiry-into-child-sexual
    -exploitation-in-rotherham.
3. Jane Martinson, "Why the Rochdale 'Grooming Trial' Wasn't About Race," *The Guard-
    ian*, May 9, 2012, https://www.theguardian.com/society/2012/may/09/rochdale
    -grooming-trial-race.
4. Haras Rafiq and Muna Adil, "Group-Based Child Sexual Exploitation: Dissecting
    'Grooming Gangs,'" Quilliam, December 2017, https://www.quilliaminternational.com
    /shop/e-publications/group-based-child-sexual-exploitation-dissecting-grooming
    -gangs/, 53.
5. Ibid.
6. Rafiq and Adil, "Group-Based Child Sexual Exploitation," 32.
7. Ibid.
8. Ella Hill, "As a Rotherham Grooming Gang Survivor, I Want People to Know About
    the Religious Extremism Which Inspired My Abusers," *Independent*, March 18, 2018,
    https://www.independent.co.uk/voices/rotherham-grooming-gang-sexual-abuse-muslim
    -islamist-racism-white-girls-religious-extremism-a8261831.html.
9. Rafiq and Adil, "Group-Based Child Sexual Exploitation."
10. Nazir Afzal, personal interview, March 28, 2018.
11. Martinson, "Why the Rochdale 'Grooming Trial' Wasn't About Race."
12. Ann Cryer, personal interview, March 27, 2018.
13. Allison Pearson, "Rotherham: In the Face of Such Evil, Who Is the Racist Now?,"
    The Telegraph, August 27, 2014, https://www.telegraph.co.uk/news/uknews/crime
    /11059138/Rotherham-In-the-face-of-such-evil-who-is-the-racist-now.html.
14. Martinson, "Why the Rochdale 'Grooming Trial' Wasn't About Race."
15. Andrew Norfolk, "Sarah Champion Interview: 'I'd Rather Be Called a Racist than
    Turn a Blind Eye to Child Abuse,'" *The Sunday Times*, September 2, 2017, https://www
    .thetimes.co.uk/article/sarah-champion-mp-i-d-rather-be-called-a-racist-than-turn-a
    -blind-eye-to-child-abuse-96s0fbm22.
16. Ibid.
17. Jay, *Independent Inquiry into Child Sexual Exploitation in Rotherham 1997–2013*, https://
    www.rotherham.gov.uk/downloads/file/279/independent-inquiry-into-child-sexual
    -exploitation-in-rotherham.
18. Julie Bindel, "Why Are So Many Left-Wing Progressives Silent About Islam's T
    otalitarian Tendencies?," UnHerd, April 3, 2018, https://unherd.com/2018/04/many
    -left-wing-progressives-protest-pope-silent-islams-totalitarian-tendencies-victims
    -cowardice-overwhelmingly-women/.
19. Louise Casey, DBE, CB, "The Casey Review: A Review into Opportunity and Integration,"
    Department for Communities and Local Government, London, December 2016, https://
    assets.publishing.service.gov.uk/government/uploads/system/uploads/attachment
    _data/file/575973/The_Casey_Review_Report.pdf, 159–60.

20. Helen Pidd, "Report Says Child Sexual Exploitation 'Normal in Parts of Greater Mancheter,'" *The Guardian*, October 30, 2014, https://www.theguardian.com/society/2014/oct/30/child-sexual-exploitation-norm-greater-manchester-ann-coffey-report.

21. Jay, *Independent Inquiry into Child Sexual Exploitation in Rotherham 1997–2003*.

22. Ibid.

23. Ann Cryer, personal interview, March 27, 2018.

24. Dearden, "Grooming Gangs Abused More than 700 Women and Girls Around Newcastle After Police Appeared to Punish Victims."

25. Richard Ford, "Rochdale sex abuse gang wins legal aid to fight deportation," *The Times*, July 29, 2017, https://www.thetimes.co.uk/article/rochdale-sex-abuse-gang-wins-legal-aid-to-fight-deportation-z0g3l7dqj.

26. Ann Cryer, personal interview, June 27, 2018.

27. "Åklagaren yrkar sex års fängelse för gruppvåldtäkten i Fittja," Botkyrka Direkt, December 6, 2017, https://www.stockholmdirekt.se/nyheter/aklagaren-yrkar-sex-ars-fangelse-for-gruppvaldtakten-i-fittja/repqld!jy2xyF5K5JtTtkv7wxQd7w/.

28. "The woman who reported five men for a group violence in Fittja in August 2016 has withdrawn her appeal, reports Omni. This means that the verdict of the District Court is fixed," (translated), in "Åklagaren yrkar sex års fängelse för gruppvåldtäkten i Fittja."

29. "Åklagaren yrkar sex års fängelse för gruppvåldtäkten i Fittja."

30. Ann Cryer, personal interview, March 27, 2018.

31. "Nazir Afzal Pledges to Make Wales 'Safest Place for Women,'" BBC News, January 21, 2018, https://www.bbc.com/news/uk-wales-42765231.

CHAPTER 16: "FOR YOU WHO ARE MARRIED TO A CHILD"

1. "Refugee Host School Bans Revealing Clothes," The Local de, June 26, 2015, https://www.thelocal.de/20150626/refugee-school-calls-for-uniform-modesty.

2. "Police Criticized for Reaction to Brutal Rape of Jogger in Leipzig Park," The Local de, September 4, 2017, https://www.thelocal.de/20170904/police-criticized-for-reaction-to-brutal-rape-of-jogger-in-leipzig.

3. Richard Orange, "Police Warn Women Not to Go Out Alone in Swedish Town After Spate of Sex Attacks," *The Telegraph*, March 8, 2016, https://www.telegraph.co.uk/news/worldnews/europe/sweden/12188274/Police-warn-women-not-to-go-out-alone-in-Swedish-town-after-spate-of-sex-attacks.html.

4. "Malmöpolisens råd till kvinnor: Gå inte ut ensamma," FriaTider, December 17, 2017, http://www.friatider.se/malm-polisens-r-d-till-kvinnor-g-inte-ut-ensamma-0.

5. Cameron Holbrook, "Sweden's Bråvalla Festival Shut Down for Good," *Mixmag*, June 26, 2018, https://mixmag.net/read/swedens-bravalla-festival-has-been-shut-down-for-good-news.

6. "Swedish police to hand out anti-groping armbands," The Local se, June 29, 2016, thelocal.se/20160629/Swedish-police-to-hand-out-anti-groping-armbands.

7. Tino Sanandaji, personal interview, April 7, 2018.

8. "Sweden's Bråvalla Music Festival Cancelled Next Year After Sex Attacks," *The Guardian*, July 3, 2017, https://www.theguardian.com/world/2017/jul/03/swedens-bravalla-music-festival-cancelled-next-year-after-sex-attacks.

9. Christina Anderson and Ceylan Yeginsu, "Tired of Sexual Assault, Music Festival for Women Stresses a 'Safe Zone,'" *New York Times*, September 1, 2018, https://www.nytimes.com/2018/09/01/world/europe/sweden-statement-festival-women.html.

10. Frank Jordans, "German Police Union Chief Slams NYE 'Safe Zone' for Women," Associated Press, December 30, 2017, https://www.apnews.com/84215e6e5ceb49d794e7e775e87b8339.

11. Flemming Rose, personal interview, April 9, 2018.
12. "Information till dig som är gift med ett barn," Migrationsverket, 2018.
13. Tomas Löwemo, "Flicka blev gravid med 20-årig make," *Östra Småland Nyheterna*, December 21, 2017.
14. "Barnäktenskap orsak till bråk," *SVT Nyheter*, January 9, 2017, https://www.svt.se/nyheter/lokalt/smaland/barnaktenskap-orsak-till-brak.
15. Unchained at Last, "Child Marriage—Shocking Statistics," https://www.unchainedatlast.org/child-marriage-shocking-statistics/.
16. *Emma*, November–December 2016, https://www.emma.de/lesesaal/61385.
17. "German Parliament Passes Law Ending Child Marriage," The Local de, June 2, 2017, https://www.thelocal.de/20170602/german-parliament-passes-law-ending-child-marriage.
18. Machteld Zee, *Choosing Sharia? Multiculturalism, Islamic Fundamentalism & Sharia Councils* (The Hague: Eleven International Publishing, 2016), 97.
19. *Integrated Communities Strategy Green Paper: Building Stronger, More United Communities*, HM Government, London, 2018, https://assets.publishing.service.gov.uk/government/uploads/system/uploads/attachment_data/file/696993/Integrated_Communities_Strategy.pdf, 56.
20. "Släng ut Sharia ur våra svenska domstolar," *Kristianstadsbladet*, March 5, 2018, http://www.kristianstadsbladet.se/ledare/slang-ut-sharia-ur-vara-svenska-domstolar/.
21. "Gender Segregation Not 'Alien to Our Culture,' Says Universities UK Chief," *The Guardian*, December 12, 2013, https://www.theguardian.com/society/2013/dec/12/gender-segregation-not-alien-culture-universities-chief.
22. May Bulman, "Top University Accepts Islamic Society's Gender-Segregated Event Was 'Unlawful,'" *Independent*, September 28, 2017, https://www.independent.co.uk/news/uk/home-news/london-university-islamic-society-gender-segregated-event-unlawful-london-school-economics-lse-a7972311.html.
23. Elin Hofverberg, "Sweden: Separate Swimming Hours by Gender Justifiable," Global Legal Monitor, January 12, 2017, http://www.loc.gov/law/foreign-news/article/sweden-separate-swimming-hours-by-gender-justifiable/.
24. Rüdiger Franz, "Neues Bonner Bad soll Vorhang für Musliminnen bekommen," *General-Anzeiger*, January 22, 2018, https://www.general-anzeiger-bonn.de/bonn/stadtbonn/neues-bonner-bad-soll-vorhang-fuer-musliminnen-bekommen_aid-43624061.
25. "Muslime fordern eigene Schwimmzeiten," IslamiQ , January 14, 2015, http://www.islamiq.de/2015/03/14/muslime-fordern-eigene-schwimmzeiten/. (Author's translation.)
26. Ibid.
27. Emma Lidman, "Pool Makes Splash with Gender Jacuzzi Split," The Local se, January 8, 2016, https://www.thelocal.se/20160108/swimming-hall-split-pools-between-men-and-women.
28. Richard Orange, "Sweden's Swimming Pool Vigilantes Accused of Neo-Nazi Links," *The Telegraph*, March 1, 2016, https://www.telegraph.co.uk/news/worldnews/europe/sweden/12179830/Swedens-swimming-pool-vigilantes-accused-of-neo-Nazi-links.html.
29. Paulina Neuding, "Sweden's Sexual Assault Crisis Presents a Feminist Paradox," Quillette, October 10, 2017, https://quillette.com/2017/10/10/swedens-sexual-assault-crisis-presents-feminist-paradox/.
30. Polizeipräsidium Krefeld, "POL-KR: Veredacht der sexuellen Belästigung im Badezentrum Bockum," Presse Portal, January 16, 2017, https://www.presseportal.de/blaulicht/pm/50667/3536390.
31. "Teenage Girls Touched at WEM Water Park, Man Charged with 6 Counts of Sexual

Assault," CBC News, February 8, 2017, https://www.cbc.ca/news/canada/edmonton /west-edmonton-mall-wem-water-park-sexual-assault-1.3972344.

32. Mikolai, personal interview, June 19, 2018.

33. Lizzie Dearden, "German Nudists Outraged at New Rules Ordering Them to Wear Swimwear as Refugee Shelter Arrives on Lake," *Independent*, June 22, 2016, https:// www.independent.co.uk/news/world/europe/german-nudists-outraged-new-rules -ordering-them-wear-swimwear-refugee-shelter-arrives-lake-a7096001.html.

34. Allan Hall, "Muslim Gang Insults 'Sluts and Infidels' at German Nudist Pool," *The Times*, July 28, 2016, https://www.thetimes.co.uk/article/muslim-gang-insults-sluts -and-infidels-at-german-nudist-pool-zk5pjqmfx.

35. "Das sagen Deutschlands Nackte zur FKK-Krise," *Bild*, August 9, 2017, https:// www.bild.de/news/inland/fkk/bild-hoerte-sich-an-fkk-straenden-in-deutschland -um-52814134.bild.html.

36. "Topless, naturisme . . . un retour de la pudeur? Observatoire mondial de la nudité feminine," IFOP, August 7, 2017, https://www.ifop.com/wp-content/uploads/2018 /03/3827-1-study_file.pdf.

37. Cecilia Rodriguez, "Nudity in Germany Losing Its Appeal," *Forbes*, July 17, 2014, https://www.forbes.com/sites/ceciliarodriguez/2014/07/17/nudity-losing-its-appeal -in-germany/#30f51bd24d79.

38. Antje Röder, "Explaining Religious Differences in Immigrants' Gender Role Attitudes: The Changing Impact of Origin Country and Individual Religiosity," *Ethnic and Racial Studies* 37, no. 14 (2014): 2615–35.

39. "Being Christian in Western Europe," Pew Research Center, May 29, 2018, https:// www.pewforum.org/2018/05/29/being-christian-in-western-europe/.

40. Haras Rafiq and Muna Adil, "Group-Based Child Sexual Exploitation: Dissecting 'Grooming Gangs,'" Quilliam, December 2017, https://www.quilliaminternational.com /shop/e-publications/group-based-child-sexual-exploitation-dissecting-grooming -gangs/, 53.

41. Daniel Schwammenthal, personal interview, March 30, 2018.

42. Til Biermann, "Weil Liam antisemitisch gemobbt wurde, flüchtet er nach Israel," *BZ*, April 7, 2018, https://www.bz-berlin.de/berlin/charlottenburg-wilmersdorf/weil -liam-antisemitisch-gemobbt-wurde-fluechtet-er-nach-israel. (Author's translation.)

43. "Antisemitsche Vorfälle 2018: Ein Bericht der Recherche-und Informationsstelle Antisemitismus Berlin (RIAS)," RIAS, 2019, https://report-antisemitism.de/media /bericht-antisemitischer-vorfaelle-2018.pdf.

44. "Germany's Jews Urged Not to Wear Kippahs After Attacks," BBC News, April 24, 2018, https://www.bbc.com/news/world-europe-43884075.

45. Cnaan Liphshiz, "In Downtown Brussels, Once Vibrant Synagogues Are Now Dying or Sold," Jewish Telegraphic Agency, February 5, 2019, https://www.jta.org/2019/02/05 /global/in-downtown-brussels-once-vibrant-synagogues-are-now-dying-or-sold.

46. Tino Sanandaji, *Mass Challenge: Economic Policy Against Social Exclusion and Antisocial Behavior* (Kuhzad Media, 2017), 81. Thomas C. Schelling, "Dynamic Models of Segregation," *Journal of Mathematical Sociology* 1 (1971): 143–86, https://www.stat .berkeley.edu/~aldous/157/Papers/Schelling_Seg_Models.pdf.

47. Paulina Neuding, "Violent Crime in Sweden Is Soaring. When Will Politicians Act?," *The Spectator*, February 10, 2018, https://www.spectator.co.uk/2018/02/violent-crime -in-sweden-is-soaring-when-will-politicians-act/.

48. "Paketjätten stoppar sina leveranser till Rosengård," *Kvällsposten*, February 23, 2019, https:// www.expressen.se/kvallsposten/paketjatten-stoppar-sina-leveranser-till-rosengard/.

49. Paulina Neuding, "Social oro ger stök på bibblan," *Svenska Dagbladet*, May 16, 2015, https://www.svd.se/social-oro-ger-stok-pa-bibblan.
50. Neuding, "Violent Crime in Sweden is Soaring."
51. Sanandaji, *Mass Challenge*, 171.
52. Cai Berger, personal interview, April 6, 2018.
53. Robert Mackey, "Paris Mayor Plans to Sue Fox over False Reports of 'No-Go Zones,'" *New York Times*, January 20, 2015, https://www.nytimes.com/2015/01/21/world/europe/paris-mayor-plans-to-sue-over-news-of-no-go-zones.html.
54. Bill de Blasio, Anne Hidalgo, and Sadiq Khan, "Our Immigrants, Our Strength," *New York Times*, September 20, 2016, https://www.nytimes.com/2016/09/20/opinion/our-immigrants-our-strength.html.
55. "Merkel Says Germany Has 'No-Go Areas;' Gov't Won't Say Where," Associated Press, February 28, 2018, https://apnews.com/438bb0ac98d04459ab2e392f3c4fc5ef.
56. Allan Hall, "'Come Here at Night? I Would Rather Order a Taxi Straight to Hell!': Women Forced to Run Gauntlet of Migrants at the Austrian Station So Risky It's Been Dubbed 'the Terminus of Fear,'" *Daily Mail*, February 23, 2016, https://www.dailymail.co.uk/news/article-3454897/Come-night-order-taxi-straight-hell-Women-forced-run-gauntlet-migrants-Austrian-station-risky-s-dubbed-terminus-fear.html.
57. Boris Palmer, personal interview, June 18, 2018.
58. Henrik Dahl, personal interview, April 10, 2018.
59. Seyran Ateş, *Der Islam braucht eine sexuelle Revolution: Eine Streitschrift* (Ullstein Taschenbuch, 2011).
60. "Death threats will not deter me from fighting extremism with enlightenment," Seyran Ateş, *New European*, September 11, 2017, https://www.theneweuropean.co.uk/top-stories/muslim-feminist-seyran-ates-1-5189908.
61. Seyran Ateş, personal interview, April 5, 2018.
62. Ibid.
63. Efgani Dönmez, personal interview, June 22, 2018.
64. Eskild Dahl Pedersen, personal interview, April 9, 2018.
65. Düzen Tekkal, personal interview, May 10, 2018.
66. Hamed Abdel-Samad, personal interview, June 27, 2018.
67. Jaleh Tavakoli, personal interview, October 4, 2017.

CHAPTER 17: THE POPULIST PROBLEM

1. "The European Commission's Eurobarometer Surveys," GESIS, https://www.gesis.org/eurobarometer-data-service/home/.
2. "Netherlands: Support for 'Migration Ban' from Muslim Countries Larger than Expected," European Commission, June 2, 2017, https://ec.europa.eu/migrant-integration/news/netherlands-support-for-migration-ban-from-muslim-countries-larger-than-expected.
3. "Six Out of Ten Voters in Sweden Want Fewer Refugees: poll," The Local se, April 21, 2018, https://www.thelocal.se/20180421/six-out-of-ten-voters-in-sweden-want-fewer-refugees-poll.
4. Charlie Duxbury, "Danish Social Democrats Win National Election," Politico, June 5, 2019, https://www.politico.eu/article/denmarks-social-democrats-on-course-to-win-election/.
5. "Poll of Polls: Germany," Politico, https://www.politico.eu/europe-poll-of-polls/germany/.
6. Daniel Schwammenthal, personal interview, March 30, 2018.
7. "Head of Far-Right AfD 'Mistakenly' Votes for Refugees to Bring Bamilies to Germany," The Local de, February 2, 2018, https://www.thelocal.de/20180202/head-of-far-right-afd-mistakenly-votes-for-refugees-to-bring-families-to-germany.

8. "Chancellor Merkel Enters 'Germans Only' Food Bank Furore," BBC News, February 27, 2018, https://www.bbc.com/news/world-europe-43210596.
9. David Goodhart, personal interview, June 11, 2018.

CHAPTER 18: A NEW APPROACH TO INTEGRATION
1. "UNHCR Global Trends: Forced Displacement in 2018," United Nations High Commission for Refugees, https://www.unhcr.org/5d08d7ee7.pdf.
2. "Austria to Propose Soldiers for Frontex," ANSA, August 29, 2018, https://www.ansa.it /english/news/politics/2018/08/29/austria-to-propose-soldiers-for-frontex_66aa0296 -c9f6-4497-be5d-624c91a21432.html.
3. Irina Angelescu and Florian Trauner, "10,000 Border Guards for Frontex: Why the EU Risks Conflated Expectations," European Policy Centre, September 21, 2018, https:// www.ies.be/files/pub_8745_frontex.pdf.
4. "Milton Friedman—Illegal Immigration—PT 1," *LibertyPen*, YouTube, December 11, 2009, https://www.youtube.com/watch?v=3eyJIbSgdSE.
5. Ellen Barry and Martin Selsoe Sorensen, "In Denmark, Harsh New Laws for Immigrant 'Ghettos,'" *New York Times*, July 1, 2018, https://www.nytimes.com/2018/07/01/world /europe/denmark-immigrant-ghettos.html.
6. "Some proposals have been rejected as too radical, like one from the far-right Danish People's Party that would confine 'ghetto children' to their homes after 8 p.m." Barry and Sorensen, "In Denmark, Harsh New Laws for Immigrant 'Ghettos.'"
7. "Auswertung der Befragung zur Sicherheit in Tübingen," Tübingen Universitätsstadt, 2018, https://www.tuebingen.de/gemeinderat/vo0050.php?__kvonr=12512.
8. Nazir Afzal, personal interview, March 28, 2018.
9. Jess Phillips, personal interview, May 15, 2018.
10. "Zainab bint Younus from Canada," Muslima, http://muslima.globalfundforwomen .org/stories/i-am-salafi-feminist.
11. The Salafi Feminist.

CONCLUSION: THE ROAD TO GILEAD
1. Margaret Atwood, *The Handmaid's Tale* (New York: Anchor Books, 1998).
2. Alan Taylor, "Afghanistan in the 1950s and '60s," *The Atlantic*, July 2, 2013, https:// www.theatlantic.com/photo/2013/07/afghanistan-in-the-1950s-and-60s/100544/.
3. "Egyptian Leader Gamal Abdel Nasser Laughing at Hijab Requirement in 1958 (Subtitled)," *Video Clips*, YouTube, December 13, 2015, https://www.youtube.com /watch?v=_ZIqdrFeFBk.
4. Anna Clark, *Women's Silence, Men's Violence: Sexual Assault in England 1770–1845* (London: Pandora Press, 1987).
5. John Stuart Mill, "The Subjection of Women (1869)," in *Essays on Equality, Law and Education* ed. John M. Robson, introduction by Stefan Collini (Toronto: University of Toronto Press, 1984) [Collected works of John Stuart Mill Vol. XXI], 261.

INDEX

ABOUT THE AUTHOR

AYAAN HIRSI ALI is a Somali-born women's rights activist, free speech advocate, and the *New York Times* bestselling author of *Infidel*, *The Caged Virgin*, *Nomad*, *Heretic*, and *The Challenge of Dawa*. Born in Mogadishu, Somalia, she grew up in Africa and the Middle East before seeking asylum in the Netherlands, where she went on to become a member of parliament. Today she lives in the United States with her husband and two sons.